Nginx HTTP Server
Third Edition

Harness the power of Nginx to make the most of your infrastructure and serve pages faster than ever

Clément Nedelcu

[PACKT] open source*
PUBLISHING   community experience distilled

BIRMINGHAM - MUMBAI

Nginx HTTP Server
Third Edition

First published: July 2010

Second edition: July 2013

Third edition: November 2015

Production reference: 1101115

Published by Packt Publishing Ltd.
Livery Place
35 Livery Street
Birmingham B3 2PB, UK.

ISBN 978-1-78528-033-7

www.packtpub.com

Credits

Author
Clément Nedelcu

Reviewer
Amet Umerov

Acquisition Editor
Indrajit Das

Content Development Editor
Kirti Patil

Technical Editor
Siddhesh Patil

Copy Editor
Sonia Mathur

Project Coordinator
Nidhi Joshi

Proofreader
Safis Editing

Indexer
Monica Ajmera Mehta

Graphics
Disha Haria

Production Coordinator
Arvindkumar Gupta

Cover Work
Arvindkumar Gupta

About the Author

Clément Nedelcu was born in France and studied in universities in the UK, France, and China. After teaching computer science, programming, and systems administration in several eastern Chinese universities, he worked as a technology consultant in France. Here, he specialized in web and .NET software development as well as Linux server administration. Since 2005, Clément has administered a major network of websites in his spare time, which eventually led him to discover Nginx. It made such a big difference that he started his own blog about it; you can find it at `http://cnedelcu.net`.

I would like to express my gratitude to my wife, Julie; my son, Leo; and my family and friends, who were all very supportive throughout the writing process. I would like to extend special thanks to Gwenaël Oberlinger (Uptobox), Martin Fjordvald, Cliff Wells, Maxim Dounin, and all the folks at the #nginx IRC channel on Freenode.

About the Reviewer

Amet Umerov works as a Linux system administrator with hosting provider from Russia. He received his bachelor's degree from Sevastopol State University, where he studied computer science and engineering.

Amet is experienced in using Linux, virtualization, Nginx, and other useful technologies and tools. He believes that the simplicity and modularity of Nginx make it the most flexible solution for organizing reverse proxies, through caching, handling static files, and load balancing.

Amet's latest open source project is a guide to creating and managing Virtuozzo-based containers and virtual machines.

www.PacktPub.com

Support files, eBooks, discount offers, and more

For support files and downloads related to your book, please visit www.PacktPub.com.

Did you know that Packt offers eBook versions of every book published, with PDF and ePub files available? You can upgrade to the eBook version at www.PacktPub.com and as a print book customer, you are entitled to a discount on the eBook copy. Get in touch with us at service@packtpub.com for more details.

At www.PacktPub.com, you can also read a collection of free technical articles, sign up for a range of free newsletters and receive exclusive discounts and offers on Packt books and eBooks.

https://www2.packtpub.com/books/subscription/packtlib

Do you need instant solutions to your IT questions? PacktLib is Packt's online digital book library. Here, you can search, access, and read Packt's entire library of books.

Why subscribe?

- Fully searchable across every book published by Packt
- Copy and paste, print, and bookmark content
- On demand and accessible via a web browser

Free access for Packt account holders

If you have an account with Packt at www.PacktPub.com, you can use this to access PacktLib today and view 9 entirely free books. Simply use your login credentials for immediate access.

Table of Contents

Preface

It is a well-known fact that the market for web servers has a long-established leader: Apache. According to recent surveys conducted in October 2015, almost 35 percent of the World Wide Web is served by this twenty-year old open source application. However, the same reports reveal the rise of a new competitor in the past few years: Nginx, a lightweight HTTP server originating from Russia and pronounced "engine x". What has caused so many server administrators to switch to Nginx since the beginning of the 2009? Is this tiny piece of software mature enough to run a high-traffic website?

To begin with, Nginx is not as young as one might think. Originally started in 2002, the project was first carried out by a standalone developer, Igor Sysoev, for the needs of an extremely high-traffic Russian website, namely Rambler, which received, as of September 2008, over 500 million HTTP requests per day. The application is now used to serve some of the most popular websites on the Web, such as Reddit, Wikipedia, WordPress, Dropbox, and many more. Nginx has proved to be a very efficient, lightweight yet powerful web server. Throughout the chapters in this book, you will discover the numerous features of Nginx and progressively understand why so many administrators decide to place their trust in this new HTTP server, often at the expense of Apache.

There are several aspects in which Nginx is more efficient than its competitors. First, and foremost, it's faster. By making use of asynchronous sockets, Nginx does not spawn processes as many times as it receives requests. One process per core suffices to handle thousands of connections, leading to a much lighter CPU load and memory consumption. Secondly, its simplicity of use is remarkable. Configuration files are much easier to read and tweak with Nginx than with other web server solutions, such as Apache; a couple of lines are enough to set up a complete virtual host configuration.

Last but not least, server administrators appreciate it for its modularity. Not only is Nginx a completely open source project released under a BSD-like license, but it also comes with a powerful plugin system referred to as "modules". A large variety of modules are included with the original distribution archive, and a number of third-party ones can be downloaded online.

All in all, Nginx combines speed, efficiency, and power to provide you with the perfect ingredients for a successful web server. It appears to be the best Apache alternative as of today.

What this book covers

Chapter 1, Downloading and Installing Nginx, guides you through the early setup stages of downloading and configuring your own build of the program.

Chapter 2, Basic Nginx Configuration, covers the essential aspects of the Nginx configuration structure and syntax.

Chapter 3, HTTP Configuration, takes you through the configuration of HTTP server components, enabling you to serve a simple static site.

Chapter 4, Module Configuration, provides an in-depth approach to the large variety of modules available with the standard Nginx package.

Chapter 5, PHP and Python with Nginx, is a comprehensive guide to setting up backend programs to serve dynamic content through Nginx.

Chapter 6, Apache and Nginx Together, describes how both server applications can cooperate on the same architecture to improve existing websites and services.

Chapter 7, From Apache to Nginx, provides key information for fully switching your server or web infrastructure from Apache to Nginx.

Chapter 8, Introducing Load Balancing and Optimization, provides useful leads for server administrators who manage sites under heavy loads.

Chapter 9, Case Studies, offers a practical approach to several real-life examples, including some of the most common tasks performed with Nginx.

Chapter 10, Troubleshooting, covers the most common issues encountered while setting up Nginx or during the production stages.

What you need for this book

Although Nginx is available for Windows from version 0.7.52 onward, it is common knowledge that Linux- or BSD-based distributions are preferred to host production sites. During the various processes described in this book, we will assume that you are hosting your website on a Linux operating system, such as Debian, Ubuntu, CentOS, or other well-known distributions.

Who this book is for

By covering both the early setup stages and advanced topics, this book suits web administrators who are interested in solutions to optimize their infrastructure, whether you are looking into replacing your existing web server software or integrating a new tool to cooperate with applications that are already up-and-running. If you, your visitors, and your operating system have been disappointed by Apache, this book is exactly what you need.

Conventions

In this book, you will find a number of text styles that distinguish between different kinds of information. Here are some examples of these styles and an explanation of their meaning.

Code words in text, database table names, folder names, filenames, file extensions, pathnames, dummy URLs, user input, and Twitter handles are shown as follows: "Or if your system does not come with the `service` command:"

A block of code is set as follows:

```
include /file/path.conf;
include sites/*.conf;
```

When we wish to draw your attention to a particular part of a code block, the relevant lines or items are set in bold:

```
user nginx nginx;
master_process on;
worker_processes 4;
events {
  worker_connections 1024;
  use epoll;
}
```

Any command-line input or output is written as follows:

```
# cp /usr/local/nginx/conf/nginx.conf /home/user/backups/nginx.conf.bak
```

New terms and **important words** are shown in bold. Words that you see on the screen, for example, in menus or dialog boxes, appear in the text like this: "If these packages are already installed on your system, you will receive a message saying something like **Nothing to do**."

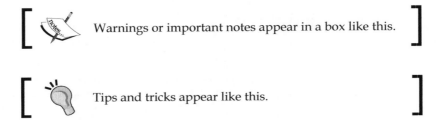

Warnings or important notes appear in a box like this.

Tips and tricks appear like this.

Reader feedback

Feedback from our readers is always welcome. Let us know what you think about this book—what you liked or disliked. Reader feedback is important for us as it helps us develop titles that you will really get the most out of.

To send us general feedback, simply e-mail feedback@packtpub.com, and mention the book's title in the subject of your message.

If there is a topic that you have expertise in and you are interested in either writing or contributing to a book, see our author guide at www.packtpub.com/authors.

Customer support

Now that you are the proud owner of a Packt book, we have a number of things to help you to get the most from your purchase.

Downloading the example code

You can download the example code files from your account at http://www.packtpub.com for all the Packt Publishing books you have purchased. If you purchased this book elsewhere, you can visit http://www.packtpub.com/support and register to have the files e-mailed directly to you.

Errata

Although we have taken every care to ensure the accuracy of our content, mistakes do happen. If you find a mistake in one of our books—maybe a mistake in the text or the code—we would be grateful if you could report this to us. By doing so, you can save other readers from frustration and help us improve subsequent versions of this book. If you find any errata, please report them by visiting http://www.packtpub.com/submit-errata, selecting your book, clicking on the **Errata Submission Form** link, and entering the details of your errata. Once your errata are verified, your submission will be accepted and the errata will be uploaded to our website or added to any list of existing errata under the Errata section of that title.

To view the previously submitted errata, go to https://www.packtpub.com/books/content/support and enter the name of the book in the search field. The required information will appear under the **Errata** section.

Piracy

Piracy of copyrighted material on the Internet is an ongoing problem across all media. At Packt, we take the protection of our copyright and licenses very seriously. If you come across any illegal copies of our works in any form on the Internet, please provide us with the location address or website name immediately so that we can pursue a remedy.

Please contact us at copyright@packtpub.com with a link to the suspected pirated material.

We appreciate your help in protecting our authors and our ability to bring you valuable content.

Questions

If you have a problem with any aspect of this book, you can contact us at questions@packtpub.com, and we will do our best to address the problem.

1
Downloading and Installing Nginx

In this chapter, we will begin with the steps necessary to establish a functional setup of Nginx. This process is crucial for the smooth functioning of your web server. There are some required libraries and tools to install the program, some parameters that you will have to decide upon when compiling the binaries, and there may also be some configuration changes to perform on your system.

This chapter covers the following topics:

- Downloading and installing the prerequisites to compile the Nginx binaries
- Downloading a suitable version of the Nginx source code
- Configuring Nginx compile-time options
- Controlling the application with an `init` script
- Configuring the system to launch Nginx automatically on startup
- A quick overview of the possibilities offered by the Nginx Plus platform

Setting up the prerequisites

We have chosen to download the source code of the application and compile it manually, as opposed to installing it using a package manager, such as `Yum`, `Aptitude`, or `Yast`. There are two reasons for this choice. First, the package may not be available in the enabled repositories of your Linux distribution. In addition, the repositories that offer to download and install Nginx automatically often contain outdated versions. More importantly, you need to configure a variety of significant compile-time options. As a result of this choice of manual setup, your system will require some tools and libraries for the compilation process.

Depending on the optional modules that you select at compile time, you will perhaps need different prerequisites. You will be guided through the process of installing the most common ones, such as GCC, PCRE, zlib, and OpenSSL.

> If your operating system offers the possibility to install the Nginx package from a repository, and you are confident enough that the available version will suit all of your needs with the modules included by default, you could consider skipping this chapter altogether and simply run one the following commands. We still recommend getting the latest version and building it from source seeing as it contains the latest bug fixes and security patches. For a Debian-based operating system, run the following command:
>
> **apt-get install nginx**
>
> For Red Hat–based operating systems, use the following command:
>
> **yum install nginx**
>
> Alternatively, you can download and install prebuilt packages from the official Nginx website at https://www.nginx.org.

The GNU Compiler Collection

Nginx is a program written in C, so you will first need to install a compiler tool, such as the **GNU Compiler Collection (GCC)**, on your system. GCC may already be present on your system, but if that is not the case, you will have to install it before going any further.

> GCC is a collection of free open source compilers for various languages: C, C++, Java, Ada, FORTRAN, and so on. It is the most commonly used compiler suite in the Linux world, and Windows versions are also available. It supports a vast number of processors such as x86, AMD64, PowerPC, ARM, MIPS, and more.

First, make sure GCC isn't already installed on your system by running the following command:

```
[alex@example.com ~]$ gcc
```

If you get the following output, it means that GCC is correctly installed on your system and you can skip to the next section:

```
gcc: no input files
```

If you receive the following message, you will have to proceed with the installation of the compiler:

```
~bash: gcc: command not found
```

GCC can be installed using the default repositories of your package manager. Depending on your distribution, the package manager will vary—yum for a Red Hat-based distribution, apt for Debian and Ubuntu, yast for SuSE Linux, and so on. Here is the typical way to proceed with the download and installation of the GCC package:

```
[root@example.com ~]# yum groupinstall "Development Tools"
```

If you use apt-get to install software packages, run the following command:

```
[root@example.com ~]# apt-get install build-essentials
```

If you use another package manager with a different syntax, you will probably find the documentation with the man utility. Either way, your package manager should be able to download and install GCC correctly after having solved the dependencies automatically. Note that this command not only installs GCC, it also proceeds with downloading and installing all common requirements to build applications from source, such as code headers and other compilation tools.

The PCRE library

The **Perl Compatible Regular Expression (PCRE)** library is required to compile Nginx. The Rewrite and HTTP core modules of Nginx use PCRE for the syntax of their regular expressions, as you will discover in later chapters. You will need to install two packages: pcre and pcre-devel. The first package provides the compiled version of the library, whereas the second one provides development headers and sources to compile projects, which are required in our case. Here are example commands that you can run in order to install both the packages.

If you are using yum, run the following command:

```
[root@example.com ~]# yum install pcre pcre-devel
```

Or you can install all of the PCRE-related packages by using the following command:

```
[root@example.com ~]# yum install pcre*
```

If you use apt-get, run the following command:

```
[root@example.com ~]# apt-get install libpcre3 libpcre3-dev
```

If these packages are already installed on your system, you will receive a message saying something like **Nothing to do**. In other words, the package manager did not install or update any component, as both components are already present on the system.

```
root@example:~# apt-get install libpcre3 libpcre3-dev
Reading package lists... Done
Building dependency tree
Reading state information... Done
libpcre3 is already the newest version.
libpcre3-dev is already the newest version.
0 upgraded, 0 newly installed, 0 to remove and 0 not upgraded.
root@example:~#
```

The zlib library

The `zlib` library provides developers with compression algorithms. It is required for the use of `gzip` compression in various modules of Nginx. Again, you can use your package manager to install this component, as it is part of the default repositories. Similar to PCRE, you will need both the library and its source for installation: `zlib` and `zlib-devel`.

If using `yum`, run the following command:

```
[root@example.com ~]# yum install zlib zlib-devel
```

Using `apt-get`, run the following command:

```
[root@example.com ~]# apt-get install zlib1g zlib1g-dev
```

These packages install quickly and have no known dependency issues.

OpenSSL

> *The OpenSSL project is a collaborative effort to develop a robust, commercial-grade, full-featured, and open source toolkit implementing the Secure Sockets Layer (SSL v2/v3) and Transport Layer Security (TLS v1) protocols, as well as a full-strength general purpose cryptography library. The project is managed by a worldwide community of volunteers that use the Internet to communicate, plan, and develop the OpenSSL toolkit and its related documentation. For more information, visit* http://www.openssl.org.

The OpenSSL library will be used by Nginx to serve web pages over a secure connection. We thus need to install the library and its development package. The process remains the same here—you install `openssl` and `openssl`-devel:

If using `yum`, run the following command:

```
[root@example.com ~]# yum install openssl openssl-devel
```

If using `apt-get`, run the following command:

```
[root@example.com ~]# apt-get install openssl openssl-dev
```

 Please be aware of the laws and regulations in your own country. Some countries do not allow usage of a strong cryptography. The author, publisher, and the developers of the OpenSSL and Nginx projects will not be held liable for any violations or law infringements on your part.

Now that you have installed all of the prerequisites, you are ready to download and compile the Nginx source code.

Downloading Nginx

This approach to the download process will lead us to discover the various resources at the disposal of server administrators—websites, communities, and wikis - all relating to Nginx. We will also quickly discuss the different version branches available, and eventually select the most appropriate one for our setup.

Websites and resources

Although Nginx is a relatively new and growing project, there are already a good number of resources available on the **World Wide Web (WWW)** along with an active community of administrators and developers.

The official website, `http://nginx.org`, currently serves as official documentation reference and provides links to download the latest version of the application source code and binaries. A wiki is also available at `http://wiki.nginx.org`, which offers a wide selection of additional resources, such as installation guides for various operating systems, tutorials related to the different modules of Nginx, and more.

There are several ways to get help in case you should need it. If you have a specific question, you may want to try posting on the Nginx forum: `http://forum.nginx.org`. An active community of users will answer your questions in no time. Additionally, the Nginx mailing list, which is relayed on the Nginx forum, will also prove to be an excellent resource for any question you may have. If you need direct assistance, there is always a group of regulars helping each other out on the IRC channel `#Nginx` on `irc.freenode.net`.

Another interesting source of information is the **blogosphere**. A simple query on your favorite search engine should return a good number of blog articles documenting Nginx, its configuration, and its modules.

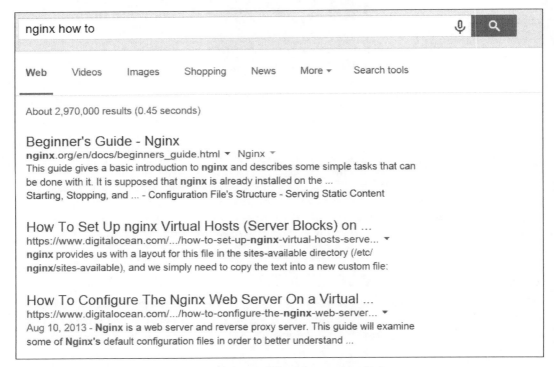

Personal websites and blogs documenting Nginx

It's now time to head over to the official website and get started with downloading the source code to compile and install Nginx. Before you do so, let's take a quick look at a summary of the available versions and features that come with them.

Version branches

Igor Sysoev, a talented Russian developer and server administrator, initiated the project back in 2002. Between the first release in 2004 and the current version, the market share of Nginx has been growing steadily. It now serves nearly 15 percent of websites on the Internet, according to a October 2015 http://netcraft.com survey. The features are plenty and render the application both powerful and flexible at the same time.

There are currently three version branches of the project:

- **Stable version**: This version is usually recommended, as it is approved by both developers and users, but is usually a little behind the mainline version in terms of bugfixes and features.

- **Mainline version**: This is the latest version available for download and comes with the newest developments and bug fixes. It was formerly known as the development version. Although it is generally solid enough to be installed on production servers, there is a tiny chance that you will run into the occasional bug. Thus, if you favor stability over novelty, going for the stable version is recommended.

- **Legacy version**: If, for some reason, you are interested in looking at the older versions, you will find them in the download area at http://www.nginx.org.

A recurring question regarding mainline versions is, *are they stable enough to be used on production servers?* Cliff Wells, original founder and maintainer of the http://www.nginx.org wiki, believes so: *I generally use and recommend the latest development version. It's only bitten me once!* Early adopters rarely report critical problems. It is up to you to select the version you will be using on your server, knowing that the instructions given in this book should be valid regardless of the release, as the Nginx developers have decided to maintain overall backward compatibility in new versions. You can find more information on version changes, new additions, and bug fixes in the dedicated change log page on the official website.

Features

As of the stable version 1.8.0, Nginx offers an impressive variety of features, which, contrary to what the title of this book indicates, are not all related to serving HTTP content. Here is a list of the main features of the web branch, quoted from the official website `http://www.nginx.org`:

- Serving static and index files; autoindexing; open file descriptor cache; accelerated reverse proxying with caching; load balancing and fault tolerance.

- Accelerated support with caching of FastCGI, uwsgi, **Simple Common Gateway Interface (SCGI)**, and memcached servers; load balancing and fault tolerance; modular architecture. Filters include gzipping, byte ranges, chunked responses, XSLT, SSI, and image transformation filter. Multiple SSI inclusions within a single page can be processed in parallel if they are handled by proxied or FastCGI/uwsgi/SCGI servers.

- SSL and TLS SNI support.

Nginx can also be used as a mail proxy server, although this aspect is not closely documented in the book:

- User redirection to IMAP/POP3 backend using an external HTTP authentication server

- User authentication using an external HTTP authentication server and connection redirection to an internal SMTP backend

- Authentication methods:
  - ° POP3: USER/PASS, APOP, AUTH LOGIN/PLAIN/CRAM-MD5
  - ° IMAP: LOGIN, AUTH LOGIN/PLAIN/CRAM-MD5
  - ° SMTP: AUTH LOGIN/PLAIN/CRAM-MD5

- SSL support

- STARTTLS and STLS support

Nginx is compatible with most computer architectures and operating systems, including Windows, Linux, Mac OS, FreeBSD, and Solaris. The application runs well on 32- and 64-bit architectures.

Downloading and extracting

Once you have made your choice about which version you will be using, head over to `http://www.nginx.org` and find the URL of the file you wish to download. Position yourself in your home directory, which will contain the source code to be compiled, and download the file using `wget`:

```
[alex@example.com ~]$ mkdir src && cd src

[alex@example.com src]$ wget http://nginx.org/download/nginx-1.8.0.tar.gz
```

We will be using version 1.8.0, the latest stable version as of April, 2015. Once downloaded, extract the archive contents in the current folder:

```
[alex@example.com src]$ tar zxf nginx-1.8.0.tar.gz
```

You have successfully downloaded and extracted Nginx. Now, the next step will be to configure the compilation process in order to obtain a binary that perfectly fits your operating system.

Configure options

There are usually three steps when building an application from source: the configuration, the compilation, and the installation. The configuration step allows you to select a number of options that will not be *editable* after the program is built, as it has a direct impact on the project binaries. Consequently, it is a very important stage that you need to follow carefully if you want to avoid surprises later, such as the lack of a specific module or having configuration files located in a random folder.

The process consists of appending certain switches to the `configure` command that comes with the source code. The three types of switches that you can activate will be covered later, but let's first study the easiest way to proceed.

The easy way

If, for some reason, you do not want to bother with the configuration step, such as for testing purposes or simply because you will be recompiling the application in the future, you may simply use the `configure` command with no switches. Execute the following three commands to build and install a working version of Nginx, starting with the `configure` command:

```
[alex@example.com nginx-1.8.0]# ./configure
```

Running this command should initiate a long procedure of verifications to ensure that your system contains all of the necessary components. If the configuration process fails, check the prerequisites section again, as it is the most common cause of errors. For information about why the command failed, you may also refer to the `objs/autoconf.err` file, which provides a more detailed report. The `make` command will compile the application. This step should not cause any errors as long as the configuration went fine.

```
[alex@example.com nginx-1.8.0]# make

[root@example.com nginx-1.8.0]# make install
```

This last step will copy the compiled files as well as other resources to the installation directory, by default, `/usr/local/nginx`. You may need to be logged in as root to perform this operation, depending on permissions granted to the `/usr/local` directory.

Again, if you build the application without configuring it, you take the risk of missing out on a lot of features, such as the optional modules and others that we are about to discover.

Path options

When running the `configure` command, you are offered the possibility to enable some switches that let you specify the directory or file paths for a variety of elements. Note that the options offered by the configuration switches may change according to the version you downloaded. The options listed below are valid with the stable version, as of release 1.8.0. If you use another version, run the `./configure --help` command to list the available switches for your setup.

Using a switch typically consists of appending some text to the command line, for instance, using the `--conf-path` switch:

```
[alex@example.com nginx-1.8.0]# ./configure --conf-path=/etc/nginx/nginx.
conf
```

Here is an exhaustive list of the configuration switches for configuring paths:

Switch	Usage	Default Value
`--prefix=`...	The base folder in which Nginx will be installed.	`/usr/local/nginx` Note: If you configure other switches using relative paths, they will connect to the base folder. For example, specifying `--conf-path=conf/nginx.conf` will result in your configuration file being found at `/usr/local/nginx/conf/nginx.conf`.
`--sbin-path=`...	The path where the Nginx binary file should be installed.	`<prefix>/sbin/nginx`.
`--conf-path=`...	The path of the main configuration file.	`<prefix>/conf/nginx.conf`.
`--error-log-path=`...	The location of your error log. Error logs can be configured very accurately in the configuration files. This path only applies in case you do not specify any error logging directive in your configuration.	`<prefix>/logs/error.log`.
`--pid-path=`...	The path of the Nginx `pid` file. You can specify the `pid` file path in the configuration file. If that's not the case, the value you specify for this switch will be used.	`<prefix>/logs/nginx.pid`. Note: The `pid` file is a simple text file containing the process identifier. It is placed in a predefined location so that other applications can easily find the `pid` of a running program.
`--lock-path=`...	The location of the lock file. Again, it can be specified in the configuration file, but if it isn't, this value will be used.	`<prefix>/logs/nginx.lock`. Note: The lock file allows other applications to determine whether or not the program is running. In the case of Nginx, it is used to make sure that the process is not started twice.

Switch	Usage	Default Value
`--with-perl_ modules_path=...`	Defines the path to the Perl modules. This switch must be defined if you want to include additional Perl modules.	
`--with-perl=...`	Path to the Perl binary file; used to execute Perl scripts. This path must be set if you want to allow execution of Perl scripts.	
`--http-log- path=...`	Defines the location of the access logs. This path is used only if the access log directive is unspecified in the configuration files.	`<prefix>/logs/access.log`.
`--http-client- body-temp-path=...`	Directory used for storing temporary files generated by client requests.	`<prefix>/client_body_temp`.
`--http-proxy- temp-path=...`	Location of the temporary files used by the proxy.	`<prefix>/proxy_temp`.
`--http-fastcgi- temp-path=...` `--http-uwsgi- temp-path=...` `--http-scgi- temp-path=...`	Location of the temporary files used by the HTTP FastCGI, uWSGI, and SCGI modules.	Respectively `<prefix>/ fastcgi_temp`, `<prefix>/uwsgi_temp`, and `<prefix>/scgi_temp`.
`--builddir=...`	Location of the application build.	

Prerequisites options

Prerequisites come in the form of libraries and binaries. You should, by now, have them all installed on your system. However, even though they are present on your system, there may be occasions where the configuration script is unable to locate them. The reasons might be diverse, for example, if they were installed in non-standard directories.

In order to solve such problems, you are given the option to specify the path of prerequisites using the following switches (miscellaneous prerequisite-related options have been grouped together):

Compiler options	Description
`--with-cc=...`	Specifies an alternate location for the C compiler.
`--with-cpp=...`	Specifies an alternate location for the C preprocessor.
`--with-cc-opt=...`	Defines additional options to be passed to the C compiler command line.
`--with-ld-opt=...`	Defines additional options to be passed to the C linker command line.
`--with-cpu-opt=...`	Specifies a different target processor architecture among the following values: `pentium`, `pentiumpro`, `pentium3`, `pentium4`, `athlon`, `opteron`, `sparc32`, `sparc64`, and `ppc64`.
PCRE options	**Description**
`--without-pcre`	Disables usage of the PCRE library. This setting is not recommended, as it will remove support for regular expressions, consequently disabling the Rewrite module.
`--with-pcre`	Forces usage of the PCRE library.
`--with-pcre=...`	Allows you to specify the path of the PCRE library source code.
`--with-pcre-opt=...`	Additional options to build the PCRE library.
`--with-pcre-jit=...`	Build PCRE with JIT compilation support.
MD5 options	**Description**
`--with-md5=...`	Specifies the path to the MD5 library sources.
`--with-md5-opt=...`	Additional options to build the MD5 library.
`--with-md5-asm`	Uses assembler sources for the MD5 library.
SHA1 options	**Description**
`--with-sha1=...`	Specifies the path to the SHA1 library sources.
`--with-sha1-opt=...`	Additional options to build the SHA1 library.
`--with-sha1-asm`	Uses assembler sources for the SHA1 library.
zlib options	**Description**
`--with-zlib=...`	Specifies the path to the `zlib` library sources.
`--with-zlib-opt=...`	Additional options to build the `zlib` library.
`--with-zlib-asm=...`	Uses assembler optimizations for the target architectures `pentium` and `pentiumpro`.

OpenSSL options	Description
`--with-openssl=...`	Specifies the path of the OpenSSL library sources.
`--with-openssl-opt=...`	Additional options to build the OpenSSL library.
Libatomic	**Description**
`--with-libatomic=...`	Forces usage of the `libatomic_ops` library on systems other than `x86`, `amd64`, and `sparc`. This library allows Nginx to perform atomic operations directly instead of resorting to lock files. Depending on your system, it may result in a decrease in `SEGFAULT` errors and possibly higher request serving rate.
`--with-libatomic=...`	Specifies the path of the `Libatomic` library sources.

Module options

Modules, which will be detailed in *Chapter 4, Module Configuration*, need to be selected before compiling the application. Some are enabled by default and some need to be enabled manually, as you will see in the following table.

Modules enabled by default

The following switches allow you to disable modules that are enabled by default:

Modules enabled by default	Description
`--without-http_charset_module`	Disables the `Charset` module to re-encode web pages.
`--without-http_gzip_module`	Disables the `Gzip` compression module.
`--without-http_ssi_module`	Disables the `Server Side Include` module.
`--without-http_userid_module`	Disables the `User ID` module providing user identification via cookies.
`--without-http_access_module`	Disables the `Access` module allowing access configuration for IP address ranges.
`--without-http_auth_basic_module`	Disables the `Basic Authentication` module.
`--without-http_autoindex_module`	Disables the `Automatic Index` module.
`--without-http_geo_module`	Disables the `Geo` module allowing you to define variables depending on IP address ranges.

Modules enabled by default	Description
`--without-http_map_module`	Disables the `Map` module that allows you to declare map blocks.
`--without-http_referer_module`	Disables the `Referer control` module.
`--without-http_rewrite_module`	Disables the `Rewrite` module.
`--without-http_proxy_module`	Disables the `Proxy` module to transfer requests to other servers.

`--without-http_fastcgi_module`
`--without-http_uwsgi_module`
`--without-http_scgi_module`
	Disables the FastCGI, uWSGI, or SCGI modules to interact with FastCGI, uWSGI, or SCGI processes respectively.

`--without-http_memcached_module`	Disables the `Memcached` module to interact with the *memcache daemon*.
`--without-http_limit_conn_module`	Disables the `Limit Connections` module to restrict resource usage according to defined zones.
`--without-http_limit_req_module`	Disables the `Limit Requests` module allowing you to limit the number of requests per user.
`--without-http_empty_gif_module`	Disables the `Empty GIF` module to serve a blank GIF image from memory.
`--without-http_browser_module`	Disables the `Browser` module to interpret the `User Agent` string.
`--without-http_upstream_ip_hash_module`	Disables the `Upstream IP Hash` module providing the `ip_hash` directive in upstream blocks.
`--without-http_upstream_least_conn_module`	Disables the `Upstream Least Conn` module providing the `least_conn` directive in upstream blocks.
`--without-http_split_clients_module`	Disables the `Split Clients` module

Modules disabled by default

The following switches allow you to enable modules that are disabled by default:

Modules disabled by default	Description
`--with-http_ssl_module`	Enables the `SSL` module to serve pages over HTTPS.
`--with-http_realip_module`	Enables the `Real IP` module to read the real IP address from the request header data.

Modules disabled by default	Description
`--with-http_addition_module`	Enables the `Addition` module, which lets you append or prepend data to the response body.
`--with-http_xslt_module`	Enables the `XSLT` module to apply XSL transformations to XML documents. Note: You will need to install the `libxml2` and `libxslt` libraries on your system if you wish to compile these modules.
`--with-http_image_filter_module`	Enables the `Image Filter` module that lets you apply modification to images. Note: You will need to install the `libgd` library on your system if you wish to compile this module.
`--with-http_geoip_module`	Enables the `GeoIP` module to achieve geographic localization using MaxMind's GeoIP binary database. Note: You will need to install the `libgeoip` library on your system if you wish to compile this module.
`--with-http_sub_module`	Enables the `Substitution` module to replace text in web pages.
`--with-http_dav_module`	Enables the `WebDAV` module (Distributed Authoring and Versioning via Web).
`--with-http_flv_module`	Enables the `FLV` module for special handling of `.flv` (Flash video) files.
`--with-http_mp4_module`	Enables the `MP4` module for special handling of `.mp4` video files.
`--with-http_gzip_static_module`	Enables the `Gzip Static` module to send pre-compressed files.
`--with-http_random_index_module`	Enables the `Random Index` module to pick a random file as the directory index.
`--with-http_secure_link_module`	Enables the `Secure Link` module to check the presence of a keyword in the URL.
`--with-http_stub_status_module`	Enables the `Stub Status` module, which generates a server statistics and information page.
`--with-google_perftools_module`	Enables the `Google Performance Tools` module.
`--with-http_degradation_module`	Enables the `Degradation` module that controls the behavior of your server depending on current resource usage.
`--with-http_perl_module`	Enables the `Perl` module, allowing you to insert Perl code directly into your Nginx configuration files and to make Perl calls from SSI.

Modules disabled by default	Description
--with-http_spdy_module	Enables the SPDY module allowing clients to communicate with Nginx over the SPDY protocol.
--with-http_gunzip_module	Enables the Gunzip module, which offers to decompress a gzip-encoded response from a backend server before forwarding it to the client.
--with-http_auth_request_ module	Enables the Auth Request module. This module allows you to delegate the HTTP authentication mechanism to a backend server via a subrequest. The status code of the response can be stored in a variable.

Miscellaneous options

Other options are available in the configuration script, for example, regarding the mail server proxy feature or event management. These have been enlisted as follows:

Mail server proxy options	Description
--with-mail	Enables mail server proxy module. Supports POP3, IMAP4, SMTP. It is disabled by default.
--with-mail_ssl_module	Enables SSL support for the mail server proxy. It is disabled by default.
--without-mail_pop3_module	Disables the POP3 module for the mail server proxy. It is enabled by default when the mail server proxy module is enabled.
--without-mail_imap_module	Disables the IMAP4 module for the mail server proxy. It is enabled by default when the mail server proxy module is enabled.
--without-mail_smtp_module	Disables the SMTP module for the mail server proxy. It is enabled by default when the mail server proxy module is enabled.
Event management:	Allows you to select the event notification system for the Nginx sequencer. For advanced users only.
--with-rtsig_module	Enables the rtsig module to use rtsig as event notification mechanism.
--with-select_module	Enables the select module to use select as event notification mechanism. By default, this module is enabled unless a better method is found on the system—kqueue, epoll, rtsig, or poll.
--without-select_module	Disables the select module.

Mail server proxy options	Description
`--with-poll_module`	Enables the `poll` module to use poll as event notification mechanism. By default, this module is enabled if available, unless a better method is found on the system— `kqueue`, `epoll`, or `rtsig`.
`--without-poll_module`	Disables the `poll` module.

User and group options	Description
`--user=...`	Default user account to start the Nginx worker processes. This setting is used only if you do not specify the user directive in the configuration file.
`--group=...`	Default user group to start the Nginx worker processes. This setting is used only if you do not specify the group directive in the configuration file.

Other options	Description
`--with-ipv6`	Enables IPv6 support.
`--without-http`	Disables the HTTP server.
`--without-http-cache`	Disables HTTP caching features.
`--add-module=PATH`	Adds a third-party module to the compile process by specifying its path. This switch can be repeated indefinitely if you wish to compile multiple modules.
`--with-debug`	Enables additional debugging information to be logged.
`--with-file-aio`	Enables support for AIO (Asynchronous IO disk operations).

Configuration examples

Here are a few examples of configuration commands that may be used for various cases. In these examples, the path switches have been omitted, as they are specific to each system and leaving the default values may simply function correctly.

Be aware that these configurations do not include additional third-party modules. Please refer to *Chapter 4, Module Configuration*, for more information about installing add-ons.

About the prefix switch

During the configuration, you should take particular care of the `--prefix` switch. Many of the future configuration directives (that will be approached in further chapters) will be based on the path you select at this point. While it is not a definitive problem since absolute paths can still be employed, you should know that the prefix cannot be changed once the binaries have been compiled.

There is also another issue that you may run into if you plan to keep up with the times and update Nginx as new versions are released. The default prefix (if you do not override the setting by using the `--prefix` switch) is `/usr/local/nginx`. This is a path that does not include the version number. Consequently, when you upgrade Nginx, if you do not specify a different prefix, the new install files will override the previous ones, which among other problems, could potentially erase your currently running binaries.

It is thus recommended to use a different prefix for each version you will be using. Use the following command to specify a prefix that is specific to version 1.8.0:

```
./configure --prefix=/usr/local/nginx-1.8.0
```

Additionally, to make future changes simpler, you may create a symbolic link `/usr/local/nginx` pointing to `/usr/local/nginx-1.8.0`. Once you upgrade, you can update the link to make it point to `/usr/local/nginx-newer.version`. This will allow the `init` script to always make use of the latest installed version of Nginx.

Regular HTTP and HTTPS servers

The first example describes a situation where the most important features and modules to serve HTTP and HTTPS content are enabled, and the mail-related options are disabled:

```
./configure --user=www-data --group=www-data --with-http_ssl_module
--with-http_realip_module
```

As you can see, the command is rather simple and most switches have been left out. The reason for this is that the default configuration is rather efficient, and most of the important modules are enabled. You will only need to include the `http_ssl` module to serve HTTPS content, and optionally, the *real IP* module to retrieve your visitors' IP addresses in case you are running Nginx as backend server.

All modules enabled

The next situation includes all available modules, and it is up to you whether you want to use them or not at runtime:

```
./configure --user=www-data --group=www-data --with-http_ssl_module
--with-http_realip_module --with-http_addition_module --with-http_xslt_
module --with-http_image_filter_module --with-http_geoip_module --with-
http_sub_module --with-http_dav_module --with-http_flv_module --with-
http_mp4_module --with-http_gzip_static_module --with-http_random_index_
module --with-http_secure_link_module --with-http_stub_status_module
--with-http_perl_module --with-http_degradation_module --with-http_spdy_
module --with-http_gunzip_module --with-http_auth_request_module
```

This configuration opens up a wide range of possible configuration options. *Chapter 3*, *HTTP Configuration*, to *Chapter 6*, *Apache and Nginx Together*, provide more detailed information on module configuration.

With this setup, all optional modules are enabled, thus requiring additional libraries to be installed — libgeoip for the Geo IP module, libgd for the Image Filter module, libxml2, and libxslt for the XSLT module. You may install those prerequisites using your system package manager, for example, by running yum install libxml2 or apt-get install libxml2.

Mail server proxy

This last build configuration is somewhat special, as it is dedicated to enabling mail server proxy features — a darker and less documented side of Nginx. You can enable all mail related features through the following command:

```
./configure --user=www-data --group=www-data --with-mail.--with-mail_ssl_
module
```

If you wish to completely disable the HTTP serving features and only dedicate Nginx to mail proxying, you may add the --without-http switch.

 Note that in the preceding commands, the user and group used to run the Nginx worker processes will be www-data, which implies that this user and group must exist on your system.

Build configuration issues

In some cases, the configure command may fail — after a long list of checks, you may receive a few error messages on your terminal. In most (if not all) cases, these errors are related to missing prerequisites or unspecified paths.

In such cases, proceed with the following verifications carefully to make sure you have all it takes to compile the application, and optionally, consult the `objs/autoconf.err` file for more details about the compilation problem. This file is generated during the configure process and will tell you exactly which part of the process failed.

Make sure you installed the prerequisites

There are basically four main prerequisites: GCC, PCRE, zlib, and OpenSSL. The last three are libraries that must be installed in two packages: the library itself and its development sources. Make sure you have installed both for each of them. Refer to the prerequisites section at the beginning of this chapter for additional information. Note that other prerequisites such as LibXML2 or LibXSLT may be required to enable extra modules (for example, in the case of the HTTP XSLT module).

If you are positive that all of the prerequisites were installed correctly, perhaps the issue comes from the fact that the `configure` script is unable to locate the prerequisite files. In that case, make sure that you include the configuration switches related to file paths, as described earlier.

For example, the following switch allows you to specify the location of the OpenSSL library files:

```
./configure [...] --with-openssl=/usr/lib64
```

The OpenSSL library file will be looked for in the specified folder.

Directories exist and must be writable

Always remember to check the obvious; everyone makes even the simplest of mistakes sooner or later. Make sure that the directory you placed the Nginx files in has *read and write* permissions for the user running the configuration and compilation scripts. Also ensure that all paths specified in the `configure` script switches are existing, valid paths.

Compiling and installing the program

The configuration process is of utmost importance — it generates a makefile for the application depending on the selected switches and performs a long list of requirement checks on your system. Once the `configure` script is successfully executed, you can proceed with compiling Nginx.

Compiling the project equates to executing the `make` command in the project source directory:

```
[alex@example.com nginx-1.8.0]$ make
```

A successful build should result in the appearance of a final message: `make[1]: leaving directory`. This should be followed by the project source path.

Again, problems might occur at compile time. Most of these problems can originate in missing prerequisites or the specification of invalid paths. If this occurs, run the `configure` command again and triple-check the switches and all of the prerequisite options. It may also so happen that you downloaded an overly recent version of the prerequisites, which may not be backwards compatible. In such cases, the best option is to visit the official website of the missing component and download an older version.

If the compilation process was successful, you are ready for the next step: installing the application. The following command must be executed with root privileges:

```
[root@example.com nginx-1.8.0]# make install
```

The `make install` command executes the `install` section of the `make` file. In other words, it performs a few simple operations, such as copying binaries and configuration files to the specified `install` folder. It also creates directories to store log and HTML files if these do not already exist. The `make install` step is not generally a source of problems, unless your system encounters an exceptional error, such as a lack of storage space or memory.

 You may require root privileges to install the application in the `/usr/local/` folder, depending on the folder permissions.

Controlling the Nginx service

At this stage, you should have successfully built and installed Nginx. The default location for the output files is `/usr/local/nginx`, so we will be basing future examples on this.

Daemons and services

The next step is obviously run Nginx for the first time. However, before doing so, it's important to understand the nature of this application. There are two types of computer applications—those that require immediate user input, thus running in the *foreground*, and those that do not, thus running in the *background*. Nginx is of the latter type, often referred to as **daemon**. Daemon names usually come with a trailing "d" and a couple of examples can be mentioned here—`httpd`, the HTTP server daemon, is the name given to Apache under several Linux distributions; `named`, the name server daemon; or `crond` the task scheduler—although, as you will notice, this is not the case for Nginx. When started from the command line, a daemon immediately returns the prompt, and in most cases, does not even bother outputting data to the terminal.

Consequently, when starting Nginx, you will not see any text appear on the screen, and the prompt will return immediately. While this might seem startling, it is, on the contrary, a good sign. It means the daemon was started correctly and the configuration did not contain any errors.

User and group

It is of utmost importance to understand the process architecture of Nginx, and particularly the user and groups under which its various processes run. A very common source of trouble when setting up Nginx is invalid file access permissions—due to a user or group misconfiguration, you often end up getting **403 Forbidden** HTTP errors because Nginx cannot access the requested files.

There are two levels of processes with possibly different permission sets:

- The **Nginx master process**: This should be started as root. In most Unix-like systems, processes started with the root account are allowed to open TCP sockets on any port, whereas other users can only open listening sockets on a port above 1024. If you do not start Nginx as root, standard ports such as 80 or 443 will not be accessible. Note that the `user` directive that allows you to specify a different user and group for the worker processes will not be taken into consideration for the master process.

- The **Nginx worker processes**: These are automatically spawned by the master process under the account you specified in the configuration file with the user directive (detailed in *Chapter 2, Basic Nginx Configuration*). The configuration setting takes precedence over the configuration switch you may have specified at compile time. If you did not specify any of those, the worker processes will be started as user `nobody` and group `nobody` (or `nogroup` depending on your OS).

Nginx command-line switches

The Nginx binary accepts command-line arguments to perform various operations, among which is controlling the background processes. To get the full list of commands, you may invoke the help screen using the following commands:

```
[alex@example.com ~]$ cd /usr/local/nginx/sbin
[alex@example.com sbin]$ ./nginx -h
```

The next few sections will describe the purpose of these switches. Some allow you to control the daemon and some let you perform various operations on the application configuration.

Starting and stopping the daemon

You can start Nginx by running the Nginx binary without any switches. If the daemon is already running, a message will show up indicating that a socket is already listening on the specified port:

```
[emerg]: bind() to 0.0.0.0:80 failed (98: Address already in use) [...]
[emerg]: still could not bind().
```

Beyond this point, you may control the daemon by stopping it, restarting it, or simply reloading its configuration. Controlling is done by sending signals to the process using the nginx -s command.

Command	Description
nginx -s stop	Stops the daemon immediately (using the TERM signal).
nginx -s quit	Stops the daemon gracefully (using the QUIT signal).
nginx -s reopen	Reopens the log files.
nginx -s reload	Reloads the configuration.

Note that when starting the daemon, stopping it, or performing any of the preceding operations, the configuration file is first *parsed* and verified. If the configuration is invalid, whatever command you have submitted will fail, even when trying to stop the daemon. In other words, in some cases you will not be able to even stop Nginx if the configuration file is invalid.

An alternate way to terminate the process, in desperate cases only, is to use the kill or killall commands with root privileges:

```
[root@example.com ~]# killall nginx
```

Testing the configuration

As you can imagine, testing the validity of your configuration will become crucial if you constantly tweak your server setup . The slightest mistake in any of the configuration files can result in a loss of control over the service—you will then be unable to stop it via regular `init` control commands, and obviously, it will refuse to start again.

Consequently, the following command will be useful to you in many occasions; it allows you to check the syntax, validity, and integrity of your configuration:

```
[alex@example.com ~]$ /usr/local/nginx/sbin/nginx -t
```

The -t switch stands for *test configuration*. Nginx will parse the configuration anew and let you know whether it is valid or not. A valid configuration file does not necessarily mean Nginx will start, though, as there might be additional problems such as socket issues, invalid paths, or incorrect access permissions.

Obviously, manipulating your configuration files while your server is in production is a dangerous thing to do and should be avoided when possible. The best practice, in this case, is to place your new configuration into a separate temporary file and run the test on that file. Nginx makes it possible by offering the -c switch:

```
[alex@example.com sbin]$ ./nginx -t -c /home/alex/test.conf
```

This command will parse /home/alex/test.conf and make sure it is a valid Nginx configuration file. When you are done, after making sure that your new file is valid, proceed to replacing your current configuration file and reload the server configuration:

```
[alex@example.com sbin]$ cp -i /home/alex/test.conf /usr/local/nginx/
conf/nginx.conf
cp: erase 'nginx.conf' ? yes
[alex@example.com sbin]$ ./nginx -s reload
```

Other switches

Another switch that might come in handy in many situations is -v. Not only does it tell you the current Nginx build version, but more importantly, it also reminds you about the arguments that you used during the configuration step—in other words, the command switches that you passed to the configure script before compilation.

```
[alex@example.com sbin]$ ./nginx -V
nginx version: nginx/1.8.0 (Ubuntu)
built by gcc 4.8.4 (Ubuntu 4.8.4-2ubuntu1~14.04)
```

```
TLS SNI support enabled
configure arguments: --with-http_ssl_module
```

In this case, Nginx was configured with the `--with-http_ssl_module` switch only.

Why is this so important? Well, if you ever try to use a module that was not included with the `configure` script during the precompilation process, the directive enabling the module will result in a configuration error. Your first reaction will be to wonder where the syntax error comes from. Your second reaction will be to wonder if you even built the module in the first place! Running `nginx -V` will answer this question.

Additionally, the `-g` option lets you specify additional configuration directives in case they were not included in the configuration file:

```
[alex@example.com sbin]$ ./nginx -g "timer_resolution 200ms";
```

Adding Nginx as a system service

In this section, we will create a script that will transform the Nginx daemon into an actual system service. This will result mainly in two outcomes: the daemon will be controllable using standard commands, and more importantly, it will be launched automatically on system startup and stopped on system shutdown.

System V scripts

Most Linux-based operating systems to date use a System-V style *init daemon*. In other words, their startup process is managed by a daemon called `init`, which functions in a way that is inherited from the old **System V** Unix-based operating system.

This daemon functions on the principle of *runlevels*, which represent the state of the computer. Here is a table representing the various runlevels and their signification:

Runlevel	State
0	System is halted
1	Single-user mode (rescue mode)
2	Multiuser mode, without NFS support
3	Full multiuser mode
4	Not used
5	Graphical interface mode
6	System reboot

You can manually initiate a runlevel transition: use the `telinit 0` command to shut down your computer or `telinit 6` to reboot it.

For each runlevel transition, a set of services are executed. This is the key concept to understand here: when your computer is stopped, its runlevel is 0. When you turn it on, there will be a transition from runlevel 0 to the default computer startup runlevel. The default startup runlevel is defined by your own system configuration (in the `/etc/inittab` file), and the default value depends on the distribution you are using. Debian and Ubuntu use runlevel 2, Red Hat and Fedora use runlevel 3 or 5, CentOS and Gentoo use runlevel 3, and so on — the list is long.

So, in summary, when you start your computer running CentOS, it operates a transition from runlevel 0 to runlevel 3. That transition consists of starting all services that are scheduled for runlevel 3. The question that remains is how to schedule a service to be started at a specific runlevel.

Name	Ext	Size	Changed	Rights	Owner
rc0.d			15/01/2015 18:16:55	rwxr-xr-x	root
rc1.d			15/01/2015 18:16:55	rwxr-xr-x	root
rc2.d			15/01/2015 18:16:55	rwxr-xr-x	root
rc3.d			15/01/2015 18:16:55	rwxr-xr-x	root
rc4.d			15/01/2015 18:16:55	rwxr-xr-x	root
rc5.d			15/01/2015 18:16:55	rwxr-xr-x	root
rc6.d			15/01/2015 18:16:55	rwxr-xr-x	root
rcS.d			15/01/2015 16:37:38	rwxr-xr-x	root

For each runlevel, there is a directory containing scripts to be executed. If you enter these directories (`rc0.d`, `rc1.d`, to `rc6.d`), you will not find actual files, but rather symbolic links referring to scripts located in the `init.d` directory. Service startup scripts will indeed be placed in `init.d`, and links will be created by tools placing them in the proper directories.

About init scripts

An `init` script, also known as a service startup script or even *sysv script*, is a shell script respecting a certain standard. The script controls a daemon application by responding to commands such as `start`, `stop`, and others, which are triggered at two levels. First, when the computer starts, if the service is scheduled to be started for the system runlevel, the `init` daemon will run the script with the `start` argument. The other possibility for you is to manually execute the script by calling it from the shell:

```
[root@example.com ~]# service httpd start
```

Or if your system does not come with the `service` command:

```
[root@example.com ~]# /etc/init.d/httpd start
```

The script must accept at least the `start`, `stop`, `restart`, `force-reload`, and `status` commands, as they will be used by the system to respectively start up, shut down, restart, forcefully reload the service, or inquire its status. However, to enlarge your field of action as a system administrator, it is often interesting to provide further options, such as a `reload` argument to reload the service configuration or a `try-restart` argument to stop and start the service again.

Note that since `service httpd start` and `/etc/init.d/httpd start` essentially do the same thing, with the exception that the second command will work on all operating systems, we will make no further mention of the `service` command and will exclusively use the `/etc/init.d/` method.

The init script for Debian-based distributions

We will thus create a shell script to start and stop our Nginx daemon and also to restart and reload it. The purpose here is not to discuss Linux shell script programming, so we will merely provide the source code of an existing `init` script, along with some comments to help you understand it.

Due to differences in the format of the `init` scripts from one distribution to another, we will discover two separate scripts here. The first one is meant for Debian-based distributions such as Debian, Ubuntu, Knoppix, and so forth.

First, create a file called `nginx` with the text editor of your choice, and save it in the `/etc/init.d/` directory (on some systems, `/etc/init.d/` is actually a symbolic link to `/etc/rc.d/init.d/`). In the file you just created, insert the script provided in the code bundle supplied with this book. Make sure that you change the paths to make them correspond to your actual setup.

You will need root permissions to save the script into the `init.d` directory.

 The complete `init` script for Debian-based distributions can be found in the code bundle.

The init script for Red Hat–based distributions

Due to the system tools, shell programming functions, and specific formatting that it requires, the preceding script is only compatible with Debian-based distributions. If your server is operated by a Red Hat–based distribution such as CentOS, Fedora, and many more, you will need an entirely different script.

 The complete `init` script for Red Hat–based distributions can be found in the code bundle.

Installing the script

Placing the file in the `init.d` directory does not complete our work. There are additional steps that will be required to enable the service. First, make the script executable. So far, it is only a piece of text that the system refuses to run. Granting executable permissions on the script is done with the `chmod` command:

```
[root@example.com ~]# chmod +x /etc/init.d/nginx
```

Note that if you created the file as the root user, you will need to be logged in as root to change the file permissions.

At this point, you should already be able to start the service using `service nginx start` or `/etc/init.d/nginx start`, as well as stopping, restarting, or reloading the service.

The last step here will be to make it so the script is automatically started at the proper runlevels. Unfortunately, doing this entirely depends on what operating system you are using. We will cover the two most popular families—Debian, Ubuntu, or other Debian-based distributions and Red Hat/Fedora/CentOS, or other Red Hat–derived systems.

Debian-based distributions

For the Debian-based distribution, a simple command will enable the `init` script for the system runlevel:

```
[root@example.com ~]# update-rc.d -f nginx defaults
```

This command will create links in the default system `runlevel` folders. For the reboot and shutdown runlevels, the script will be executed with the `stop` argument; for all other runlevels, the script will be executed with `start`. You can now restart your system and see your Nginx service being launched during the boot sequence.

Red Hat–based distributions

For the Red Hat–based systems family, the command differs, but you get an additional tool to manage system startup. Adding the service can be done via the following command:

```
[root@example.com ~]# chkconfig nginx on
```

Once that is done, you can then verify the runlevels for the service:

```
[root@example.com ~]# chkconfig --list nginx
Nginx  0:off   1:off   2:on    3:off   4:on    5:on    6:off
```

Another tool will be useful to you to manage system services, namely, `ntsysv`. It lists all services scheduled to be executed on system startup and allows you to enable or disable them at will.

 The tool `ntsysv` requires root privileges to be executed.

Note that prior to using `ntsysv`, you must first run the `chkconfig nginx on` command, otherwise Nginx will not appear in the list of services.

Downloading the example code

You can download the example code files for all Packt books you have purchased from your account at http://www.packtpub.com. If you purchased this book elsewhere, you can visit http://www.packtpub.com/support and register to have the files e-mailed to you directly.

NGINX Plus

Since mid-2013, NGINX, Inc., the company behind the Nginx project, also offers a paid subscription called NGINX Plus. The announcement came as a surprise for the open source community, but several companies quickly jumped on the bandwagon and reported amazing improvements in terms of performance and scalability after using NGINX Plus.

> *NGINX, Inc., the high performance web company, today announced the availability of NGINX Plus, a fully-supported version of the popular NGINX open source software complete with advanced features and offered with professional services. The product is developed and supported by the core engineering team at Nginx Inc., and is available immediately on a subscription basis.*
>
> *As business requirements continue to evolve rapidly, such as the shift to mobile and the explosion of dynamic content on the Web, CIOs are continuously looking for opportunities to increase application performance and development agility, while reducing dependencies on their infrastructure. NGINX Plus provides a flexible, scalable, uniformly applicable solution that was purpose built for these modern, distributed application architectures.*

Considering the pricing plans ($1,500 per year per instance) and the additional features made available, this platform is indeed clearly aimed at large corporations looking to integrate Nginx into their global architecture seamlessly and effortlessly. Professional support from the Nginx team is included and discounts can be offered for multiple-instance subscriptions. This book covers the open source version of Nginx only and does not detail advanced functionality offered by NGINX Plus. For more information about the paid subscription, take a look at http://www.nginx.com.

Summary

This chapter covered a number of critical steps. You first made sure that your system contained all the required components for compiling Nginx. You then proceeded to select the proper version branch for your usage—will you be using the stable version or a more advanced, yet potentially less stable, one? After downloading the source and configuring the compilation process by enabling or disabling features and modules such as SSL, GeoIP, and more, you compiled the application and installed it on the system in the directory of your choice. You created an *init script* and modified the system boot sequence to schedule for the service to be started.

From this point on, Nginx is installed on your server and automatically starts with the system. Your web server is functional, though it does not yet answer the most basic functionality: serving a website. The first step towards hosting a website will be to prepare a suitable configuration file. The next chapter will cover the basic configuration of Nginx and will teach you how to optimize performance based on the expected audience and system resources.

2
Basic Nginx Configuration

In this chapter, we will establish an appropriate configuration for your web server. For this purpose, we begin to discover the syntax that is used in the Nginx configuration files. Then, we need to understand the various directives that will let you prepare and optimize your web server for the different traffic patterns and hardware setups. Finally, we will create some test pages to make sure that everything has been done correctly and that the configuration is valid. We will only approach the basic configuration directives here. The following chapters will explore more advanced topics such as HTTP module configuration and usage, creating virtual hosts, and more.

This chapter covers the following topics:

- The presentation of the configuration syntax
- An overview of basic configuration directives
- Establishing an appropriate configuration for your profile
- Serving a test website
- Testing and maintaining your web server

Configuration file syntax

A configuration file is generally a text file that is edited by the administrator and parsed by a program. By specifying a set of values, you define the behavior of the program. In Linux-based operating systems, a large share of the applications rely on vast, complex configuration files, which often turn out to be a nightmare to manage. Apache, Qmail, and Bind—all these names bring up bad memories in the mind of a Linux system administrator. The fact is that all these applications use their own configuration file with different syntaxes and styles. PHP works with a Windows-style .ini file, *sendmail* uses the *M4 macro-processor* to compile the configuration files, *Zabbix* pulls its configuration from a MySQL database, and so on. There is, unfortunately, no well-established standard, and the same applies to Nginx—you will be required to study a new syntax with its own particularities and its own vocabulary.

Why isn't there a universal standard for configuration file syntax? A possible explanation by
Randall Munroe (xkcd.com – reproduced with authorization)

On the other hand (and this is one of its advantages), configuring Nginx turns out to be rather simple—at least in comparison to Apache or other mainstream web servers. There are only a few mechanisms that need to be mastered—directives, blocks, and the overall logical structure. Most of the actual configuration process will consist of writing values for the directives.

Configuration directives

The Nginx configuration file can be described as a list of directives organized in a logical structure. The entire behavior of the application is defined by the values that you give to those directives.

By default, Nginx makes use of one main configuration file. The path of this file was defined in the steps described in *Chapter 1, Downloading and Installing Nginx*, under the *Build configuration* section. If you did not edit the configuration file path and prefix options, it should be located at `/usr/local/nginx/conf/nginx.conf`. However, if you installed Nginx with a package manager, your configuration file will likely be located in the `/etc/nginx` folder, and the contents of the file may be quite different from the version that comes in the original Nginx source code package. Now, let's take a quick peek at the first few lines of this initial setup:

```
nginx.conf - Notepad
File  Edit  Format  View  Help

#user    nobody;
worker_processes    1;

#error_log    logs/error.log;
#error_log    logs/error.log    notice;
#error_log    logs/error.log    info;

#pid          logs/nginx.pid;


events {
    worker_connections    1024;
}


http {
    include          mime.types;
```

The default configuration file bundled with the Nginx 1.8.0 source code package

Let's take a closer look at the first two lines:

```
#user nobody;
worker_processes 1;
```

As you can probably make out from the # character, the first line is a *comment*. In other words, a piece of text that is not interpreted and has no value whatsoever. Its sole purpose is to be read by whoever opens the file, or to temporarily disable parts of an existing configuration section. You may use the # character at the beginning of a line or following a directive.

The second line is an actual statement—a *directive*. The first bit (`worker_processes`) represents a setting key to which you append one or more values. In this case, the value is `1`, indicating that Nginx should function with a single worker process (more information about this particular directive is given in later sections).

Directives always end with a semicolon (;).

Each directive has a unique meaning and defines a particular feature of the application. It may also have a particular syntax. For example, the `worker_process` directive only accepts one numeric value, whereas the `user` directive lets you specify up to two character strings—one for the *user account* (that the Nginx worker processes should run as) and a second for the *user group*.

Nginx works in a modular way, and as such, each module comes with a specific set of directives. The most fundamental directives are part of the Nginx Core module and will be detailed in this chapter. As for the directives brought in by other modules, they will be explored in the later chapters.

Organization and inclusions

In the preceding screenshot, you may have noticed a particular directive—`include`.

```
include mime.types;
```

As the name suggests, this directive will perform an inclusion of the specified file. In other words, the contents of the file will be inserted at this exact location. Here is a practical example that will help you understand this concept:

`nginx.conf`:

```
user nginx nginx;
worker_processes 4;
include other_settings.conf;
```

`other_settings.conf`:

```
error_log logs/error.log;
pid logs/nginx.pid;
```

The final result, as interpreted by Nginx, is as follows:

```
user nginx nginx;
worker_processes 4;
error_log logs/error.log;
pid logs/nginx.pid;
```

Inclusions are processed recursively. In this case, you have the possibility to use the `include` directive again in the `other_settings.conf` file in order to include yet another file.

In the initial configuration setup, there are two files in use—`nginx.conf` and `mime.types`. However, in the case of a more advanced configuration, there may be five or more files, as described in the following table:

Standard name	Description
`nginx.conf`	Base configuration of the application.
`mime.types`	A list of file extensions and their associated MIME types.
`fastcgi_params`	Fast CGI-related configuration.
`proxy.conf`	Proxy-related configuration.
`sites.conf`	Configuration of the websites served by Nginx, also known as virtual hosts. It's recommended to create separate files for each domain.

These filenames were defined conventionally; nothing actually prevents you from regrouping your FastCGI and proxy settings into a common file named `proxy_and_fastcgi_config.conf`.

Note that the `include` directive supports filename `globbing`, that is, filenames referenced with the * wildcard, where * may match zero, one, or more consecutive characters:

```
include sites/*.conf;
```

This will include all the files with a name that ends with `.conf` in the `sites` folder. This mechanism allows you to create a separate file for each of your websites and include them all at once.

Be careful when including a file—if the specified file does not exist, the configuration checks will fail, and Nginx will not start:

```
[alex@example sbin]# ./nginx -t
[emerg]: open() "/usr/local/nginx/conf/dummyfile.conf" failed (2: No such file or directory) in /usr/local/nginx/conf/nginx.conf:48
```

The previous statement is not true for the inclusions with wildcards. If you insert `include dummy*.conf` in your configuration file and test it (whether there is any file matching this pattern on your system or not), the following is what should happen:

```
[alex@example sbin]# ./nginx -t

the configuration file /usr/local/nginx/conf/nginx.conf syntax is ok
configuration file /usr/local/nginx/conf/nginx.conf test is successful
```

Directive blocks

Directives are brought in by modules—if you activate a new module, a specific set of directives becomes available. Modules may also enable *directive blocks*, which allow for a logical construction of the configuration:

```
events {
    worker_connections 1024;
}
```

The `events` block that you can find in the default configuration file is brought in by the *Events module*. The directives that the module enables can only be used within that block—in the preceding example, `worker_connections` will only make sense in the context of the `events` block. On the other hand, some directives must be placed at the root of the configuration file, because they have a global effect on the server. The root of the configuration file is also known as the `main` block.

For the most part, blocks can be nested into each other, following a specific logic. The following sequence demonstrates the structure of a simple website setup, making use of nested blocks:

```
http {
    server {
        listen 80;
        server_name example.com;
        access_log /var/log/nginx/example.com.log;
        location ^~ /admin/ {
            index index.php;
        }
    }
}
```

The topmost directive block is the `http` block, in which you may declare a variety of configuration directives as well as one or more `server` blocks. A `server` block allows you to configure a virtual host, in other words, a website that is to be hosted on your machine. The `server` block, in this example, contains some configuration that applies to all HTTP requests with a `Host` header exactly matching `example.com`.

Within this `server` block, you may insert one or more `location` blocks. These allow you to enable settings only when the requested URI matches the specified path. More information is provided in the *The Location block* section of *Chapter 3, HTTP Configuration*.

Last but not least, configuration is inherited within children blocks. The `access_log` directive (defined at the `server` block level in this example) specifies that all HTTP requests for this server should be logged into a text file. This is still true within the `location` child block, although you have the option of disabling it by reusing the `access_log` directive:

```
[...]
    location ^~ /admin/ {
        index index.php;
        access_log off;
    }
[...]
```

In this case, logging will be enabled everywhere on the website except for the `/admin/` location path. The value set for the `access_log` directive at the `server` block level is overridden by the one at the `location` block level.

Advanced language rules

There are a number of important observations regarding the Nginx configuration file syntax. These will help you understand certain language rules that may seem confusing if you have never worked with Nginx before.

Directives accept specific syntaxes

You may indeed stumble upon complex syntaxes that can be confusing at first sight, like the following one:

```
rewrite ^/(.*)\.(png|jpg|gif)$ /image.php? file=$1&format=$2 last;
```

Syntaxes are directive-specific. While the `root` directive only accepts a simple character string defining the folder containing the files that should be served for a website, the `location` block and the `rewrite` directive support complex expressions in order to match particular patterns. Some other directives such as `listen` accept up to 17 different parameters. Syntaxes will be explained along with directives in their respective chapters.

Later on, we will detail a module (the *Rewrite* module) which allows for a much more advanced logical structure through the `if`, `set`, `break`, and `return` blocks and directives, and the use of variables. With all these new elements, configuration files will begin to look like programming scripts. You will find that, the more modules we discover, the richer the syntax becomes.

Diminutives in directive values

Finally, you may use the following diminutives for specifying a file size in the context of a directive value:

- k or K: Kilobytes
- m or M: Megabytes
- g or G: Gigabytes

As a result, the following three syntaxes are correct and equal:

```
client_max_body_size 2G;
client_max_body_size 2048M;
client_max_body_size 2097152k;
```

Note that Nginx does not allow you to insert the same directive more than once within the same block (although there are a few exceptions, such as `allow` or `deny`); should you do so, the configuration will be considered invalid, and Nginx will refuse to start up or reload.

Additionally, when specifying a time value, you may use the following shortcuts:

- ms: Milliseconds
- s: Seconds
- m: Minutes
- h: Hours
- d: Days
- w: Weeks
- M: Months (30 days)
- y: Years (365 days)

This becomes especially useful in the case of directives accepting a period of time as a value:

```
client_body_timeout 3m;
client_body_timeout 180s;
client_body_timeout 180;
```

Note that the default time unit is seconds; the last two lines in the preceding list thus result in an identical behavior. It is also possible to combine two values with different units:

```
client_body_timeout 1m30s;
client_body_timeout '1m 30s 500ms';
```

The latter variant is enclosed in quotes since values are separated by spaces.

Variables

Modules also provide variables that can be used in the definition of directive values. For example, the Nginx HTTP core module defines the `$nginx_version` variable. Variables in Nginx always start with $ — the dollar sign. When setting the `log_format` directive, you may include all kinds of variables in the format string:

```
[...]
location ^~ /admin/ {
    access_log logs/main.log;
    log_format main '$pid - $nginx_version - $remote_addr';
}
[...]
```

Note that some directives do not allow you to use variables:

```
error_log logs/error-$nginx_version.log;
```

The preceding directive is valid, syntax-wise. However, it simply generates a file named `error-$nginx_version.log` without parsing the variable.

String values

Character strings that you use as directive values can be written in three forms. First, you may enter the value without quotes:

```
root /home/example.com/www;
```

However, if you want to use a particular character, such as a blank space (" "), a semicolon (;), or curly braces ({ and }), you will need to either prefix the said character with a backslash (\), or enclose the entire value in single or double quotes:

```
root '/home/example.com/my web pages';
```

In Nginx, it makes no difference whether you use single or double quotes. Note that the variables inserted in strings within quotes will be expanded normally, unless you prefix the $ character with a backslash (\).

Base module directives

In this section, we will take a closer look at the base modules. We are particularly interested in answering two questions: what are base modules? What are the directives that are available?

What are base modules?

The base modules offer directives that allow you to define the parameters of the basic functionality of Nginx. They cannot be disabled at compile time, and as a result, the directives and blocks that they offer are always available. Three base modules have been distinguished:

- **Core module**: Consists of essential features and directives such as process management and security
- **Events module**: Lets you configure the inner mechanisms of the networking capabilities
- **Configuration module**: Enables the inclusion mechanism

These modules offer a large range of directives; we will be detailing them individually with their syntaxes and default values.

The Nginx process architecture

Before we start detailing the basic configuration directives, it is necessary to understand the overall process architecture, that is, the way that the Nginx daemon works behind the scenes. Although the application comes as a simple binary file (and a somewhat lightweight background process), the way it functions at runtime can be relatively complex.

A unique process—the *Master Process*—exists in memory from the very moment that Nginx starts. It is launched with the current user and group permissions—usually root/root if the service is launched at boot time by an `init` script. The master process itself does not process any client request; instead, it spawns the processes that do, that is, the *Worker Processes*, which are affected to a customizable user and group.

From the configuration file, you can define the number of worker processes, the maximum connections per worker process, the user and group that the worker processes are running under, and more. The following screenshot shows an example of a running instance of Nginx with eight worker processes running under the `www-data` user account.

```
root@example:~# ps fuax | grep nginx
root     17485  0.0  0.0   7772    852 pts/0    S+   03:15   0:00         \_ grep nginx
root     20286  0.0  0.0  35752   3840 ?        Ss   Apr10   0:00 nginx: master process /usr/local/nginx/sbin/nginx
www-data  8910  0.0  0.0  37052   5460 ?        S    Apr24   1:26  \_ nginx: worker process
www-data  8911  0.0  0.0  37316   5756 ?        S    Apr24   1:28   \_ nginx: worker process
www-data  8912  0.0  0.0  36960   5668 ?        S    Apr24   1:29   \_ nginx: worker process
www-data  8913  0.0  0.0  37052   5492 ?        S    Apr24   1:27   \_ nginx: worker process
www-data  8914  0.0  0.0  37316   5756 ?        S    Apr24   1:35   \_ nginx: worker process
www-data  8915  0.0  0.0  36788   5232 ?        S    Apr24   1:30   \_ nginx: worker process
www-data  8916  0.0  0.0  37052   5492 ?        S    Apr24   1:30   \_ nginx: worker process
www-data  8917  0.0  0.0  37316   5748 ?        S    Apr24   1:26   \_ nginx: worker process
root@example:~#
```

Core module directives

The following is the list of directives made available by the core module. Most of these directives must be placed at the root of the configuration file, and can only be used once. However, some of them are valid in multiple contexts. If that is the case, the following is the list of valid contexts under the directive name:

Name and context	Syntax and description
daemon	Accepted values: on or off
	Syntax:
	`daemon on;`
	Default value: on
	Enables or disables daemon mode. If you disable it, the program will not be started in the background; it will stay in the foreground when launched from the shell. This may come in handy for debugging, in situations where you need to know what causes Nginx to crash and when.
debug_points	Accepted values: stop or abort
	Syntax:
	`debug_points stop;`
	Default value: None
	Activates debug points in Nginx. Use stop to interrupt the application when a debug point comes about in order to attach a debugger. Use abort to abort the debug point and create a core dump file.
	To disable this feature, simply do not use the directive.

Name and context	Syntax and description

`env`	Syntax:
	
	`env MY_VARIABLE;`
	`env MY_VARIABLE=my_value;`
	
	Allows you to define or redefine environment variables.

`error_log`
 	
Context: `main,`
`http, server,` and
`location`
	Syntax:
	
	`error_log /file/path level;`
	
	Default value: `logs/error.log error`.
	
	Where `level` is one of the following values: `debug`, `info`, `notice`, `warn`, `error`, `crit`, `alert`, `emerg` (from the most to least detailed: `debug` provides frequent log entries, `emerg` reports only the most critical errors).
	
	Enables error logging at different levels: Application, HTTP server, virtual host, and virtual host directory.
	
	By redirecting the log output to `/dev/null`, you can disable error logging. Use the following directive at the root of the configuration file:
	
	`error_log /dev/null crit;`
	
	Instead of specifying a file path, you might also select one of the following alternatives: `stderr` will send log entries to the standard error file, `syslog` to the system log, and `memory` will store the log entries in the memory.

`lock_file`	Syntax: File path `lock_file logs/nginx.lock;` Default value: Defined at compile time Use a lock file for mutual exclusion. This is disabled by default, unless you enabled it at compile time. On most operating systems, locks are implemented using atomic operations, so this directive is ignored anyway.

`log_not_found`
 	
Context: `main,`
`http, server,` and
`location`
	Accepted values: `on` or `off`
	
	`log_not_found on;`
	
	Default value: `on`
	
	Enables or disables the logging of **404 not found** HTTP errors. If your logs get filled with 404 errors due to missing `favicon.ico` or `robots.txt` files, you might want to turn this off.

Name and context	Syntax and description
`master_process`	Accepted values: `on` or `off` `master_process on;` Default value: `on` If enabled, Nginx will start multiple processes: a main process (the master process) and worker processes. If disabled, Nginx works with a unique process. This directive should be used for testing purposes only, as it disables the master process—thus, clients will not be able to connect to your server.
`pcre_jit`	Accepted values: `on` or `off` `pcre_jit on;` Enables or disables the Just-In-Time compilation for regular expressions (PCRE from version 8.20 and above), which may speed up their processing significantly. For this to work, the PCRE libraries on your system must be specifically built with the `--enable-jit` configuration argument. When configuring your Nginx build, you must also add the `--with-pcre-jit` argument.
`pid`	Syntax: File path `pid logs/nginx.pid;` Default value: Defined at compile time. Path of the `pid` file for the Nginx daemon. The default value can be configured at compile time. Make sure to enable this directive, and set its value properly, since the `pid` file may be used by the Nginx `init` script depending on your operating system.

`ssl_engine`	Syntax: Character string
	
	`ssl_engine enginename;`
	
	Default value: None
	
	Where `enginename` is the name of an available hardware SSL accelerator on your system. To check for the available hardware SSL accelerators, run this command from the shell:
	
	`openssl engine -t`

Name and context	Syntax and description

`thread_pool`	Syntax:
	
	`thread_pool name threads=number [max_queue=number];`
	
	Default value:
	
	`thread_pool default threads=32 max_queue=65536;`
	
	Defines a thread pool reference that can be used with the `aio` directive for serving larger files asynchronously. Further details are provided in *Chapter 8, Introducing Load Balancing and Optimization.*

`timer_resolution`	Syntax: Numeric (time) `timer_resolution 100ms;` Default value: None Controls the interval between system calls to `gettimeofday()` for synchronizing the internal clock. If this value is not specified, the clock is refreshed after each kernel event notification.

`user`	Syntax:
	
	`user username groupname;`
	`user username;`
	
	Default value: Defined at compile time. If still undefined, the user and the group of the Nginx master process are used.
	
	Allows you to define the user account, and optionally, the user group used for starting the Nginx worker processes. For security reasons, you should make sure to specify a user and a group with limited privileges. For example, create a new user and a group dedicated to Nginx, and remember to apply proper permissions on the files that will be served.

Name and context	Syntax and description

`worker_cpu_affinity`	Syntax:
	
	`worker_cpu_affinity 1000 0100 0010 0001;`
	`worker_cpu_affinity 10 10 01 01;`
	`worker_cpu_affinity;`
	
	Default value: None
	
	This directive works in conjunction with `worker_processes`. It lets you affect the worker processes to CPU cores.
	
	There are as many series of digit blocks as worker processes; there are as many digits in a block as your CPU has cores.
	
	If you configure Nginx to use three worker processes, there are three blocks of digits. For a dual-core CPU, each block has two digits:
	
	`worker_cpu_affinity 01 01 10;`
	
	The first block (`01`) indicates that the first worker process should be affected to the second core.
	
	The second block (`01`) indicates that the second worker process should be affected to the second core.
	
	The third block (`10`) indicates that the third worker process should be affected to the first core.
	
	Note that affinity is only recommended for multi-core CPUs, not for processors with hyper-treading or similar technologies.

`worker_priority`	Syntax: Numeric `worker_priority 0;` Default value: 0 Defines the priority of the worker processes, from `-20` (highest) to `19` (lowest). The default value is `0`. Note that the kernel processes run at priority level `-5`, so it's not recommended that you set the priority to `-5` or less.

Name and context	Syntax and description
`worker_processes`	Syntax: Numeric or auto `worker_processes 4;` Default value: 1 Defines the number of worker processes. Nginx offers to separate the treatment of requests into multiple processes. The default value is 1, but it's recommended to increase this value if your CPU has more than one core. Besides, if a process gets blocked due to slow I/O operations, the incoming requests can be delegated to the other worker processes. Alternatively, you may use the `auto` value, which will let Nginx select an appropriate value for this directive. By default, it is the amount of CPU cores detected on the system.
`worker_rlimit_ core`	Syntax: Numeric (size) `worker_rlimit_core 100m;` Default value: None Defines the size of core files per worker process.
`worker_rlimit_ nofile`	Syntax: Numeric `worker_rlimit_nofile 10000;` Default value: None Defines the number of files that a worker process may use simultaneously.
`working_directory`	Syntax: Directory path `working_directory /usr/local/nginx/;` Default value: The prefix switch defined at compile time. A working directory used for worker processes, it is only used to define the location of the core files. The worker process user account (`user` directive) must have write permissions on this folder in order to be able to write core files.
`worker_aio_ requests`	Syntax: Numeric `worker_aio_requests 10000;` If you are using `aio` with the `epoll` connection processing method, this directive sets the maximum number of outstanding asynchronous I/O operations for a single worker process.

The Events module

The Events module comes with directives that allow you to configure the
network mechanisms. Some of the parameters have an important impact
on the application's performance.

All the directives listed in the following table must be placed in the `events` block,
which is located at the root of the configuration file:

```
user nginx nginx;
master_process on;
worker_processes 4;
events {
  worker_connections 1024;
  use epoll;
}
[...]
```

These directives cannot be placed elsewhere (if you do so, the configuration test
will fail).

Directive name	Syntax and description
`accept_mutex`	Accepted values: `on` or `off` `accept_mutex on;` Default value: `on` Enables or disables the use of an accept `mutex` (mutual exclusion) to open the listening sockets.
`accept_mutex_delay`	Syntax: Numeric (time) `accept_mutex_delay 500ms;` Default value: `500` milliseconds Defines the amount of time that a worker process should wait for before trying to acquire the resource again. This value is not used if the `accept_mutex` directive is set to off.

`debug_connection`	Syntax: IP address or CIDR block.
	
	`debug_connection 172.63.155.21;`
	`debug_connection 172.63.155.0/24;`
	
	Default value: None
	
	Writes detailed logs for clients matching this IP address or address block. The debug information is stored in the file specified with the `error_log` directive, enabled with the debug level.
	
	Note: Nginx must be compiled with the `--debug` switch in order to enable this feature.

Directive name	Syntax and description
multi_accept	Syntax: on or off `multi_accept off;` Default value: off Defines whether or not Nginx should accept all the incoming connections at once from the listening queue.
use	Accepted values: /dev/poll, epoll, eventport, kqueue, rtsig, or select `use kqueue;` Default value: Defined at compile time Selects the event model among the available ones (the ones that you enabled at compile time). Nginx automatically selects the most appropriate one, so you should not have to modify this value. The supported models are: • select: The default and standard module, it is used if the OS does not support a more efficient one (it's the only available method under Windows). This method is not recommended for servers that expect to be under high load. • poll: It is automatically preferred over select, but is not available on all systems. • kqueue: An efficient method for the FreeBSD 4.1+, OpenBSD 2.9+, NetBSD 2.0, and MacOS X operating systems. • epoll: An efficient method for Linux 2.6+ based operating systems. • rtsig: Real-time signals, available as of Linux 2.2.19, but unsuited for high-traffic profiles, as the default system settings allow only 1,024 queued signals. • /dev/poll: An efficient method for the Solaris 7 11/99+, HP/UX 11.22+, IRIX 6.5.15+, and Tru64 UNIX 5.1A+ operating systems. • eventport: An efficient method for Solaris 10, though a security patch is required.
worker_connections	Syntax: Numeric `worker_connections 1024;` Default value: None Defines the number of connections that a worker process may treat simultaneously.

The Configuration module

The Nginx Configuration module is a simple module enabling file inclusions with the `include` directive, as previously described in the *Organization and inclusions* section. The directive can be inserted anywhere in the configuration file and accepts a single parameter—a file path.

```
include /file/path.conf;
include sites/*.conf;
```

 Note that if you do not specify an absolute path, the file path is relative to the configuration directory. By default, `include sites/example.conf` will include the following file: `/usr/local/nginx/conf/sites/example.conf`

Necessary adjustments

Several core directives deserve to be adjusted carefully upon preparing the initial setup of Nginx on your server. We will review several of these directives and the possible values that you may set:

- `user root root;`

  This directive specifies that the worker processes is started as root. This is dangerous from the security point of view, as it grants Nginx full permissions over your file system. You need to create a new user account on your system and make use of it there.

  Recommended value (granted that a `www-data` user account and group exist on the system): `user www-data www-data;`

- `worker_processes 1;`

  With this setting, only one worker process is started, which implies that all the requests will be processed by a unique execution flow. This also implies that the execution is delegated to only one core of your CPU. It is highly recommended to increase this value; you should have at least one process per CPU core. Alternatively, just set this to auto to leave it up to Nginx to determine the optimal value. Recommended value: `worker_processes auto;`

- `worker_priority 0;`

  By default, the worker processes are started with a regular priority. If your system performs other tasks simultaneously, you might want to grant a higher priority to the Nginx worker processes. In this case, you should decrease the value—the smaller the value, the higher the priority. Values range from `-20` (highest priority) to `19` (lowest priority). There is no recommended value here, as it completely depends on your situation. However, you should not set it under `-5`, as it is the default priority for kernel processes.

- `log_not_found on;`

  This directive specifies whether Nginx should log `404 errors` or not. While these errors may, of course, provide useful information about the missing resources, a lot of them may be generated by web browsers trying to reach the *favicon* (the conventional `/favicon.ico` of a website), or robots trying to access the indexing instructions (`robots.txt`). Set this to `off` if you want to ensure that your log files don't get cluttered by *Error 404* entries, but keep in mind that this could deprive you from potentially important information about other pages that visitors failed to reach. Note that this directive is part of the HTTP core module. Refer to the next chapter for more information.

- `worker_connections 1024;`

  This setting, combined with the number of worker processes, allows you to define the total number of connections accepted by the server simultaneously. If you enable four worker processes, each accepting 1,024 connections, your server will treat a total of 4,096 simultaneous connections. You need to adjust this setting to match your hardware: the more RAM and CPU power your server relies on, the more connections you can accept concurrently. If your server is a huge monster meant to host high traffic sites, you will want to increase this value.

Testing your server

At this point, you have configured several basic directives that affect the core functioning of Nginx. We will perform a simple test to ensure that all is working as expected, and that you are ready to further configure and deploy your websites.

Creating a test server

In order to perform simple tests, such as connecting to the server with a web browser, we need to set up a website for Nginx to serve. A test page comes with the default package in the `html` folder (`/usr/local/nginx/html/index.html`) and the original `nginx.conf` is configured to serve this page. The following is the section that we are interested in for now:

```
http {
    include       mime.types;
    default_type  application/octet-stream;
    sendfile      on;
    keepalive_timeout  65;
    server {
        listen       80;
        server_name  localhost;
        location / {
            root   html;
            index  index.html index.htm;
        }
        error_page   500 502 503 504   /50x.html;
        location = /50x.html {
            root   html;
        }
    }
}
```

As you can perhaps already tell, this segment configures Nginx to serve a website:

- By opening a listening socket on port `80`
- Accessible at the address: `http://localhost/`
- With the index page, `index.html`

For more details about these directives, please refer to *Chapter 3, HTTP Configuration,* and go to the *HTTP module configuration* section. Anyhow, fire up your favorite web browser and visit `http://localhost/`:

You should be greeted with a welcome message; if you aren't, then check the configuration again, and make sure you reload Nginx in order to apply the changes.

Performance tests

Having configured the basic functioning and the architecture of your Nginx setup, you may want to proceed with running some tests. The methodology here is experimental — run the tests, edit the configuration, reload the server, run the tests again, edit the configuration again, and so on. Ideally, you should avoid running the testing tool on the same computer that is used to run Nginx, as it may give biased results.

One could question the pertinence of running performance tests at this stage. On one hand, virtual hosts and modules are not fully configured yet, and your website might use FastCGI applications (PHP, Python, and so on). On the other hand, we are testing the raw performance of the server without additional components (for example, to make sure that it fully makes use of all the CPU cores). Besides, it's always better to come up with a polished configuration before the server is put into production.

We have retained three tools to evaluate the server performance here. All three applications were specifically designed for load tests on web servers and have different approaches due to their origin:

- httperf: A relatively well-known open source utility developed by HP for Linux operating systems only

- Autobench: Perl wrapper for httperf, for improving the testing mechanisms and generating detailed reports

- OpenWebLoad: Smaller scale open source load testing application that supports both the Windows and Linux platforms

The principle behind each of these tools is to generate a massive amount of HTTP requests in order to clutter the server and study the results.

Httperf

Httperf is a simple command-line tool that can be downloaded from its official website at http://www.hpl.hp.com/research/linux/httperf/ (it might also be available in the default repositories of your operating system). The source comes as a tar.gz archive and needs to be compiled using the standard methods: ./configure, make, and make install.

Once installed, you may execute the following command:

```
[alex@example ~]$ httperf --server 192.168.1.10 --port 80 --uri /index.
html --rate 300 --num-conn 30000 --num-call 1 --timeout 5
```

Replace the values in the preceding command with your own:

- --server: The website hostname that you wish to test

- --uri: The path of the file that will be downloaded

- --rate: The number of requests that should be sent every second

- --num-conn: The total number of connections

- --num-call: The number of requests that should be sent per connection

- --timeout: The number of seconds elapsed before a request is considered as lost

In this example, `httperf` will download `http://192.168.1.10/index.html` repeatedly, `300` times per second, resulting in a total of `30000` requests.

```
alex@example: /home/alex                                           _ □ x
Maximum connect burst length: 6298

Total: connections 21767 requests 21710 replies 21710 test-duration 14.692 s

Connection rate: 1481.6 conn/s (0.7 ms/conn, <=1022 concurrent connections)
Connection time [ms]: min 1.4 avg 563.4 max 3922.6 median 197.5 stddev 988.4
Connection time [ms]: connect 397.6
Connection length [replies/conn]: 1.000

Request rate: 1477.7 req/s (0.7 ms/req)
Request size [B]: 72.0

Reply rate [replies/s]: min 1942.8 avg 2077.3 max 2211.8 stddev 190.2 (2 samples)
Reply time [ms]: response 165.7 transfer 0.0
Reply size [B]: header 215.0 content 151.0 footer 0.0 (total 366.0)
Reply status: 1xx=0 2xx=21702 3xx=0 4xx=0 5xx=8

CPU time [s]: user 0.22 system 8.88 (user 1.5% system 60.5% total 62.0%)
Net I/O: 633.5 KB/s (5.2*10^6 bps)

Errors: total 78290 client-timo 57 socket-timo 0 connrefused 0 connreset 0
Errors: fd-unavail 78233 addrunavail 0 ftab-full 0 other 0
```

The results indicate the response times and the number of successful requests. If the success ratio is 100 percent, or the response time near 0 ms, increase the request rate, and run the test again until the server shows signs of weakness. Once the results begin to look a little less perfect, tweak the appropriate configuration directives, and run the test again.

Autobench

Autobench is a Perl script that makes use of `httperf` more efficiently — it runs continuous tests the and automatically increases request rates until your server gets saturated. One of the interesting features of Autobench is that it generates a `.tsv` report that you can open with various applications to generate graphs. You may download the source code from the author's personal website: `http://www.xenoclast.org/autobench/`. Once again, extract the files from the archive, run `make`, then `make install`.

Although it supports testing of multiple hosts at once, we will only be using the single host test for more simplicity. The command that we will execute resembles the `httperf` one:

```
[alex@example ~]$ autobench --single_host --host1 192.168.1.10 --uri1
/index.html --quiet --low_rate 20 --high_rate 200 --rate_step 20
--num_call 10 --num_conn 5000 --timeout 5 --file results.tsv
```

The switches can be configured as follows:

- `--host1`: The website host name that you wish to test
- `--uri1`: The path of the file that will be downloaded
- `--quiet`: Does not display the `httperf` information on the screen
- `--low_rate`: Connections per second at the beginning of the test
- `--high_rate`: Connections per second at the end of the test
- `--rate_step`: The number of connections by which to increase the rate after each test
- `--num_call`: The number of requests that should be sent per connection
- `--num_conn`: Total number of connections
- `--timeout`: The number of seconds elapsed before a request is considered as lost
- `--file`: Export results as specified (`.tsv` file)

Once the test terminates, you end up with a `.tsv` file that you can import in applications such as Microsoft Excel. The following is a graph generated from results on a test server (note that the report file contains up to 10 series of statistics):

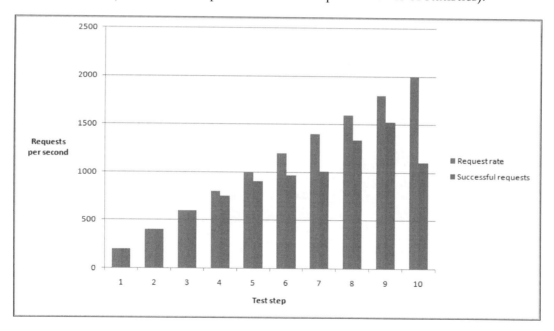

As you can tell from the graph, this test server supports up to 600 requests per second without a loss. Past this limit, some connections get dropped as Nginx cannot handle the load. It stills gets up to over 1500 successful requests per second at step 9.

OpenWebLoad

OpenWebLoad is a free open source application. It is available for both the Linux and Windows platforms and was developed in the first few years of the 21st century, back in the days of Web 1.0. A different approach is offered here. Instead of throwing loads of requests at the server and seeing how many are handled correctly, it will simply send as many requests as possible using a variable number of connections and report to you every second.

You may download OpenWebLoad from its official website at http://openwebload. sourceforge.net. Extract the source from the .tar.gz archive, run ./configure, make, and make install.

Its usage is simpler than the previous two utilities:

```
[alex@example ~]$ openload example.com/index.html 10
```

The first argument is the URL of the website that you want to test. The second one is the number of connections that should be opened.

```
C:\WINDOWS\system32\cmd.exe

C:\>openload.exe example.com/index.html 10
URL: http://example.com:80/index.html
Clients: 10
MaTps 210.37, Tps 210.37, Resp Time 0.046, Err 0%, Count 211
MaTps 211.51, Tps 221.78, Resp Time 0.045, Err 0%, Count 433
MaTps 212.69, Tps 223.33, Resp Time 0.045, Err 0%, Count 657
MaTps 213.38, Tps 219.56, Resp Time 0.046, Err 0%, Count 877
MaTps 214.63, Tps 225.87, Resp Time 0.044, Err 0%, Count 1104
MaTps 215.20, Tps 220.34, Resp Time 0.045, Err 0%, Count 1325
Total TPS: 216.40
Avg. Response time:   0.045 sec.
Max Response time:    0.097 sec
Total Requests:      1325
Total Errors:           0

C:\>
```

A new result line is produced every second. Requests are sent continuously until you press the *Enter* key; following that, a result summary is displayed. Here is how to decipher the output:

- **Tps** (transactions per second): A transaction corresponds to a completed request (back and forth)
- **MaTps**: Average TPS over the last 20 seconds

- **Resp Time**: Average response time for the elapsed second
- **Err** (error rate): Errors occur when the server returns a response that is not the expected `HTTP 200 OK`
- **Count**: Total transaction count

You can fiddle with the number of simultaneous connections, and see how your server performs in order to establish a balanced configuration for your setup. Three tests were run here with different numbers of connections. The results speak for themselves:

	Test 1	Test 2	Test 3
Simultaneous connections	1	20	1000
Transactions per second (Tps)	67.54	205.87	185.07
Average response time	14 ms	91 ms	596 ms

Too few connections result in a low Tps rate; however, the response times are optimal. Too many connections produce a relatively high Tps, but the response times are critically high. You thus need to find a happy medium.

Upgrading Nginx gracefully

There are many situations where you need to replace the Nginx binary, for example, when you compile a new version and wish to put it in production, or simply after having enabled new modules and rebuilt the application. What most administrators would do in this situation is stop the server, copy the new binary over the old one, and start Nginx again. While this is not considered to be a problem for most websites, there may be some cases where the uptime is critical, and connection losses should be avoided at all costs. Fortunately, Nginx embeds a mechanism allowing you to switch binaries with uninterrupted uptime—zero percent request loss is guaranteed if you follow these steps carefully:

1. Replace the old Nginx binary (by default, `/usr/local/nginx/sbin/nginx`) with the new one.
2. Find the `pid` of the Nginx master process, for example, with `ps x | grep nginx | grep master`, or by looking at the value found in the pid file.
3. Send a `USR2` (12) signal to the master process—`kill -USR2 1234`, replacing `1234` with the pid found in *step 2*. This will initiate the upgrade by renaming the old `.pid` file and running the new binary.

4. Send a WINCH (28) signal to the old master process—kill -WINCH 1234, replacing 1234 with the pid found in *step 2*. This will engage a graceful shutdown of the old worker processes.

5. Make sure that all the old worker processes are terminated, and then send a QUIT signal to the old master process—kill -QUIT 1234, replacing 1234 with the pid found in *step 2*.

Congratulations! You have successfully upgraded Nginx and have not lost a single connection.

Summary

This chapter provided an overview of the configuration architecture by studying the syntax and the core module directives that have an impact on the overall server performance. We then went through a series of adjustments in order to fit your profile, followed by performance tests that have probably led you to fine-tune some more.

This is just the beginning though. Practically everything that we will be doing from now on is to prepare configuration sections. The next chapter will detail more advanced directives by further exploring the module system and the exciting possibilities that are offered to you.

3
HTTP Configuration

At this stage, we have a working Nginx setup. Not only is it installed on the system and launched automatically on startup, but it's also organized and optimized with the help of basic directives. It's now time to go one step further into the configuration and discover the HTTP Core module. This module constitutes the essential component of the HTTP configuration—it allows you to set up websites to be served, also referred to as *virtual hosts*.

This chapter will cover the following topics:

- An introduction to the HTTP Core module
- The http / server / location structure
- HTTP Core module directives, organized thematically
- HTTP Core module variables
- The in-depths of the location block

The HTTP Core module

The HTTP Core module is the component that contains all the fundamental blocks, directives, and variables of the HTTP server. It's enabled by default when you configure the build (as described in *Chapter 1, Downloading and Installing Nginx*), but as it turns out, it's actually optional—you can decide not to include it in your custom build. Doing so will completely disable all the HTTP functionalities, and all the other HTTP modules will not be compiled. However, if you've purchased this book it's highly likely that you are interested in the web-serving capacities of Nginx, so you will have this enabled.

This module is the largest of all the standard Nginx modules — it provides an impressive amount of directives and variables. In order to understand all these new elements and how they come into play, we first need to understand the logical organization introduced by the three main blocks — http, server, and location.

Structure blocks

In the previous chapter, we discovered the Core module by studying the default Nginx configuration file, which includes a sequence of directives and values with no apparent organization. Then came the Events module, which introduced the first block (events). This block would be the only placeholder for all of the directives brought in by the Events module.

As it turns out, the HTTP module introduces three new logical blocks:

- http: This block is inserted at the root of the configuration file. It allows you to start defining the directives and blocks from all the modules related to the HTTP facet of Nginx. Although there is no real purpose in doing so, the block can be inserted multiple times, in which case the directive values inserted in the last block will override the previous ones.

- server: This block allows you to *declare a website*. In other words, a specific website (identified by one or more hostnames, for example, www.mywebsite.com) becomes acknowledged by Nginx and receives its own configuration. This block can only be used within the http block.

- location: The location block lets you define a group of settings to be applied to a particular location on a website. This block can be used within a server block or nested within another location block.

The following diagram summarizes the final structure by providing a couple of basic examples corresponding to actual situations:

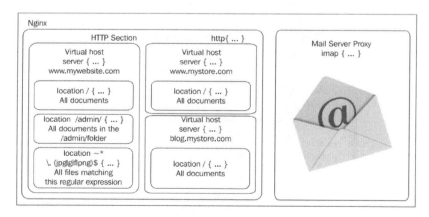

The HTTP section, defined by the `http` block, encompasses the entire web-related configuration. It may contain one or more `server` blocks, defining the domains and sub-domains that you are hosting. For each of these websites, you have the possibility of defining `location` blocks that let you apply additional settings to a particular request URI or request URIs matching a pattern.

Remember that the principle of setting inheritance applies here. If you define a setting at the `http` block level (for example, `gzip on` to enable gzip compression), the setting preserves its value in the potentially incorporated `server` and `location` blocks:

```
http {
    # Enable gzip compression at the http block level
    gzip on;

    server {
       server_name localhost;
        listen 80;

       # At this stage, gzip still set to on

       location /downloads/ {
           gzip off;
    #      This directive only applies to documents found
    #      in /downloads/
        }
    }
}
```

Module directives

At each of the three levels, directives can be inserted in order to affect the behavior of the web server. The following is the list of all directives that are introduced by the main HTTP module, grouped thematically. For each directive, an indication regarding the context is given. Some cannot be used at certain levels. For instance, it would make no sense to insert a `server_name` directive at the `http` block level, since `server_name` is a directive directly affecting a virtual host — it should only be inserted in the `server` block. For this purpose, the table indicates the possible levels where each directive is allowed — the `http` block, the `server` block, the `location` block, and additionally the `if` block, later introduced by the *Rewrite module*.

 Note that this documentation is valid as of the stable version 1.8.0. Future updates may alter the syntax of some directives or provide new features that are not discussed here.

Socket and host configuration

This set of directives allows you to configure your virtual hosts. In practice, this materializes by creating `server` blocks that you identify either by a hostname or by an IP address and port combination. In addition, some directives let you fine-tune your network settings by configuring the TCP socket options.

listen

Context: `server`

Specifies the IP address and/or the port to be used by the listening socket that serves the website. Sites are generally served on port `80` (the default value) via HTTP, or `443` via HTTPS.

Syntax: `listen [address] [:port] [additional options];`

Additional options:

- `default_server`: Specifies this `server` block to be used as the default website for any request received at the specified IP address and port
- `ssl`: Specifies that the website should be served over SSL
- `spdy`: Enables support for the SPDY protocol if the SPDY module is present
- `proxy_protocol`: Enables the PROXY protocol for all the connections accepted on this port
- Other options are related to the `bind` and `listen` system calls: `backlog=num`, `rcvbuf=size`, `sndbuf=size`, `accept_filter=filter`, `deferred`, `setfib=number`, and `bind`

Examples:

```
listen 192.168.1.1:80;
listen 127.0.0.1;
listen 80 default;
listen [:::a8c9:1234]:80; # IPv6 addresses must be put between square
brackets
listen 443 ssl;
```

This directive also allows Unix sockets:

```
listen unix:/tmp/nginx.sock;
```

server_name

Context: `server`

This assigns one or more hostnames to the `server` block. When Nginx receives an HTTP request, it matches the `Host` header of the request against all the `server` blocks. The first `server` block to match this hostname is selected.

Plan B: if no `server` block matches the desired host, Nginx selects the first `server` block that matches the parameters of the `listen` directive (such as `listen *:80` would be a catch-all for all the requests received on port `80`), giving priority to the first block that has the `default` option enabled on the `listen` directive.

Note that this directive accepts wildcards as well as regular expressions (in which case, the hostname should start with the ~ character).

Syntax: `server_name hostname1 [hostname2...];`

Examples:

```
server_name www.website.com;
server_name www.website.com website.com;
server_name *.website.com;
server_name .website.com; # combines both *.website.com and website.
com
server_name *.website.*;
server_name ~^(www)\.example\.com$; # $1 = www
```

Note that you may use an empty string as the directive value in order to catch all the requests that do not come with a `Host` header, but only after at least one regular name (or " _ " for a dummy hostname):

```
server_name website.com "";
server_name _ "";
```

server_name_in_redirect

Context: `http`, `server`, `location`

This directive applies to the case of internal redirects (for more information about internal redirects, check the *Rewrite Module* section given further on in this chapter). If set to `on`, Nginx uses the first hostname specified in the `server_name` directive. If set to `off`, Nginx uses the value of the `Host` header from the HTTP request.

Syntax: `on` or `off`

Default value: `off`

server_names_hash_max_size

Context: `http`

Nginx uses hash tables for various data collections in order to speed up the processing of requests. This directive defines the maximum size of the server names hash table. The default value fits with most configurations. If this needs to be changed, Nginx automatically tells you so on startup, or when you reload its configuration.

Syntax: Numeric value

Default value: `512`

server_names_hash_bucket_size

Context: `http`

Sets the bucket size for server names hash tables. You should only change this value if Nginx tells you to.

Syntax: Numeric value

Default value: `32` (or `64`, or `128`, depending on your processor cache specifications)

port_in_redirect

Context: `http`, `server`, `location`

In case of a redirect, this directive defines whether or not Nginx should append the port number to the redirection URL.

Syntax: `on` or `off`

Default value: `on`

tcp_nodelay

Context: `http`, `server`, `location`

Enables or disables the `TCP_NODELAY` socket option for keep-alive connections only. Quoting the Linux documentation on sockets programming:

> *"TCP_NODELAY is for a specific purpose; to disable the Nagle buffering algorithm. It should only be set for applications that send frequent small bursts of information without getting an immediate response, where timely delivery of data is required (the canonical example is mouse movements)."*

Syntax: on or off

Default value: on

tcp_nopush

Context: http, server, location

Enables or disables the TCP_NOPUSH (FreeBSD) or TCP_CORK (Linux) socket option. Note that this option applies only if the sendfile directive is enabled. If tcp_nopush is set to on, Nginx attempts to transmit all the HTTP response headers in a single TCP packet.

Syntax: on or off

Default value: off

sendfile

Context: http, server, location

If this directive is enabled, Nginx uses the sendfile kernel call to handle file transmission. If disabled, Nginx handles the file transfer by itself. Depending on the physical location of the file being transmitted (such as NFS), this option may affect the server performance.

Syntax: on or off

Default value: off

sendfile_max_chunk

Context: http, server

This directive defines the maximum size of data to be used for each call to sendfile (read the previous section).

Syntax: Numeric value (size)

Default value: 0

send_lowat

Context: `http, server`

This is an option that allows you to make use of the `SO_SNDLOWAT` flag for TCP sockets under FreeBSD only. This value defines the minimum number of bytes in the buffer for output operations.

Syntax: Numeric value (size)

Default value: `0`

reset_timedout_connection

Context: `http, server, location`

When a client connection times out, its associated information may remain in memory depending on its state. Enabling this directive will erase all memory associated with the connection after it times out.

Syntax: `on` or `off`

Default value: `off`

Paths and documents

This section describes the directives that configure the documents that should be served for each website, such as the document root, the site index, error pages, and so on.

root

Context: `http, server, location, if`. Variables are accepted.

This directive defines the document root containing the files that you wish to serve to your visitors.

Syntax: Directory path

Default value: `html`

```
root /home/website.com/public_html;
```

alias

Context: `location`. Variables are accepted.

`alias` is a directive that you place in a `location` block only. It assigns a different path for Nginx to retrieve documents for a specific request. As an example, consider the following configuration:

```
http {
    server {
        server_name localhost;
        root /var/www/website.com/html;
        location /admin/ {
          alias /var/www/locked/;
        }
    }
}
```

When a request for `http://localhost/` is received, files are served from the `/var/www/website.com/html/` folder. However, if Nginx receives a request for `http://localhost/admin/`, the path used to retrieve the files is `var/www/locked/`. Moreover, the value of the document root directive (`root`) is not altered. This procedure is invisible in the eyes of dynamic scripts.

Syntax: Directory (do not forget the trailing /) or file path

error_page

Context: `http`, `server`, `location`, `if`. Variables are accepted.

This allows you to affect URIs to the HTTP response code and optionally, to substitute the code with another.

Syntax: `error_page code1 [code2...] [=replacement code] [=@block | URI]`

Examples :

```
error_page 404 /not_found.html;
error_page 500 501 502 503 504 /server_error.html;
error_page 403 http://website.com/;
error_page 404 @notfound; # jump to a named location block
error_page 404 =200 /index.html; # in case of 404 error, redirect to
index.html with a 200 OK response code
```

if_modified_since

Context: `http, server, location`

This defines the way Nginx handles the `If-Modified-Since` HTTP header. This header is mostly used by search engine spiders (such as Google web crawling bots). The robot indicates the date and time of the last pass. If the requested file has not been modified since that time, the server simply returns a `304 Not Modified` response code with no body.

This directive accepts the following three values:

- `off`: Ignores the `If-Modified-Since` header.
- `exact`: Returns `304 Not Modified` if the date and time specified in the HTTP header are an exact match with the actual requested file modification date. If the file modification date is anterior or ulterior, the file is served normally (`200 OK` response).
- `before`: Returns `304 Not Modified` if the date and time specified in the HTTP header is anterior or equal to the requested file modification date.

Syntax: `if_modified_since off | exact | before`

Default value: `exact`

index

Context: `http, server, location`. Variables are accepted.

This defines the default page that Nginx will serve if no filename is specified in the request (in other words, the index page). You may specify multiple filenames, and the first file to be found will be served. If none of the specified files are found, and if the `autoindex` directive is enabled (check the `HTTP Autoindex` module), Nginx will attempt to generate an automatic index of the files. Otherwise, it will return a `403 Forbidden` error page. Optionally, you may insert an absolute filename (such as `/page.html`, based from the document root directory) but only as the last argument of the directive.

Syntax: `index file1 [file2…] [absolute_file];`

Default value: `index.html`

```
index index.php index.html index.htm;
index index.php index2.php /catchall.php;
```

recursive_error_pages

Context: `http`, `server`, `location`

Sometimes, an error page itself served by the `error_page` directive may trigger an error; in this case, the `error_page` directive is used again (recursively). This directive enables or disables recursive error pages.

Syntax: on or `off`

Default value: `off`

try_files

Context: `server`, `location`. Variables are accepted.

This attempts to serve the specified files (arguments 1 to N-1). If none of these files exist, it jumps to the respective named `location` block (last argument) or serves the specified URI.

Syntax: Multiple file paths followed by a named `location` block or a URI

Example:

```
location / {
    try_files $uri $uri.html $uri.php $uri.xml @proxy;
}
# the following is a "named location block"
location @proxy {
    proxy_pass 127.0.0.1:8080;
}
```

In this example, Nginx tries to serve files normally. If the requested URI does not correspond to any existing file, Nginx appends `.html` to the URI and tries to serve the file again. If it fails again, it tries with `.php`, and then with `.xml`. Eventually, if all of these possibilities fail, another `location` block (@proxy) handles the request.

> You may also specify `$uri/` in the list of values in order to test for the existence of a directory with that name.

Client requests

This section documents the way that Nginx handles client requests. Among other things, you are allowed to configure the keep-alive mechanism behavior and, possibly, logging the client requests into files.

keepalive_requests

Context: `http, server, location`

This specifies the maximum number of requests served over a single keep-alive connection.

Syntax: Numeric value

Default value: `100`

keepalive_timeout

Context: `http, server, location`

This directive defines the number of seconds the server will wait before closing a keep-alive connection. The second (optional) parameter is transmitted as the value of the `Keep-Alive: timeout=` HTTP response header. The intended effect is to let the client browser close the connection itself after this period has elapsed. Note that some browsers ignore this setting. Internet Explorer, for instance, automatically closes the connection after around `60` seconds.

Syntax: `keepalive_timeout time1 [time2];`

Default value: `75`

```
keepalive_timeout 75;
keepalive_timeout 75 60;
```

keepalive_disable

Context: `http, server, location`

This option allows you to disable the `keepalive` functionality for the browser families of your choice.

Syntax: `keepalive_disable browser1 browser2;`

Default value: `msie6`

send_timeout

Context: `http, server, location`

This specifies the amount of time after which Nginx closes an inactive connection. A connection becomes inactive the moment a client stops transmitting data.

Syntax: Time value (in seconds)

Default value: 60

client_body_in_file_only

Context: http, server, location

If this directive is enabled, the body of the incoming HTTP requests will be stored into actual files on the disk. The *client body* corresponds to the client HTTP request raw data, minus the headers (in other words, the content transmitted in POST requests). Files are stored as plain text documents.

This directive accepts three values:

- off: Does not store the request body in a file
- clean: Stores the request body in a file, and removes the file after a request is processed
- on: Stores the request body in a file, but does not remove the file after the request is processed (not recommended unless for debugging purposes)

Syntax: client_body_in_file_only on | clean | off

Default value: off

client_body_in_single_buffer

Context: http, server, location

This directive defines whether or not Nginx should store the request body in a single buffer in memory.

Syntax: on or off

Default value: off

client_body_buffer_size

Context: http, server, location

The client_body_buffer_size directive specifies the size of the buffer holding the body of client requests. If this size is exceeded, the body (or at least a part of it) will be written to the disk. Note that if the client_body_in_file_only directive is enabled, request bodies are always stored to a file on the disk, regardless of their size (whether they fit in the buffer or not).

Syntax: Size value

Default value: `8k` or `16k` (2 memory pages) depending on your computer architecture

client_body_temp_path

Context: `http, server, location`

This option allows you to define the path of the directory that will store the client request body files. An additional option lets you separate those files into a folder hierarchy of up to three levels.

Syntax: `client_body_temp_path path [level1] [level2] [level3]`

Default value: `client_body_temp`

```
client_body_temp_path /tmp/nginx_rbf;
client_body_temp_path temp 2; # Nginx will create 2-digit folders to
hold request body files
client_body_temp_path temp 1 2 4; # Nginx will create 3 levels of
folders (first level: 1 digit, second level: 2 digits, third level: 4
digits)
```

client_body_timeout

Context: `http, server, location`

This directive defines the inactivity timeout while reading a client request body. A connection becomes inactive the moment the client stops transmitting data. If the delay is reached, Nginx returns a `408 Request timeout` HTTP error.

Syntax: Time value (in seconds)

Default value: `60`

client_header_buffer_size

Context: `http, server, location`

This directive allows you to define the size of the buffer that Nginx allocates to request headers. Usually, `1k` is enough. However, in some cases, the headers contain large chunks of cookie data or the request URI is lengthy. If that is the case, then Nginx allocates one or more larger buffers (the size of larger buffers is defined by the `large_client_header_buffers` directive).

Syntax: Size value

Default value: `1k`

client_header_timeout

Context: `http, server, location`

This defines the inactivity timeout while reading a client request header. A connection becomes inactive the moment the client stops transmitting data. If the delay is reached, Nginx returns a `408 Request timeout` HTTP error.

Syntax: Time value (in seconds)

Default value: `60`

client_max_body_size

Context: `http, server, location`

This is the maximum size of a client request body. If this size is exceeded, Nginx returns a `413 Request entity too large` HTTP error. This setting is particularly important if you are going to allow users to upload files to your server over HTTP.

Syntax: Size value

Default value: `1m`

large_client_header_buffers

Context: `http, server, location`

This defines the amount and size of the larger buffers to be used for storing client requests in case the default buffer (`client_header_buffer_size`) is insufficient. Each line of the header must fit in the size of a single buffer. If the request URI line is greater than the size of a single buffer, Nginx returns the `414 Request URI too large` error. If another header line exceeds the size of a single buffer, Nginx returns a `400 Bad request` error.

Syntax: `large_client_header_buffers amount size`

Default value: 4*8 kilobytes

lingering_time

Context: http, server, location

This directive applies to the client requests with a request body. As soon as the amount of uploaded data exceeds max_client_body_size, Nginx immediately sends a 413 Request entity too large HTTP error response. However, most browsers continue uploading data regardless of that notification. This directive defines the amount of time Nginx should wait for after sending this error response before it closes the connection.

Syntax: Numeric value (time)

Default value: 30 seconds

lingering_timeout

Context: http, server, location

This directive defines the amount of time that Nginx should wait between two read operations before it closes the client connection.

Syntax: Numeric value (time)

Default value: 5 seconds

lingering_close

Context: http, server, location

The lingering_close directive controls the way Nginx closes client connections. Set this to off to immediately close connections after all the request data has been received. The default value (on) allows Nginx to wait and process additional data if necessary. If set to always, Nginx will always wait to close the connection. The amount of waiting time is defined by the lingering_timeout directive.

Syntax: on, off, or always

Default value: on

ignore_invalid_headers

Context: http, server

If this directive is disabled, Nginx returns a 400 Bad Request HTTP error in case the request headers are malformed.

Syntax: on or off

Default value: on

chunked_transfer_encoding

Context: http, server, location

This directive enables or disables chunked transfer encoding for HTTP 1.1 requests.

Syntax: on or off

Default value: on

max_ranges

Context: http, server, location

This directive defines the number of byte ranges that Nginx will accept to serve when a client requests partial content from a file. If you do not specify a value, there is no limit. If you set this to 0, the byte range functionality is disabled.

Syntax: Size value

MIME types

Nginx offers two particular directives that help you configure the MIME types: types and default_type, which defines the default MIME types for documents. This will affect the *Content-Type* HTTP header sent within responses. Read on.

types

Context: http, server, location

This directive allows you to establish correlations between the MIME types and file extensions. It's actually a block accepting a particular syntax:

```
types {
  mimetype1   extension1;
  mimetype2   extension2 [extension3...];
  [...]
}
```

When Nginx serves a file, it checks the file extension in order to determine the MIME type. The MIME type is then sent as the value of the `Content-Type HTTP` header in the response. This header may affect the way in which browsers handle files. For example, if the MIME type of the file you are requesting is `application/pdf`, your browser may, for instance, attempt to render the file using a plugin associated to that MIME type instead of merely downloading it.

Nginx includes a basic set of MIME types as a standalone file (`mime.types`) to be included with the `include` directive:

```
include mime.types;
```

This file already covers the most important file extensions, so you will probably not need to edit it. If the extension of the served file is not found within the listed types, the default type is used, as defined by the `default_type` directive (read below).

Note that you may override the list of types by re-declaring the `types` block. A useful example would be to force all the files in a folder to be downloaded instead of being displayed:

```
http {
    include mime.types;
    [...]
    location /downloads/ {
        # removes all MIME types
        types { }
        default_type application/octet-stream;
    }
    [...]
}
```

Note that some browsers ignore the MIME types and may still display files if their filename ends with a known extension such as `.html` or `.txt`.

> To control the way files are handled by your visitors' browsers in a more certain and definitive manner, you should make use of the `Content-Disposition` HTTP header via the `add_header` directive—detailed in the HTTP Headers module (*Chapter 4, Module Configuration*).

The default values, if the `mime.types` file is not included, are:

```
types {
  text/html html;
  image/gif gif;
  image/jpeg jpg;
}
```

default_type

Context: `http`, `server`, `location`

This defines the default MIME type. When Nginx serves a file, the file extension is matched against the known types declared within the `types` block in order to return the proper MIME type as the value of the `Content-Type` HTTP response header. If the extension doesn't match any of the known MIME types, the value of the `default_type` directive is used.

Syntax: MIME type

Default value: `text/plain`

types_hash_max_size

Context: `http`, `server`, `location`

This defines the maximum size of an entry in the MIME types hash tables.

Syntax: Numeric value.

Default value: `4k` or `8k` (1 line of CPU cache)

types_hash_bucket_size

Context: `http`, `server`, `location`

This directive sets the bucket size for the MIME types hash tables. You should only change this value if Nginx tells you to.

Syntax: Numeric value.

Default value: `64`

Limits and restrictions

This set of directives allow you to add restrictions to be applied when a client attempts to access a particular location or document on your server. Note that you will find additional directives for restricting access in the next chapter.

limit_except

Context: `location`

This directive allows you to prevent the use of all the HTTP methods except the ones that you explicitly allow. Within a `location` block, you may want to restrict the use of some HTTP methods, for instance by forbidding clients from sending POST requests. You need to define two elements—first, the methods that are not forbidden (the allowed methods; all others will be forbidden), and second, the audience that is affected by the restriction:

```
location /admin/ {
    limit_except GET {
        allow 192.168.1.0/24;
        deny all;
    }
}
```

The preceding example applies a restriction to the `/admin/` location—all visitors are only allowed to use the GET method. Visitors that have a local IP address, as specified with the `allow` directive (detailed in the HTTP Access module), are not affected by this restriction. If a visitor uses a forbidden method, Nginx will return a `403 Forbidden` HTTP error. Note that the GET method implies the HEAD method (if you allow GET, both GET and HEAD are allowed).

The syntax for this is as follows:

```
limit_except METHOD1 [METHOD2...] {
    allow | deny | auth_basic | auth_basic_user_file | proxy_pass |
    perl;
}
```

The directives that you are allowed to insert within the block are documented in their respective module section in *Chapter 4, Module Configuration*.

limit_rate

Context: `http, server, location, if`

This directive allows you to limit the transfer rate of individual client connections. The rate is expressed in bytes per second:

```
limit_rate 500k;
```

This will limit the connection transfer rates to 500 kilobytes per second. If a client opens two connections, the client will be allowed 2 * 500 kilobytes.

Syntax: Size value

Default value: No limit

limit_rate_after

Context: `http, server, location, if`

This defines the amount of data transferred before the `limit_rate` directive takes effect.

```
limit_rate 10m;
```

Nginx sends the first `10` megabytes at the maximum speed. Past this size, the transfer rate is limited by the value specified with the `limit_rate` directive (see preceding section). Similarly to the `limit_rate` directive, this setting applies only to a single connection.

Syntax: Size value

Default: None

satisfy

Context: `location`

The `satisfy` directive defines whether clients require all access conditions to be valid (`satisfy all`) or at least one (`satisfy any`).

```
location /admin/ {
    allow 192.168.1.0/24;
    deny all;
    auth_basic "Authentication required";
    auth_basic_user_file conf/htpasswd;
}
```

In the preceding example, there are two conditions for clients to be able to access the resource:

- Through the `allow` and `deny` directives (HTTP Access module), we only allow clients that have a local IP address; all other clients are denied access.
- Through the `auth_basic` and `auth_basic_user_file` directives (HTTP Auth Basic module), we only allow clients that provide a valid username and password.

With `satisfy all`, the client must satisfy both the conditions in order to gain access to the resource. With `satisfy any`, if the client satisfies either condition, they are granted access.

Syntax: `satisfy any | all`

Default value: `all`

internal

Context: `location`

This directive specifies that the `location` block is internal. In other words, the specified resource cannot be accessed by external requests.

```
server {
    [...]
    server_name .website.com;
    location /admin/ {
        internal;
    }
}
```

With the preceding configuration, clients will not be able to browse `http://website.com/admin/`. Such requests will be met with `404 Not Found` errors. The only way to access the resource is via internal redirects (check the *Rewrite module* section for more information on internal redirects).

File processing and caching

It's important for your websites to be built upon solid foundations. File access and caching is a critical aspect of web serving. In this instance, Nginx lets you perform precise tweaking with the use of the following directives.

disable_symlinks

This directive allows you to control the way Nginx handles symbolic links when they are to be served. By default (the directive value is `off`), symbolic links are allowed and Nginx follows them. You may decide to disable the following symbolic links under different conditions by specifying one of these values:

- `on`: If any part of the requested URI is a symbolic link, access to it is denied, and Nginx returns a `403 HTTP` error page.

- `if_not_owner`: Similar to the preceding value, but access is denied only if the link and the object it points to have different owners.

- The optional parameter `from=` allows you to specify a part of the URL that will not be checked for symbolic links. For example, `disable_symlinks on from=$document_root` will tell Nginx to normally follow the symbolic links in the URI up to the `$document_root` folder. If a symbolic link is found in the URI parts after that, access to the requested file will be denied.

directio

Context: `http`, `server`, `location`

If this directive is enabled, files with a size greater than the specified value will be read with the Direct I/O system mechanism. This allows Nginx to read data from the storage device and place it directly in memory with no intermediary caching process involved.

Syntax: Size value, or off

Default value: `off`

directio_alignment

Context: `http`, `server`, `location`

This directive sets the byte alignment when using `directio`. Set this value to `4k` if you use XFS under Linux.

Syntax: Size value

Default value: 512

open_file_cache

Context: `http, server, location`

This directive allows you to enable the cache, which stores information about open files. It does not actually store the file contents but only information such as:

- File descriptors (file size, modification time, and so on).
- The existence of files and directories.
- File errors, such as Permission denied, File not found, and so on. Note that this can be disabled with the `open_file_cache_errors` directive.

This directive accepts two arguments:

- `max=X`, where `X` is the number of entries that the cache can store. If this number is reached, older entries will be deleted in order to leave room for newer entries.
- `inactive=Y`, where `Y` is the number of seconds that a cache entry should be stored. By default, Nginx will wait for 60 seconds before clearing a cache entry. If the cache entry is accessed, the timer is reset. If the cache entry is accessed more often than the value defined by `open_file_cache_min_uses`, the cache entry will not be cleared (until Nginx runs out of space and decides to clear out the older entries).

Syntax: `open_file_cache max=X [inactive=Y] | off`

Default value: `off`

Example:

```
open_file_cache max=5000 inactive=180;
```

open_file_cache_errors

Context: `http, server, location`

This directive enables or disables the caching of file errors with the `open_file_cache` directive (read the preceding directive).

Syntax: on or `off`

Default value: `off`

open_file_cache_min_uses

Context: http, server, location

By default, entries in the open_file_cache are cleared after a period of inactivity (60 seconds, by default). However, if there is any activity, you can prevent Nginx from removing the cache entry. This directive defines the number of times an entry must be accessed in order to be eligible for protection.

```
open_file_cache_min_uses 3;
```

If the cache entry is accessed more than three times, it becomes permanently active and is not removed until Nginx decides to clear out the older entries to clear some space.

Syntax: Numeric value

Default value: 1

open_file_cache_valid

Context: http, server, location

The open file cache mechanism is important, but the cached information quickly becomes obsolete, especially in the case of a fast-moving filesystem. From that perspective, information needs to be re-verified after a short period of time. This directive specifies the number of seconds that Nginx will wait before revalidating a cache entry.

Syntax: Time value (in seconds)

Default value: 60

read_ahead

Context: http, server, location

The read_ahead directive defines the number of bytes to be pre-read from the files. Under Linux-based operating systems, setting this directive to a value above 0 will enable reading ahead, but the actual value that you specify has no effect. Set this to 0 to disable pre-reading.

Syntax: Size value

Default value: 0

Other directives

The following directives relate to various aspects of the web server—logging, URI composition, DNS, and so on.

log_not_found

Context: `http, server, location`

This directive enables or disables the logging of `404 Not Found` HTTP errors. If your logs get filled with 404 errors due to missing `favicon.ico` or `robots.txt` files, you might want to turn this off.

Syntax: `on` or `off`

Default value: `on`

log_subrequest

Context: `http, server, location`

This directive enables or disables the logging of sub-requests triggered by internal redirects (see *The Rewrite module* section) or SSI requests (see the *Server Side Includes* module section).

Syntax: `on` or `off`

Default value: `off`

merge_slashes

Context: `http, server, location`

Enabling this directive will have the effect of merging multiple consecutive slashes in a URI. It turns out to be particularly useful in situations resembling the following:

```
server {
    [...]
    server_name website.com;
    location /documents/ {
        type { }
        default_type text/plain;
    }
}
```

By default, if the client attempts to access `http://website.com//documents/` (note the `//` in the middle of the URI), Nginx will return a `404 Not found` HTTP error. If you enable this directive, the two slashes will be merged into one, and the location pattern will be matched.

Syntax: `on` or `off`

Default value: `off`

msie_padding

Context: `http`, `server`, `location`

This directive functions with the Microsoft Internet Explorer (MSIE) and Google Chrome browser families. In the case of error pages (with error code 400 or higher), if the length of the response body is less than 512 bytes, these browsers will display their own error page, sometimes at the expense of a more informative page provided by the server. If you enable this option, the body of responses with a status code of 400 or higher will be padded to 512 bytes.

Syntax: `on` or `off`

Default value: `off`

msie_refresh

Context: `http`, `server`, `location`

This is another MSIE-specific directive that takes effect in the case of HTTP response codes `301 Moved permanently` and `302 Moved temporarily`. When enabled, Nginx sends a response body containing a refresh meta tag (`<meta http-equiv="Refresh"...>`) to the clients running an MSIE browser in order to redirect the browser to the new location of the requested resource.

Syntax: `on` or `off`

Default value: `off`

resolver

Context: `http`, `server`, `location`

This directive specifies the name servers that should be employed by Nginx to resolve hostnames to IP addresses and vice versa. DNS query results are cached for some time, either by respecting the TTL provided by the DNS server, or by specifying a time value to the valid argument.

Syntax: one or more IPv4 or IPv6 addresses, `valid=Time value, ipv6=on|off`

Default value: None (system default)

```
resolver 127.0.0.1; # use local DNS
resolver 8.8.8.8 8.8.4.4 valid=1h; # use Google DNS and cache results
for 1 hour
```

resolver_timeout

Context: `http, server, location`

Timeout for a hostname resolution query.

Syntax: Time value (in seconds)

Default value: 30

server_tokens

Context: `http, server, location`

This directive allows you to define whether or not Nginx should inform clients of the running version number. There are two situations where Nginx indicates its version number:

- In the server header of HTTP responses (such as `nginx/1.8.0`). If you set `server_tokens` to `off`, the server header will only indicate `Nginx`.
- On error pages, Nginx indicates the version number in the footer. If you set `server_tokens` to `off`, the footer of error pages will only indicate `Nginx`.

If you are running an older version of Nginx and do not plan to update it, it might be a good idea to hide your version number for security reasons.

Syntax: `on` or `off`

Default value: `on`

underscores_in_headers

Context: `http`, `server`

This directive allows or disallows underscores in custom HTTP header names. If this directive is set to `on`, the following example header is considered valid by `Nginx`: `test_header: value`.

Syntax: `on` or `off`

Default value: `off`

variables_hash_max_size

Context: `http`

This directive defines the maximum size of the variables hash tables. If your server configuration uses a total of more than 1024 variables, you will have to increase this value.

Syntax: Numeric value

Default value: `1024`

variables_hash_bucket_size

Context: `http`

This directive allows you to set the bucket size for the variables hash tables.

Syntax: Numeric value

Default value: `64` (or `32` or `128`, depending on your processor cache specifications)

post_action

Context: `http`, `server`, `location`, `if`

The `post_action` directive defines a post-completion action, a URI that will be called by Nginx after the request has been completed.

Syntax: URI or named `location` block.

Example:

```
location /payment/ {
    post_action /scripts/done.php;
}
```

Module variables

The HTTP Core module introduces a large set of variables that you can use within the value of directives. Be careful though, as only a handful of directives accept variables in the definition of their value. If you insert a variable in the value of a directive that does not accept variables, no error is reported; instead, the variable name appears as raw text.

There are three different kinds of variables that you will come across. The first set represents the values transmitted in the headers of the client request. The second set corresponds to the headers of the response sent to the client. Finally, the third set comprises variables that are completely generated by Nginx.

Request headers

Nginx lets you access client request headers under the form of variables that you will be able to employ later on in the configuration:

Variable	Description
$http_host	Value of the *Host* HTTP header, a string indicating the hostname that the client is trying to reach.
$http_user_agent	Value of the *User-Agent* HTTP header, a string indicating the web browser of the client.
$http_referer	Value of the *Referer* HTTP header, a string indicating the URL of the previous page from which the client comes.
$http_via	Value of the *Via* HTTP header, which informs us about the possible proxies used by the client.
$http_x_forwarded_for	Value of the *X-Forwarded-For* HTTP header, which shows the actual IP address of the client if the client is behind a proxy.
$http_cookie	Value of the *Cookie* HTTP header, which contains the cookie data sent by the client.
$http_...	Additional headers sent by the client can be retrieved using $http_ followed by the header name in lowercase and with dashes (-) replaced by underscores (_).

Response headers

In a similar fashion, you are allowed to access the HTTP headers of the response that was sent to the client. These variables are not available at all times—they will only carry a value after the response is sent, for instance, at the time of writing messages in the logs.

Variable	Description
$sent_http_content_type	Value of the *Content-Type* HTTP header indicating the MIME type of the resource being transmitted.
$sent_http_content_length	Value of the *Content-Length* HTTP header informing the client of the response body length.
$sent_http_location	Value of the *Location* HTTP header, which indicates that the location of the desired resource is different from the one specified in the original request.
$sent_http_last_modified	Value of the *Last-Modified* HTTP header corresponding to the modification date of the requested resource.
$sent_http_connection	Value of the *Connection* HTTP header defining whether the connection will be kept alive or closed.
$sent_http_keep_alive	Value of the *Keep-Alive* HTTP header that defines the amount of time a connection will be kept alive.
$sent_http_transfer_encoding	Value of the *Transfer-Encoding* HTTP header giving information about the response body encoding method (such as compress, gzip).
$sent_http_cache_control	Value of the *Cache-Control* HTTP header, telling us whether the client browser should cache the resource or not.
$sent_http_...	Additional headers sent to the client can be retrieved using $sent_http_ followed by the header name in lowercase and with dashes (-) replaced by underscores (_).

Nginx generated

Apart from the HTTP headers, Nginx provides a large number of variables concerning the request, the way it was and will be handled, as well as the settings in use with the current configuration.

Variable	Description
$arg_XXX	Allows you to access the query string (GET parameters), where XXX is the name of the parameter that you wish to utilize.
$args	All the arguments of the query string combined together.

Variable	Description
$binary_remote_addr	IP address of the client as binary data (4 bytes).
$body_bytes_sent	The number of bytes sent in the body of the response (does not include the response headers).
$bytes_sent	The number of bytes sent to the client.
$connection	Serial number identifying a connection.
$connection_requests	The number of requests already served by the current connection.
$content_length	Equates to the *Content-Length* HTTP header.
$content_type	Equates to the *Content-Type* HTTP header.
$cookie_XXX	Allows you to access cookie data, where XXX is the name of the parameter that you wish to utilize.
$document_root	Returns the value of the root directive for the current request.
$document_uri	Returns the current URI of the request. This may differ from the original request URI if internal redirects were performed. It is identical to the $uri variable.
$host	This variable equates to the *Host* HTTP header of the request. Nginx itself gives this variable a value for cases where the *Host* header is not provided in the original request.
$hostname	Returns the system hostname of the server computer
$https	Set to on for HTTPS connections, empty otherwise.
$is_args	If the $args variable is defined, $is_args equates to ?. If $args is empty, $is_args is empty as well. You may use this variable for constructing a URI that comes with a query string option, such as index.phpis_argsargs. If there is any query string argument in the request, $is_args is set to ?, making this a valid URI.
$limit_rate	Returns the per-connection transfer rate limit as defined by the limit_rate directive. You are allowed to edit this variable by using set (directive from *The Rewrite module*): `    set $limit_rate 128k;`
$msec	Returns the current time (in seconds + milliseconds).
$nginx_version	Returns the version of Nginx that you are running.
$pid	Returns the Nginx process identifier.
$pipe	If the current request is pipelined, this variable is set to p, otherwise the value is ".".

Variable	Description
`$proxy_protocol_addr`	If the `proxy_protocol` parameter is enabled on the `listen` directive, this variable will contain the client address.
`$query_string`	Identical to `$args`.
`$remote_addr`	Returns the IP address of the client.
`$remote_port`	Returns the port of the client socket.
`$remote_user`	Returns the client username if they use authentication.
`$realpath_root`	Returns the document root in the client request with symbolic links resolved into the actual path.
`$request_body`	Returns the body of the client request, or - if the body is empty.
`$request_body_file`	If the request body was saved (see the `client_body_in_file_only` directive), this variable indicates the path of the temporary file.
`$request_completion`	Returns OK if the request is completed, an empty string otherwise.
`$request_filename`	Returns the full filename served in the current request.
`$request_length`	Returns the total length of the client request.
`$request_method`	Indicates the HTTP method used in the request, such as GET or POST.
`$request_time`	Returns the amount of time elapsed since the first byte was read from the client (seconds + milliseconds value).
`$request_uri`	Corresponds to the original URI of the request, remains unmodified throughout the process (unlike `$document_uri`/`$uri`).
`$scheme`	Returns either `http` or `https` depending on the request.
`$server_addr`	Returns the IP address of the server. Beware while using this, as each use of the variable requires a system call, which could potentially affect the overall performance in the case of high-traffic setups.
`$server_name`	Indicates the value of the `server_name` directive that was used while processing the request.
`$server_port`	Indicates the port of the server socket that received the request data.
`$server_protocol`	Returns the protocol and version, usually `HTTP/1.0` or `HTTP/1.1`.
`$status`	Returns the response status code.

Variable	Description

`$tcpinfo_rtt,`
`$tcpinfo_rttvar,`
`$tcpinfo_snd_`
`cwnd, $tcpinfo_`
`rcv_space`
	If your operating system supports the `TCP_INFO` socket option, these variables will be populated with information on the current client TCP connection.

`$time_iso8601,` `$time_local`	Provides the current time in ISO 8601 and local formats respectively for use with the `access_log` directive.
`$uri`	Identical to `$document_uri`.

The location block

We have established that Nginx offers you the possibility to fine-tune your configuration down to three levels—at the *protocol* level (`http` block), the server level (`server` block), and the requested URI level (`location` block). Let us now detail the latter.

Location modifier

Nginx allows you to define `location` blocks by specifying a pattern that will be matched against the requested document URI.

```
server {
    server_name website.com;
    location /admin/ {
    # The configuration you place here only applies to
    # http://website.com/admin/
    }
}
```

Instead of a simple folder name, you can indeed insert complex patterns. The syntax of the `location` block is:

```
location [=|~|~*|^~|@] pattern { ... }
```

The first optional argument is a symbol called **location modifier** that defines the way Nginx matches the specified pattern, and also defines the very nature of the pattern (simple string or regular expression). The following paragraphs detail the different modifiers and their behavior.

The = modifier

The requested document URI must match the specified pattern exactly. The pattern here is limited to a simple literal string; you cannot use a regular expression:

```
server {
    server_name website.com;
    location = /abcd {
    […]
    }
}
```

The configuration in the `location` block:

- Applies to `http://website.com/abcd` (exact match)
- May apply to `http://website.com/ABCD` (it is only case-sensitive if your operating system uses a case-sensitive filesystem)
- Applies to `http://website.com/abcd?param1&param2` (regardless of the query string arguments)
- Does not apply to `http://website.com/abcd/` (trailing slash)
- Does not apply to `http://website.com/abcde` (extra characters after the specified pattern)

No modifier

The requested document URI must begin with the specified pattern. You may not use regular expressions:

```
server {
    server_name website.com;
    location /abcd {
    […]
    }
}
```

The configuration in the `location` block:

- Applies to `http://website.com/abcd` (exact match)
- May apply to `http://website.com/ABCD` (it is only case-sensitive if your operating system uses a case-sensitive filesystem)
- Applies to `http://website.com/abcd?param1&param2` (regardless of the query string arguments)

- Applies to `http://website.com/abcd/` (trailing slash)
- Applies to `http://website.com/abcde` (extra characters after the specified pattern)

The ~ modifier

The requested URI must be a case-sensitive match to the specified regular expression:

```
server {
    server_name website.com;
    location ~ ^/abcd$ {
    [...]
    }
}
```

The `^/abcd$` regular expression used in this example specifies that the pattern must begin (^) with /, be followed by `abc`, and finish ($) with `d`. Consequently, the configuration in the `location` block:

- Applies to `http://website.com/abcd` (exact match)
- Does not apply to `http://website.com/ABCD` (case-sensitive)
- Applies to `http://website.com/abcd?param1&param2` (regardless of the query string arguments)
- Does not apply to `http://website.com/abcd/` (trailing slash) due to the specified regular expression
- Does not apply to `http://website.com/abcde` (extra characters) due to the specified regular expression

 With operating systems such as Microsoft Windows, ~ and ~* are both case-insensitive, as the OS uses a case-insensitive filesystem.

The ~* modifier

The requested URI must be a case-insensitive match to the specified regular expression:

```
server {
    server_name website.com;
    location ~* ^/abcd$ {
    [...]
    }
}
```

The regular expression used in the example is similar to the previous one. Consequently, the configuration in the `location` block:

- Applies to `http://website.com/abcd` (exact match)
- Applies to `http://website.com/ABCD` (case-insensitive)
- Applies to `http://website.com/abcd?param1&param2` (regardless of the query string arguments)
- Does not apply to `http://website.com/abcd/` (trailing slash) due to the specified regular expression
- Does not apply to `http://website.com/abcde` (extra characters) due to the specified regular expression

The ^~ modifier

Similar to the no-symbol behavior, the location URI must begin with the specified pattern. The difference is that if the pattern is matched, Nginx stops searching for other patterns (read the following section about search order and priority).

The @ modifier

Defines a named location block. These blocks cannot be accessed by the client but only by internal requests generated by other directives such as `try_files` or `error_page`.

Search order and priority

Since it's possible to define multiple `location` blocks with different patterns, you need to understand that when Nginx receives a request, it searches for the `location` block that best matches the requested URI:

```
server {
    server_name website.com;
    location /files/ {
    # applies to any request starting with "/files/"
    # for example /files/doc.txt, /files/, /files/temp/
    }
    location = /files/ {
    # applies to the exact request to "/files/"
    # and as such does not apply to /files/doc.txt
    # but only /files/
    }
}
```

When a client visits `http://website.com/files/doc.txt`, the first `location` block applies. However, when they visit `http://website.com/files/`, the second block applies (even though the first one matches), because it has priority over the first one (it is an exact match).

The order you established in the configuration file (placing the `/files/` block before the `= /files/` block) is irrelevant. Nginx will search for matching patterns in a specific order:

- `location` blocks with the `=` modifier: If the specified string exactly matches the requested URI, Nginx retains the `location` block.

- `location` blocks with no modifier: If the specified string *exactly* matches the requested URI, Nginx retains the `location` block.

- `location` blocks with the `^~` modifier: If the specified string matches the beginning of the requested URI, Nginx retains the `location` block.

- `location` blocks with `~` or `~*` modifier: If the regular expression matches the requested URI, Nginx retains the `location` block.

- `location` blocks with no modifier: If the specified string matches the *beginning* of the requested URI, Nginx retains the `location` block.

In that context, the `^~` modifier begins to make sense, and we can envision cases where it would be useful.

Case 1

Let's begin by a simple example:

```
server {
    server_name website.com;
    location /doc {
    [...] # requests beginning with "/doc"
    }
    location ~* ^/document$ {
    [...] # requests exactly matching "/document"
    }
}
```

You might wonder: when a client requests `http://website.com/document`, which of these two `location` blocks applies? Indeed, both blocks match this request. Again, the answer does not lie in the order in which the blocks appear in the configuration files. In this case, the second `location` block will apply as the `~*` modifier has priority over the other.

Case 2

We will now take a look at this second example:

```
server {
    server_name website.com;
    location /document {
    [...] # requests beginning with "/document"
    }
    location ~* ^/document$ {
    [...] # requests exactly matching "/document"
    }
}
```

The question remains the same — what happens when a client sends a request to download `http://website.com/document`? There is a trick here. The string specified in the first block now exactly matches the requested URI. As a result, Nginx prefers it over the regular expression.

Case 3

Finally, let's go over a third and last scenario:

```
server {
    server_name website.com;
    location ^~ /doc {
    [...] # requests beginning with "/doc"
    }
    location ~* ^/document$ {
    [...] # requests exactly matching "/document"
    }
}
```

This last case makes use of the `^~` modifier. Which block applies when a client visits `http://website.com/document`? The answer is: the first block. The reason being that `^~` has priority over `~*`. As a result, any request with a URI beginning with `/doc` will be affected to the first block, even if the request URI matches the regular expression defined in the second block.

Summary

All through this chapter, we studied the key concepts of the Nginx HTTP configuration. First, you learned about creating virtual hosts by declaring `server` blocks. Then you discovered the directives and variables of the HTTP Core module that can be inserted within those blocks, and eventually, understood the mechanisms governing the `location` block.

The job is done—your server now actually serves websites. We are going to take it one step further by exploring the modules that truly form the power of Nginx. The next chapter will deal with advanced topics such as the Rewrite and SSI modules as well as additional components of the HTTP server.

Module Configuration

4

The true power of Nginx lies within its modules. The entire application is built on a modular system, and each module can be enabled or disabled at compile time. Some bring up simple functionality, such as the *Autoindex* module that generates a listing of the files in a directory. Others will transform your perception of a web server (such as the *Rewrite* module). Developers are also invited to create their own modules. A quick overview of the third-party module system can be found at the end of this chapter.

This chapter covers:

- The Rewrite module, which does more than just rewriting URIs
- The SSI module, a server-side scripting language
- Additional modules enabled in the default Nginx build
- Optional modules that must be enabled at compile time
- A quick note on third-party modules

The Rewrite module

This module, in particular, brings much more functionality to Nginx than a simple set of directives. It defines a whole new level of request processing that will be explained throughout this section.

Basically, the purpose of this module (as the name suggests) is to perform URL rewriting. This mechanism allows you to get rid of ugly URLs containing multiple parameters. For instance, `http://example.com/article.php?id=1234&comment=32` — such URLs are particularly uninformative and meaningless for a regular visitor. Instead, links to your website will contain useful information that indicates the nature of the page the visitor is about to visit. The URL given in the example becomes `http://website.com/article-1234-32-US-economy-strengthens.html`. This solution is not only more interesting for your visitors, but also for search engines — URL rewriting is a key element of **Search Engine Optimization (SEO)**.

The principle behind this mechanism is simple — it consists of rewriting the URI of the client request after it is received and before serving the file. Once rewritten, the URI is matched against the location blocks in order to find the configuration that should be applied to the request. The technique is further detailed in the coming sections.

Reminder on regular expressions

First and foremost, this module requires a certain understanding of *regular expressions*, also known as *regexes* or *regexps*. Indeed, URL rewriting is performed by the `rewrite` directive, which accepts a pattern followed by the replacement URI.

It is a vast topic — entire books are dedicated to explaining the ins and outs of regular expressions. However, the simplified approach that we are about to examine should be more than sufficient to make the most of the mechanism.

Purpose

The first question we must answer is: what is the purpose of regular expressions? To put it simply, the main purpose is to verify that a string of characters matches a given pattern. The pattern is written in a particular language that allows the defining of extremely complex and accurate rules.

String	Pattern	Does it match?	Explanation
hello	^hello$	Yes	The string begins with the character h (^h), followed by e, l, l, and then finishes with o (o$).
hell	^hello$	No	The string begins with the character h (^h), followed by e, l, and l, but does not finish with o.
Hello	^hello$	Depends	If the engine performing the match is case-sensitive, the string doesn't match the pattern.

This concept becomes a lot more interesting when complex patterns are employed, such as one that validates e-mail addresses: `^[A-Z0-9._%+-]+@[A-Z0-9.-]+\.[A-Z]{2,4}$`. Programmatically validating if an e-mail address is well-formed would require a great deal of code, while all the work can be done with a single regular expression in pattern matching.

PCRE syntax

The syntax that Nginx employs originates from the **Perl Compatible Regular Expression (PCRE)** library, which (if you remember *Chapter 2, Basic Nginx Configuration*) is a pre-requisite for making your own build, unless you disable the modules that make use of it. It's the most commonly used form of regular expressions, and nearly everything you learn here remains valid for other language variations.

In its simplest form, a pattern is composed of one character, for example, x. We can match strings against this pattern. Does `example` match the pattern x? Yes, `example` contains the character x. It can be more than one specific character — the pattern `[a-z]` matches any character between a and z, or even a combination of letters and digits: `[a-z0-9]`. In consequence, the pattern `hell[a-z0-9]` validates the following strings: `hello` and `hell4` but not `hell` or `hell!`.

You probably noticed that we employed the brackets `[` and `]`. They are part of what we call *metacharacters* and have a special effect on the pattern. There are a total of 11 metacharacters, and all play a different role. If you want to create a pattern that actually contains one of these characters, you need to escape the character with a `\` (backslash).

Metacharacter	Description
`^` Beginning	The entity after this character must be found at the beginning. Example pattern: `^h` Matching strings: `hello`, `h`, `hh` (anything beginning with h) Non-matching strings: `character`, `ssh`
`$` End	The entity before this character must be found at the end. Example pattern: `e$` Matching strings: `sample`, `e`, `file` (anything ending with e) Non-matching strings: `extra`, `shell`
`.` (dot) Any	Matches any character. Example pattern: `hell.` Matching strings: `hello`, `hellx`, `hell5`, `hell!` Non-matching strings: `hell`, `helo`

Metacharacter	Description
[ ] Set	Matches any character within the specified set. Syntax: `[a-z]` for a range, `[abcd]` for a set, and `[a-z0-9]` for two ranges. Note that if you want to include the – character in a range, you need to insert it right after `[` or just before `]`. Example pattern: `hell[a-y123-]` Matching strings: `hello, hell1, hell2, hell3, hell-` Non-matching strings: `hellz, hell4, heloo, he-llo`
[^] Negate set	Matches any character that is not within the specified set. Example pattern: `hell[^a-np-z0-9]` Matching strings: `hello, hell!` Non-matching strings: `hella, hell5`
| Alternation	Matches the entity placed either before or after |. Example pattern: `hello|welcome` Matching strings: `hello, welcome, helloes, awelcome` Non-matching strings: `hell, ellow, owelcom`
( ) Grouping	Groups a set of entities, often used in conjunction with |. Also *captures* the matched entities; captures are detailed further on. Example pattern: `^(hello|hi) there$` Matching strings: `hello there, hi there.` Non-matching strings: `hey there, ahoy there`
\\ Escape	Allows you to escape special characters. Example pattern: `Hello\.` Matching strings: `Hello., Hello. How are you?, Hi! Hello...` Non-matching strings: `Hello, Hello! how are you?`

Quantifiers

So far, you are able to express simple patterns with a limited number of characters. Quantifiers allow you to extend the number of accepted entities:

Quantifier	Description
* 0 or more times	The entity preceding * must be found 0 or more times. Example pattern: `he*llo` Matching strings: `hllo, hello, heeeello` Non-matching strings: `hallo, ello`

Quantifier	Description
+ 1 or more times	The entity preceding + must be found 1 or more times. Example pattern: `he+llo` Matching strings: `hello, heeeello` Non-matching strings: `hllo, helo`
? 0 or 1 time	The entity preceding ? must be found 0 or 1 time. Example pattern: `he?llo` Matching strings: `hello, hllo` Non-matching strings: `heello, heeeello`
{x} x times	The entity preceding {x} must be found x times. Example pattern: `he{3}llo` Matching strings: `heeello, oh heeello there!` Non-matching strings: `hello, heello, heeeello`
{x,} At least x times	The entity preceding {x,} must be found at least x times. Example pattern: `he{3,}llo` Matching strings: `heeello, heeeeeello` Non-matching strings: `hllo, hello, heello`
{x,y} x to y times	The entity preceding {x,y} must be found between x and y times. Example pattern: `he{2,4}llo` Matching strings: `heello, heeello, heeeello` Non-matching strings: `hello, heeeeello`

As you probably noticed, the { and } characters in the regular expressions conflict with the block delimiter of the Nginx configuration file syntax language. If you want to write a regular expression pattern that includes curly brackets, you need to place the pattern between quotes (single or double quotes):

```
rewrite hel{2,}o /hello.php; # invalid
rewrite "hel{2,}o" /hello.php; # valid
rewrite 'hel{2,}o' /hello.php; # valid
```

Captures

One last feature of the regular expression mechanism is the ability to capture sub-expressions. Whatever text is placed between the parentheses ( ) is captured and can be used after the matching process. The captured characters become available under the form of variables called $N, where N is a numeric index, in order of capture. Alternatively, you can attribute an arbitrary name to each of your captures (see the next example). The variables generated through the captures can be inserted within the directive values. The following are a couple of examples that illustrate the principle:

Pattern	Example of a matching string	Captured
`^(hello|hi) (sir|mister)$`	hello sir	$1 = hello $2 = sir
`^(hello (sir))$`	hello sir	$1 = hello sir $2 = sir
`^(.*)$`	nginx rocks	$1 = nginx rocks
`^(.{1,3})([0-9]{1,4})([?!]{1,2})$`	abc1234!?	$1 = abc $2 = 1234 $3 = !?
Named captures are also supported through the following syntax: ?<name>. Example: `^/(?<folder>[^/]+)/(?<file>.*)$`	/admin/doc	$folder = admin $file = doc

When you use a regular expression in Nginx, for example, in the context of a `location` block, the buffers that you capture can be employed in later directives:

```
server {
    server_name website.com;
    location ~* ^/(downloads|files)/(.*)$ {
        add_header Capture1 $1;
        add_header Capture2 $2;
    }
}
```

In the preceding example, the `location` block will match the request URI against a regular expression. A couple of URIs that would apply here would be /downloads/ file.txt, /files/archive.zip, or even /files/docs/report.doc. Two parts are captured: $1 will contain either downloads or files, and $2 will contain whatever comes after /downloads/ or /files/. Note that the `add_header` directive (syntax: `add_header header_name header_value`, see the *HTTP headers module* section) is employed here to append arbitrary headers to the client response for the sole purpose of demonstration.

Internal requests

Nginx differentiates external and internal requests. External requests directly originate from the client; the URI is then matched against the possible `location` blocks:

```
server {
    server_name website.com;
    location = /document.html {
        deny all; # example directive
    }
}
```

A client request to http://website.com/document.html would directly fall into the `location` block.

As opposed to this, internal requests are triggered by Nginx via specific directives. Among the directives offered by the default Nginx modules, there are several directives capable of producing internal requests: error_page, index, rewrite, try_files, add_before_body, add_after_body (from the Addition module), the include SSI command, and more.

There are two different types of internal requests:

- **Internal redirects:** Nginx redirects the client requests internally. The URI is changed, and the request may therefore match another `location` block and become eligible for different settings. The most common case of internal redirects is when using the **rewrite** directive, which allows you to rewrite the request URI.

- **Sub-requests**: These are additional requests that are triggered internally to generate content that is complementary to the main request. A simple example would be with the Addition module. The add_after_body directive allows you to specify a URI that will be processed after the original one, the resulting content being appended to the body of the original request. The SSI module also makes use of sub-requests to insert content with the include SSI command.

error_page

Detailed in the module directives of the Nginx HTTP Core module, `error_page` allows you to define the server behavior when a specific error code occurs. The simplest form is that of affecting a URI to an error code:

```
server {
    server_name website.com;
    error_page 403 /errors/forbidden.html;
    error_page 404 /errors/not_found.html;
}
```

When a client attempts to access a URI that triggers one of these errors (such as loading a document or a file that does not exist on the server, resulting in a 404 error), Nginx is supposed to serve the page associated with the error code. In fact, it does not just send the client the error page — it actually initiates a completely new request based on the new URI.

Consequently, you can end up falling back on a different configuration, like in the following example:

```
server {
    server_name website.com;
    root /var/www/vhosts/website.com/httpdocs/;
    error_page 404 /errors/404.html;
    location /errors/ {
        alias /var/www/common/errors/;
        internal;
    }
}
```

When a client attempts to load a document that does not exist, they will initially receive a 404 error. We employed the `error_page` directive to specify that 404 errors should create an internal redirect to /errors/404.html. As a result, a new request is generated by Nginx with the URI /errors/404.html. This URI falls under the location block /errors/, so the corresponding configuration applies.

 Logs can prove to be particularly useful when working with redirects and URL rewrites. Be aware that information on internal redirects will show up in the logs only if you set the `error_log` directive to `debug`. You can also get it to show up at the `notice` level, under the condition that you specify `rewrite_log on;` wherever you need it.

A raw but trimmed excerpt from the debug log summarizes the mechanism:

```
->http request line: "GET /page.html HTTP/1.1"
->http uri: "/page.html"
->test location: "/errors/"
->using configuration ""
->http filename: "/var/www/vhosts/website.com/httpdocs/page.html"
-> open() "/var/www/vhosts/website.com/httpdocs/page.html" failed (2:
No such file or directory), client: 127.0.0.1, server: website.com,
request: "GET /page.html HTTP/1.1", host:"website.com"
->http finalize request: 404, "/page.html?" 1
->http special response: 404, "/page.html?"
->internal redirect: "/errors/404.html?"
->test location: "/errors/"
->using configuration "/errors/"
->http filename: "/var/www/common/errors/404.html"
->http finalize request: 0, "/errors/404.html?" 1
```

Note that the use of the `internal` directive in the `location` block forbids clients from accessing the /errors/ directory. This location can thus only be accessed through an internal redirect.

The mechanism is the same for the `index` directive (detailed further on in the Index module) — if no file path is provided in the client request, Nginx will attempt to serve the specified index page by triggering an internal redirect.

Rewrite

While the previous directive, `error_page`, is not actually a part of the Rewrite module, detailing its functionality provides a solid introduction to the way Nginx handles client requests.

Similarly to how the `error_page` directive redirects to another location, rewriting the URI with the `rewrite` directive generates an internal redirect:

```
server {
    server_name website.com;
    root /var/www/vhosts/website.com/httpdocs/;
    location /storage/ {
        internal;
        alias /var/www/storage/;
    }
    location /documents/ {
        rewrite ^/documents/(.*)$ /storage/$1;
    }
}
```

A client query to http://website.com/documents/file.txt initially matches the second location block (location /documents/). However, the block contains a rewrite instruction that transforms the URI from /documents/file.txt to /storage/file.txt. The URI transformation reinitializes the process—the new URI is matched against the location blocks. This time, the first location block (location /storage/) matches the URI (/storage/file.txt).

Again, a quick peek at the debug log details the mechanism:

```
->http request line: "GET /documents/file.txt HTTP/1.1"
->http uri: "/documents/file.txt"
->test location: "/storage/"
->test location: "/documents/"
->using configuration "/documents/"
->http script regex: "^/documents/(.*)$"
->"^/documents/(.*)$" matches "/documents/file.txt", client:
127.0.0.1, server: website.com, request: "GET /documents/file.txt
HTTP/1.1", host: "website.com"
->rewritten data: "/storage/file.txt", args: "", client: 127.0.0.1,
server: website.com, request: "GET /documents/file.txt HTTP/1.1",
host: "website.com"
->test location: "/storage/"
->using configuration "/storage/"
->http filename: "/var/www/storage/file.txt"
->HTTP/1.1 200 OK
->http output filter "/storage/test.txt?"
```

Infinite loops

With all the different syntaxes and directives, you could easily get confused. Worse—you might get Nginx confused. This happens, for instance, when your rewrite rules are redundant, and cause internal redirects to loop infinitely:

```
server {
    server_name website.com;
    location /documents/ {
        rewrite ^(.*)$ /documents/$1;
    }
}
```

You thought you were doing well, but this configuration actually triggers internal redirects /documents/anything to /documents//documents/anything. Moreover, since the location patterns are re-evaluated after an internal redirect, /documents//documents/anything becomes /documents//documents//documents/anything.

Here is the corresponding excerpt from the debug log:

```
->test location: "/documents/"
->using configuration "/documents/"
->rewritten data: "/documents//documents/file.txt", [...]
->test location: "/documents/"
->using configuration "/documents/"
->rewritten data: "/documents//documents//documents/file.txt" [...]
->test location: "/documents/"
->using configuration "/documents/"
->rewritten data: -
>"/documents//documents//documents//documents/file.txt" [...]
->[...]
```

You probably wonder if this goes on indefinitely—the answer is no. The number of cycles is restricted to 10. You are only allowed 10 internal redirects. Anything past this limit and Nginx will produce a `500 Internal Server Error`.

Server Side Includes

A potential source of sub-requests is the **Server Side Include (SSI)** module. The purpose of SSI is for the server to parse documents before sending the response to the client in a fashion somewhat similar to PHP or other preprocessors.

Within a regular HTML file (for example), you are offered the possibility of inserting tags corresponding to the commands interpreted by Nginx:

```
<html>
<head>
  <!--# include file="header.html" -->
</head>
<body>
  <!--# include file="body.html" -->
</body>
</html>
```

Nginx processes these two commands; in this case, it reads the contents of `header.html` and `body.html` and inserts them into the document source, which is then sent to the client.

Several commands are at your disposal; they are detailed in the SSI module section in this chapter. The one we are interested in for now is the `include` command for including a file into another file:

```
<!--# include virtual="/footer.php?id=123" -->
```

The specified file is not just opened and read from a static location. Instead, a whole subrequest is processed by Nginx, and the body of the response is inserted instead of the `include` tag.

Conditional structure

The Rewrite module introduces a new set of directives and blocks among which is the `if` conditional structure:

```
server {
    if ($request_method = POST) {
        [...]
    }
}
```

This allows you to apply a configuration according to the specified condition. If the condition is true, the configuration is applied; otherwise, it isn't.

The following table describes the various syntaxes accepted when forming a condition:

Operator	Description

None	The condition is true if the specified variable or data is not equal to an empty string or a string starting with the character 0:
	
	`if ($string) {`
	`    [...]`
	`}`

=, !=	The condition is true if the argument preceding the = symbol is equal to the argument following it. The following example can be read as "if the request_method is equal to POST, then apply the configuration":
	
	`if ($request_method = POST) {`
	`    [...]`
	`}`
	
	The != operator does the opposite: "if the request method is not equal to GET, then apply the configuration":
	
	`if ($request_method != GET) {`
	`    [...]`
	`}`

Operator	Description

~, ~*, !~, !~*	The condition is true if the argument preceding the ~ symbol matches the regular expression pattern placed after it:
	
	``
	if ($request_filename ~ "\.txt$") {
	    [...]
	}
	``
	
	~ is case-sensitive, ~* is case-insensitive. Use the ! symbol to negate the matching:
	
	``
	if ($request_filename !~* "\.php$") {
	    [...]
	}
	``
	
	Note that you can insert the capture buffers in the regular expression:
	
	``
	if ($uri ~ "^/search/(.*)$") {
	    set $query $1;
	    rewrite ^ http://google.com/search?q=$query;
	}
	``

-f, !-f	Tests the existence of the specified file:
	
	``
	if (-f $request_filename) {
	    [...] # if the file exists
	}
	``
	
	Use !-f to test the non-existence of the file:
	
	``
	if (!-f $request_filename) {
	    [...] # if the file does not exist
	}
	``

-d, !-d	Similar to the -f operator, is used for testing the existence of a directory.
-e, !-e	Similar to the -f operator, is used for testing the existence of a file, directory, or symbolic link.
-x, !-x	Similar to the -f operator, is used for testing whether a file exists and is executable.

As of version 1.8, there is no else or else if-like instruction. However, other directives allowing you to control the configuration flow sequencing are available.

You might wonder: what are the advantages of using a location block over an if block? Indeed, in the following example, both seem to have the same effect:

```
if ($uri ~ /search/) {
    [...]
}
location ~ /search/ {
    [...]
}
```

As a matter of fact, the main difference lies within the directives that can be employed within either block—some can be inserted in an `if` block and some can't; on the contrary, almost all the directives are authorized within a `location` block, as you probably noticed in the directive listings so far. In general, it's best to only insert the directives from the Rewrite module within an `if` block, as other directives were not originally intended for such usage.

Directives

The Rewrite module provides you with a set of directives that do more than just rewriting a URI. The following table describes these directives, along with the context in which they can be employed:

Directive	Description
rewrite Context: server, location, if	As discussed previously, the `rewrite` directive allows you to rewrite the URI of the current request, thus resetting the treatment of the said request. Syntax: `rewrite regexp replacement [flag];` Where `regexp` is the regular expression that the URI should match in order for the replacement to apply. Flag may take one of the following values: • `last`: The current rewrite rule should be the last to be applied. After its application, the new URI is processed by Nginx, and a `location` block is searched for. However, further rewrite instructions will be disregarded. • `break`: The current rewrite rule is applied, but Nginx does not initiate a new request for the modified URI (does not restart the search for matching `location` blocks). All further rewrite directives are ignored. • `redirect`: Returns a `302 Moved temporarily` HTTP response, with the replacement URI set as the value of the `location` header. • `permanent`: Returns a `301 Moved permanently` HTTP response, with the replacement URI set as the value of the `location` header. • If you specify a URI beginning with `http://` as the replacement URI, Nginx will automatically use the `redirect` flag. • Note that the request URI processed by the directive is a relative URI: It does not contain the hostname and protocol. For a request such as `http://website.com/documents/page.html`, the request URI is `/documents/page.html`.

Directive	Description
	• Is decoded: The URI corresponding to a request such as `http://website.com/my%20page.html` would be `/my page.html` (in the encoded URI, %20 indicates a white space character).
	• Does not contain arguments: For a request such as `http://website.com/page.php?id=1&p=2`, the URI would be `/page.php`. When rewriting the URI, you don't need to consider including the arguments in the replacement URI—Nginx does it for you. If you want Nginx not to include the arguments after the rewritten URI, you must insert a ? character at the end of the replacement URI: `rewrite ^/search/(.*)$ /search.php?q=$1?`.
	• Examples:

	``
	rewrite ^/search/(.*)$ /search.php?q=$1;
	rewrite ^/search/(.*)$ /search.php?q=$1?;
	rewrite ^ http://website.com;
	rewrite ^ http://website.com permanent;
	``

`break`
Context: `server, location, if`
	The `break` directive is used to prevent further rewrite directives. Past this point, the URI is fixed and cannot be altered.
	
	Example:
	
	``
	if (-f $uri) {
	    break; # break if the file exists
	}
	if ($uri ~ ^/search/(.*)$) {
	    set $query $1;
	    rewrite ^ /search.php?q=$query?;
	}
	``
	
	This example rewrites `/search/anything`-like queries to `/search.php?q=anything`. However, if the requested file exists (such as `/search/index.html`), the break instruction prevents Nginx from rewriting the URI.

Directive	Description

`return`
 	
Context: `server,`
`location, if`
	Interrupts the processing of the request, and returns the specified HTTP status code or specified text.
	
	Syntax: `return code | text;`
	
	Where the code is one of the following status codes: 204, 400, 402 to 406, 408, 410, 411, 413, 416, and 500 to 504. In addition, you may use the Nginx-specific code 444 in order to return a `HTTP 200 OK` status code with no further response header or body. Alternatively, you may also specify a raw text value that will be returned to the user as the response body. This comes in handy when testing whether your request URIs fall within particular location blocks.
	
	Example:
	
	``
	if ($uri ~ ^/admin/) {
	    return 403;
	    # the instruction below is NOT executed
	    # as Nginx already completed the request
	    rewrite ^ http://website.com;
	}
	``

`set`
 	
Context: `server,`
`location, if`
	Initializes or redefines a variable. Note that some variables cannot be redefined, for example, you are not allowed to alter $uri.
	
	Syntax: `set $variable value;`
	
	Examples:
	
	``
	set $var1 "some text";
	if ($var1 ~ ^(.*) (.*)$) {
	    set $var2 $1$2; #concatenation
	    rewrite ^ http://website.com/$var2;
	}
	``

`uninitialized_`
`variable_warn`
 	
Context: `http,`
`server,`
`location, if`
	If set to on, Nginx will issue log messages when the configuration employs a variable that has not yet been initialized.
	
	Syntax: on or off
	
	``
	uninitialized_variable_warn on;
	``

`rewrite_log`
 	
Context: `http,`
`server,`
`location, if`
	If set to on, Nginx will issue log messages for every operation performed by the rewrite engine at the `notice` error level (see `error_log` directive).
	
	Syntax: on or off
	
	Default value: `off`
	
	``
	rewrite_log off;
	``

Common rewrite rules

Here is a set of rewrite rules that satisfy the basic needs of the dynamic websites that wish to beautify their page links, thanks to the URL rewriting mechanism. You will obviously need to adjust these rules according to your particular situation, as every website is different.

Performing a search

This rewrite rule is intended for search queries. Search keywords are included in the URL.

Input URI	`http://website.com/search/some-search-keywords`
Rewritten URI	`http://website.com/search.php?q=some-search-keywords`
Rewrite rule	`rewrite ^/search/(.*)$ /search.php?q=$1?;`

User profile page

Most dynamic websites that allow the visitors to register, offer a profile view page. URLs of this form, containing both the user ID and the username can be employed.

Input URI	`http://website.com/user/31/James`
Rewritten URI	`http://website.com/user.php?id=31&name=James`
Rewrite rule	`rewrite ^/user/([0-9]+)/(.+)$ /user.php?id=$1&name=$2?;`

Multiple parameters

Some websites may use different syntaxes for the argument string, for example, separating non-named arguments with slashes.

Input URI	`http://website.com/index.php/param1/param2/param3`
Rewritten URI	`http://website.com/index.php?p1=param1&p2=param2&p3=param3`
Rewrite rule	`rewrite ^/index.php/(.*)/(.*)/(.*)$ /index.php?p1=$1&p2=$2&p3=$3?;`

Wikipedia-like

Many websites have now adopted the URL style introduced by Wikipedia: a prefix folder, followed by an article name.

Input URI	`http:// website.com/wiki/Some_keyword`
Rewritten URI	`http://website.com/wiki/index.php?title=Some_keyword`
Rewrite rule	`rewrite ^/wiki/(.*)$ /wiki/index.php?title=$1?;`

News website article

This URL structure is often employed by news websites, as the URLs contain indications to the articles' contents. It is formed of an article identifier, followed by a slash, then a list of keywords. The keywords can usually be ignored and excluded from the rewritten URI.

Input URI	`http://website.com/33526/us-economy-strengthens`
Rewritten URI	`http://website.com/article.php?id=33526`
Rewrite rule	`rewrite ^/([0-9]+)/.*$ /article.php?id=$1?;`

Discussion board

Modern bulletin boards now mostly use *pretty URLs*. The following example shows how to create a *topic view* URL with two parameters—the topic identifier and the starting post. Once again, keywords are ignored:

Input URI	`http://website.com/topic-1234-50-some-keywords.html`
Rewritten URI	`http://website.com/viewtopic.php?topic=1234&start=50`
Rewrite rule	`rewrite ^/topic-([0-9]+)-([0-9]+)-(.*)\.html$ / viewtopic.php?topic=$1&start=$2?;`

SSI module

SSI or Server Side Includes, is actually a sort of server-side programming language interpreted by Nginx. Its name originates from the fact that the most-used functionality of the language is the `include` command. Back in the 1990s, such languages were employed in order to render web pages dynamically, from simple static `.html` files with client-side scripts to complex pages with server-processed instructions. Within the HTML source code, webmasters could now insert server-interpreted directives, which would then lead the way to much more advanced pre-processors such as PHP or ASP.

The most famous illustration of SSI is the *quote of the day* example. In order to insert a new quote every day at the top of each page of their website, webmasters would have to edit out the HTML source of every page of the site, updating the old quote manually. With Server Side Includes, a single command suffices to simplify the task:

```
<html>
<head><title>My web page</title></head>
<body>
  <h1>Quote of the day: <!--# include file="quote.txt" -->
  </h1>
</body>
</html>
```

All you would have to do to update the quote is to edit the contents of the `quote.txt` file. Automatically, all the pages would show the updated quote. As of today, most of the major web servers (Apache, IIS, Lighttpd, and so on) support Server Side Includes.

Module directives and variables

Having directives inserted within the actual content of the files that Nginx serves raises one major issue—what files should Nginx parse for the SSI commands? It would be a waste of resources to parse binary files such as images (.gif, .jpg, and .png) or other kinds of media, since they are unlikely to contain any SSI commands. You need to make sure to configure Nginx correctly with the directives introduced by this module:

Directive	Description
ssi Context: http, server, location, if	Enables parsing files for SSI commands. Nginx only parses the files corresponding to the MIME types selected with the ssi_types directive. Syntax: on or off Default value: off `ssi on;`

ssi_types
 	
Context: http, server, location
	Defines the MIME file types that should be eligible for SSI parsing. The text/html type is always included.
	
	Syntax:
	
	`ssi_types type1 [type2] [type3...];`
	`ssi_types *;`
	
	Default value: text/html
	
	`ssi_types text/plain;`

ssi_silent_errors Context: http, server, location	Some SSI commands may generate errors; in that case, Nginx outputs a message at the location of the command—'an error occurred while processing the directive'. Enabling this option silences Nginx and the message does not appear. Syntax: on or off Default value: off `ssi_silent_errors off;`
ssi_value_length Context: http, server, location	SSI commands have arguments that accept a value (for example, `<!--# include file="value" -->`). This parameter defines the maximum length accepted by Nginx. Syntax: Numeric Default: 256 (characters) `ssi_value_length 256;`

Directive	Description
`ssi_ignore_recycled_buffers` Context: `http, server, location`	When set to `on`, this directive prevents Nginx from making use of the recycled buffers. Syntax: `on` or `off` Default: `off`
`ssi_min_file_chunk` Context: `http, server, location`	If the size of a buffer is greater than `ssi_min_file_chunk`, data is stored in a file and then sent via `sendfile`. In other cases, it is transmitted directly from the memory. Syntax: Numeric value (size) Default: `1,024`
`ssi_last_modified` Context: `http, server, location`	If set to `off`, Nginx removes the `Last-modified` header from the original response during SSI processing in order to increase the caching likeliness. The `Last-modified` date is likely to change often due to dynamically generated elements contained in the response, rendering it non-cacheable. Syntax: `on` or `off` Default: `off`

A quick note regarding possible concerns about the SSI engine resource usage — by enabling the SSI module at the `location` or `server` block level, you enable parsing of at least all `text/html` files (pretty much any page to be displayed by the client browser). While the Nginx SSI module is efficiently optimized, you might want to disable parsing for the files that do not require it.

Firstly, all your pages containing the SSI commands should have the `.shtml` (Server HTML) extension. Then, in your configuration at the `location` block level, enable the SSI engine under a specific condition. The name of the served file must end with `.shtml`:

```
server {
    server_name website.com;
    location ~* \.shtml$ {
        ssi on;
    }
}
```

On one hand, all HTTP requests submitted to Nginx will go through an additional regular expression pattern matching. On the other hand, static HTML files or files to be processed by other interpreters (`.php`, for instance) will not be parsed unnecessarily.

Finally, the SSI module enables two variables:

- `$date_local`: Returns the current time according to the current system time zone

- `$date_gmt`: Returns the current GMT time, regardless of the server time zone

SSI commands

Once you have the SSI engine enabled for your web pages, you are ready to start writing your first dynamic HTML page. Again, the principle is simple—design the pages of your website using the regular HTML code, inside which you will insert the SSI commands.

These commands respect a particular syntax—at first sight, they look like regular HTML comments: `<!-- A comment -->`, and that is the good thing about it—if you accidentally disable SSI parsing of your files, the SSI commands do not appear on the client browser; they are only visible in the source code as actual HTML comments. The full syntax is as follows:

```
<!--# command param1="value1" param2="value2" … -->
```

File includes

The main command of the Server Side Include module is, obviously, the `include` command. It can be used in two different fashions.

First, you are allowed to make a simple file include:

```
<!--# include file="header.html" -->
```

This command generates an HTTP sub-request to be processed by Nginx. The body of the response that was generated is inserted instead of the command itself.

The second possibility is to use the `include virtual` command:

```
<!--# include virtual="/sources/header.php?id=123" -->
```

This also sends a sub-request to the server; the difference lies in the way that Nginx fetches the specified file (when using `include file`, the `wait` parameter is automatically enabled). Indeed, two parameters can be inserted within the `include` command tag. By default, all SSI requests are issued simultaneously, in parallel. This can cause slowdowns and timeouts in case of heavy loads. Alternatively, you can use the `wait="yes"` parameter to specify that Nginx should wait for the completion of the request before moving on to other includes:

```
<!--# include virtual="header.php" wait="yes" -->
```

If the result of your `include` command is empty or if it triggered an error (404, 500, and so on), Nginx inserts the corresponding error page with its HTML: `<html>[...]404 Not Found</body></html>`. The message is displayed at exactly the same place where you inserted the `include` command. If you wish to revise this behavior, you have the option to create a named block. By linking the block to the `include` command, the contents of the block will show at the location of the `include` command tag in case an error occurs:

```
<html>
<head><title>SSI Example</title></head>
<body>
<center>
  <!--# block name="error_footer" -->Sorry, the footer file was not
found.<!--# endblock -->
  <h1>Welcome to nginx</h1>
  <!--# include virtual="footer.html" stub="error_footer" -->
</center>
</body>
</html>
```

The result as output in the client browser is shown as follows:

As you can see, the contents of the `error_footer` block were inserted at the location of the `include` command, after the `<h1>` tag.

Working with variables

The Nginx SSI module also offers the option of working with variables. Displaying a variable (in other words, inserting the variable value into the final HTML source code) can be done with the `echo` command:

```
<!--# echo var="variable_name" -->
```

The command accepts the following three parameters:

- `var`: The name of the variable that you want to display, for example, `REMOTE_ADDR` to display the IP address of the client.
- `default`: A string to be displayed in case the variable is empty. If you don't specify this parameter, the output is (none).
- `encoding`: Encoding method for the string. The accepted values are `none` (no particular encoding), `url` (encode text like a URL—a blank space becomes %20, and so on), and `entity` (uses HTML entities: & becomes &).

You may also affect your own variables with the `set` command:

```
<!--# set var="my_variable" value="your value here" -->
```

The `value` parameter is itself parsed by the engine; as a result, you are allowed to make use of the existing variables:

```
<!--# echo var="MY_VARIABLE" -->
<!--# set var="MY_VARIABLE" value="hello" -->
<!--# echo var="MY_VARIABLE" -->
<!--# set var="MY_VARIABLE" value="$MY_VARIABLE there" -->
<!--# echo var="MY_VARIABLE" -->
```

The following is the output that Nginx displays for each of the three `echo` commands from the preceding example:

```
(none)
hello
hello there
```

Conditional structure

The following set of commands allow you to include text or other directives depending on a condition. The conditional structure can be established with the following syntax:

```
<!--# if expr="expression1" -->
[...]
<!--# elif expr="expression2" -->
```

```
[...]
<!--# else -->
[...]
<!--# endif -->
```

The expression can be formulated in three different ways:

- Inspecting a variable: `<!--# if expr="$variable" -->`. Similar to the `if` block in the Rewrite module, the condition is true if the variable is not empty.

- Comparing two strings: `<!--# if expr="$variable = hello" -->`. The condition is true if the first string is equal to the second string. Use `!=` instead of `=` to revert the condition (the condition is true if the first string is not equal to the second string).

- Matching a regular expression pattern: `<!--# if expr="$variable = /pattern/" -->`. Note that the pattern must be enclosed within `/` characters, otherwise it is considered to be a simple string (for example, `<!--# if expr="$MY_VARIABLE = /^/documents//" -->`). Similar to the comparison, use `!=` to negate the condition. The captures in regular expressions are supported.

The content that you insert within a condition block can contain regular HTML code or additional SSI directives with one exception — you cannot nest `if` blocks.

Configuration

Last and probably the least (for once) of the SSI commands offered by Nginx is the `config` command. It allows you to configure two simple parameters.

First, the message that appears when the SSI engine faces an error related to malformed tags or invalid expressions. By default, Nginx displays [an error occurred while processing the directive]. If you want it to display something else, enter the following:

```
<!--# config errmsg="Something terrible happened" -->
```

Additionally, you can configure the format of the dates that are returned by the `$date_local` and `$date_gmt` variables using the `timefmt` parameter:

```
<!--# config timefmt="%A, %d-%b-%Y %H:%M:%S %Z" -->
```

The string that you specify here is passed as the format string of the `strftime` C function. For more information about the arguments that can be used in the format string, please refer to the documentation of the `strftime` C language function at http://www.opengroup.org/onlinepubs/009695399/functions/strftime.html.

Additional modules

The first half of this chapter covered two of the most important Nginx modules: the Rewrite module and the SSI module. There are a lot more modules that will greatly enrich the functionality of the web server; they are regrouped here, thematically.

Among the modules described in this section, some are included in the default Nginx build, but some are not. This implies that unless you specifically configured your Nginx build to include these modules (as described in *Chapter 1, Downloading and Installing Nginx*), they will not be available to you. But remember that rebuilding Nginx to include additional modules is a relatively quick and easy process.

Website access and logging

The following set of modules allows you to configure the way visitors access your website and the way your server logs requests.

Index

The Index module provides a simple directive named index, which lets you define the page that Nginx will serve by default if no filename is specified in the client request (in other words, it defines the website index page). You may specify multiple filenames; the first file to be found will be served. If none of the specified files are found, Nginx will either attempt to generate an automatic index of the files (if the autoindex directive is enabled—check the HTTP Autoindex module), or return a 403 Forbidden error page.

Optionally, you may insert an absolute filename (such as /page.html), but only as the last argument of the directive.

Syntax: index file1 [file2...] [absolute_file];

Default value: index.html

```
index index.php index.html index.htm;
index index.php index2.php /catchall.php;
```

This directive is valid in the following contexts: http, server, and location.

Autoindex

If Nginx cannot provide an index page for the requested directory, the default behavior is to return a 403 Forbidden HTTP error page. With the following set of directives, you enable an automatic listing of the files that are present in the requested directory:

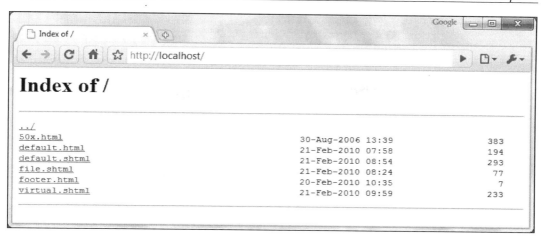

Three columns of information appear for each file—the filename, the file date and time, and the file size in bytes.

Directive	Description
`autoindex` Context: `http, server, location`	Enables or disables the automatic directory listing for directories missing an index page. Syntax: `on` or `off`
`autoindex_exact_size` Context: `http, server, location`	If set to `on`, this directive ensures that the listing displays the file sizes in bytes. Otherwise, another unit is employed, such as KB, MB, or GB. Syntax: `on` or `off` Default value: `on`
`autoindex_localtime` Context: `http, server, location`	By default, this directive is set to `off`, so the date and time of files in the listing appears as the GMT time. Set it to `on` to make use of the local server time. Syntax: `on` or `off` Default value: `off`
`autoindex_format` Context: `http, server, location`	Nginx offers to serve the directory index in different formats: HTML, XML, JSON, or JSONP (by default, HTML is used). Syntax: `autoindex_format html | xml | json | jsonp;` If you set the directive value to `jsonp`, Nginx inserts the value of the `callback` query argument as JSONP callback. For example, your script should call the following URI: `/folder/?callback=MyCallbackName`.

Random index

This module enables a simple directive, `random_index`, which can be used within a `location` block for Nginx to return an index page selected randomly among the files of the specified directory.

 This module is not included in the default Nginx build.

Syntax: `on` or `off`

Log

This module controls the behavior of Nginx regarding the access logs. It is a key module for system administrators, as it allows analyzing the runtime behavior of web applications. It is composed of three essential directives:

Directive	Description
`access_log` Context: `http`, `server`, `location`, `if` (in location), `limit_except`	This parameter defines the access log file path, the format of entries in the access log by selecting a template name, or disables access logging. Syntax: `access_log path [format [buffer=size]] | off;` Some remarks concerning the directive syntax are as follows: • Use `access_log off` to disable access logging at the current level • The format argument corresponds to a template declared with the `log_format` directive, described next • If the format argument is not specified, the default format is employed (combined) • You may use variables in the file path

Directive	Description
`log_format` Context: `http, server, location`	Defines a template to be utilized by the `access_log` directive, describing the contents that should be included in an entry of the access log. Syntax: `log_format template_name format_string;` The default template is called `combined`, and matches the following example: ```log_format combined '$remote_addr - $remote_user [$time_local] '"$request" $status $body_bytes_sent '"$http_referer" "$http_user_agent"'; # Other example log_format simple '$remote_addr $request';```
`open_log_file_cache` Context: `http, server, location`	Configures the cache for log file descriptors. Please refer to the `open_file_cache` directive of the HTTP Core module for additional information. Syntax: `open_log_file_cache max=N [inactive=time] [min_uses=N] [valid=time]	off;`  The arguments are similar to the `open_file_cache` and other related directives; the difference is that this applies to access log files only.

The Log module also enables several new variables, though they are only accessible when writing log entries:

- `$connection`: The connection number
- `$pipe`: The variable is set to "p" if the request was pipelined
- `$time_local`: Local time (at the time of writing the log entry)
- `$msec`: Local time (at the time of writing the log entry) to the microsecond
- `$request_time`: Total length of the request processing, in milliseconds
- `$status`: Response status code
- `$bytes_sent`: Total number of bytes sent to the client
- `$body_bytes_sent`: Number of bytes sent to the client for the response body
- `$apache_bytes_sent`: Similar to `$body_bytes`, which corresponds to the `%B` parameter of Apache's `mod_log_config`
- `$request_length`: Length of the request body

Limits and restrictions

The following modules allow you to regulate access to the documents of your websites—require users to authenticate, match a set of rules, or simply restrict the access to certain visitors.

Auth_basic module

The `auth_basic` module enables the basic authentication functionality. With the two directives that it brings forth, you can make it such that a specific location of your website (or your server) is restricted to users who authenticate with a username and password:

```
location /admin/ {
    auth_basic "Admin control panel"; # variables are supported
    auth_basic_user_file access/password_file;
}
```

The first directive, `auth_basic`, can be set to either `off` or a text message, usually referred to as *authentication challenge* or *authentication realm*. This message is displayed by the web browsers in a username/password box when a client attempts to access the protected resource.

The second one, `auth_basic_user_file`, defines the path of the password file relative to the directory of the configuration file. A password file is formed of lines respecting the following syntax: `username:[{SCHEME}]password[:comment]`. Where:

- `username`: a plain text user name
- `{SCHEME}`: optionally, the password hashing method. There are currently three supported schemes: `{PLAIN}` for plain text passwords, `{SHA}` for SHA-1 hashing, and `{SSHA}` for salted SHA-1 hashing.
- `password`: the password
- `comment`: a plain text comment for your own use

If you fail to specify a scheme, the password will need to be encrypted with the `crypt(3)` function, for example with the help of the `htpasswd` command-line utility from the Apache packages.

 If you aren't too keen on installing Apache on your system just for the sake of the `htpasswd` tool, you may resort to online tools, as there are plenty of them available. Fire up your favorite search engine and type `online htpasswd`.

Access

Two important directives are brought up by this module: `allow` and `deny`. They let you allow or deny access to a resource for a specific IP address or IP address range.

Both directives have the same syntax: `allow IP | CIDR | unix: | all`, where IP is an IP address, CIDR is an IP address range (CIDR syntax), unix: represents all UNIX domain sockets, and `all` specifies that the directive applies to all clients:

```
location {
    allow 127.0.0.1; # allow local IP address
    allow unix:; # allow UNIX domain sockets
    deny all; # deny all other IP addresses
}
```

Note that rules are processed from top-down—if your first instruction is `deny all`, all possible `allow` exceptions that you place afterwards will have no effect. The opposite is also true—if you start with `allow all`, all possible `deny` directives that you place afterwards will have no effect, as you already allowed all the IP addresses.

Limit connections

The mechanism induced by this module is a little more complex than the regular ones. It allows you to define the maximum number of simultaneous connections to the server for a specific *zone*.

The first step is to define the zone using the `limit_conn_zone` directive:

- Directive syntax: `limit_conn_zone $variable zone=name:size;`
- `$variable` is the variable that will be used to differentiate one client from another, typically `$binary_remote_addr`—the IP address of the client in the binary format (this is more efficient than ASCII)
- name is an arbitrary name given to the zone
- size is the maximum size you allocate to the table storing session states

The following example defines the zones based on the client IP addresses:

```
limit_conn_zone $binary_remote_addr zone=myzone:10m;
```

Now that you have defined a zone, you may limit the connections using `limit_conn`:

```
limit_conn zone_name connection_limit;
```

When applied to the previous example, it becomes:

```
location /downloads/ {
    limit_conn myzone 1;
}
```

As a result, requests that share the same `$binary_remote_addr` are subject to the connection limit (one simultaneous connection). If the limit is reached, all additional concurrent requests will be answered with a `503 Service unavailable` HTTP response. This response code can be overridden if you specify another code via the `limit_conn_status` directive. If you wish to log client requests that are affected by the limits you have set, enable the `limit_conn_log_level` directive, and specify the log level (`info | notice | warn | error`).

Limit request

In a similar fashion, the *Limit request* module allows you to limit the number of requests for a defined zone.

Defining the zone is done via the `limit_req_zone` directive; its syntax differs from the *Limit zone* equivalent directive:

```
limit_req_zone $variable zone=name:max_memory_size rate=rate;
```

The directive parameters are identical except for the trailing `rate`: expressed in requests per second (r/s) or requests per minute (r/m). It defines a request rate that will be applied to clients where the zone is enabled. To apply a zone to a location, use the `limit_req` directive:

```
limit_req zone=name burst=burst [nodelay];
```

The `burst` parameter defines the maximum possible bursts of requests — when the amount of requests received from a client exceeds the limit defined in the zone, the responses are delayed in a manner that respects the rate that you defined. To a certain extent, only a maximum of `burst` requests will be accepted simultaneously. Past this limit, Nginx returns a `503 Service Unavailable` HTTP error response. This response code can be overridden if you specify another code via the `limit_req_status` directive.

```
limit_req_zone $binary_remote_addr zone=myzone:10m rate=2r/s;
[...]
location /downloads/ {
  limit_req zone=myzone burst=10;
  limit_req_status 404; # returns a 403 error if limit is exceeded
}
```

If you wish to log client requests that are affected by the limits you have set, enable the `limit_req_log_level` directive, and specify the log level (`info` | `notice` | `warn` | `error`).

Auth_request

The **auth_request** module was implemented in the recent versions of Nginx, and allows you to allow or deny access to a resource based on the result of a sub-request. Nginx calls the URI that you specify via the `auth_request` directive: if the sub-request returns a 2XX response code (that is, `HTTP/200 OK`), access is allowed. If the sub-request returns a 401 or 403 status code, access is denied, and Nginx forwards the response code to the client. Should the backend return any other response code, Nginx will consider it to be an error and deny access to the resource.

```
location /downloads/ {
    # if the script below returns a 200 status code,
    # the download is authorized
    auth_request /authorization.php;
}
```

Additionally, the module offers a second directive called `auth_request_set`, allowing you to set a variable after the sub-request is executed. You can insert variables that originate from the sub-request upstream (`$upstream_http_*`) such as `$upstream_http_server` or other HTTP headers from the server response.

```
location /downloads/ {
    # requests authorization from PHP script
    auth_request /authorization.php;
    # assuming authorization is granted, get filename from
    # sub-request response header and redirect
    auth_request_set $filename "${upstream_http_x_filename}.zip";
    rewrite ^ /documents/$filename;
}
```

Content and encoding

The following set of modules provides functionalities having an effect on the contents served to the client, either by modifying the way the response is encoded, by affecting the headers, or by generating a response from scratch.

Empty GIF

The purpose of this module is to provide a directive that serves a *1 x 1* transparent GIF image from the memory. Such files are sometimes used by web designers to tweak the appearance of their website. With this directive, you get an empty GIF straight from the memory instead of reading and processing an actual GIF file from the storage space.

To utilize this feature, simply insert the empty_gif directive in the location of your choice:

```
location = /empty.gif {
    empty_gif;
}
```

FLV and MP4

FLV and MP4 are separate modules enabling a simple functionality that becomes useful when serving Flash (FLV) or MP4 video files. It parses a special argument of the request, start, which indicates the offset of the section that the client wishes to download or pseudo-stream. The video file must thus be accessed with the following URI: video.flv?start=XXX. This parameter is prepared automatically by mainstream video players such as JWPlayer.

 This module is not included in the default Nginx build.

To utilize this feature, simply insert the flv or mp4 directive in the location of your choice:

```
location ~* \.flv {
    flv;
}
location ~* \.mp4 {
    mp4;
}
```

Be aware that in case Nginx fails to seek the requested position within the video file, the request will result in a 500 Internal Server Error HTTP response. JWPlayer sometimes misinterprets this error, and simply displays a *Video not found* error message.

HTTP headers

Two directives are introduced by this module that affect the header of the response sent to the client.

First, `add_header Name value [always]` lets you add a new line in the response headers, respecting the following syntax: `Name: value`. The line is added only for responses with the following codes: `200`, `201`, `204`, `301`, `302`, and `304`. You may insert variables in the `value` argument. If you specify `always` at the end of the directive value, the header will always be added regardless of the response code.

Additionally, the `expires` directive allows you to control the value of the *Expires and Cache-Control HTTP header* sent to the client, affecting the requests of the codes listed previously. It accepts a single value among the following:

- `off`: Does not modify either of the headers
- A time value: The expiration date of the file is set to *the current time +, the time you specify*. For example, `expires 24h` will return an expiry date set to 24 hours from now
- `epoch`: The expiration date of the file is set to January 1, 1970. The Cache-Control header is set to `no-cache`
- `max`: The expiration date of the file is set to December 31, 2037. The Cache-Control header is set to 10 years

Addition

The Addition module allows you (through simple directives) to add content before or after the body of the HTTP response.

 This module is not included in the default Nginx build.

The two main directives are:

```
add_before_body file_uri;
add_after_body file_uri;
```

As stated previously, Nginx triggers a sub-request for fetching the specified URI. Additionally, you can define the type of files to which the content is appended in case your `location` block pattern is not specific enough (default: `text/html`):

```
addition_types mime_type1 [mime_type2...];
addition_types *;
```

Substitution

Along the same lines as that of the preceding module, the Substitution module allows you to search and replace text directly from the response body:

```
sub_filter searched_text replacement_text;
```

 This module is not included in the default Nginx build.

Two additional directives provide more flexibility:

- `sub_filter_once` (on or off, default on): Only replaces the text once, and stops after the first occurrence.
- `sub_filter_types` (default text/html): Affects the additional MIME types that are eligible for text replacement. The * wildcard is allowed.

Gzip filter

This module allows you to compress the response body with the Gzip algorithm before sending it to the client. To enable Gzip compression, use the gzip directive (on or off) at the http, server, location, and even the if level (though that is not recommended). The following directives will help you further configure the filter options:

Directive	Description
`gzip_buffers` Context: http, server, location	Defines the number and size of buffers to be used for storing the compressed response. Syntax: gzip_buffers amount size; Default: gzip_buffers 4 4k (or 8k depending on the OS).
`gzip_comp_level` Context: http, server, location	Defines the compression level of the algorithm. The specified value ranges from 1 (low compression, faster for the CPU) to 9 (high compression, slower). Syntax: Numeric value. Default: 1
`gzip_disable` Context: http, server, location	Disables Gzip compression for the requests where the User-Agent HTTP header matches the specified regular expression. Syntax: Regular expression Default: None

Directive	Description
`gzip_http_version` Context: `http, server, location`	Enables Gzip compression for the specified protocol version. Syntax: `1.0` or `1.1` Default: `1.1`
`gzip_min_length` Context: `http, server, location`	If the response body length is inferior to the specified value, it is not compressed. Syntax: Numeric value (size) Default: `0`
`gzip_proxied` Context: `http, server, location`	Enables or disables Gzip compression for the body of responses received from a proxy (see reverse-proxying mechanisms in later chapters). The directive accepts the following parameters; some can be combined: • `off`/`any`: Disables or enables compression for all requests • `expired`: Enables compression if the *Expires* header prevents caching • `no-cache`/`no-store`/`private`: Enables compression if the *Cache-Control* header is set to no-cache, no-store, or private • `no_last_modified`: Enables compression in case the *Last-Modified* header is not set • `no_etag`: Enables compression in case the *ETag* header is not set • `auth`: Enables compression in case an *Authorization* header is set

`gzip_types`
Context: `http, server, location`
	Enables compression for types other than the default `text/html` MIME type.
	Syntax:
	`gzip_types mime_type1 [mime_type2...];`
	`gzip_types *;`
	Default: `text/html` (cannot be disabled)

`gzip_vary` Context: `http, server, location`	Adds the *Vary: Accept-Encoding* HTTP header to the response. Syntax: `on` or `off` Default: `off`

Directive	Description

`gzip_window`
 	
Context: `http,`
`server, location`
	Sets the size of the window buffer (`windowBits` argument) for Gzipping operations. This directive value is used for calls to functions from the Zlib library.
	
	Syntax: Numeric value (size)
	
	Default: `MAX_WBITS` constant from the Zlib library

`gzip_hash`
 	
Context: `http,`
`server, location`
	Sets the amount of memory that should be allocated for the internal compression state (`memLevel` argument). This directive value is used for calls to functions from the Zlib library.
	
	Syntax: Numeric value (size)
	
	Default: `MAX_MEM_LEVEL` constant from the Zlib prerequisite library

`postpone_`
`gzipping`
 	
Context: `http,`
`server, location`
	Defines a minimum data threshold to be reached before starting the Gzip compression.
	
	Syntax: Size (numeric value)
	
	Default: `0`

`gzip_no_buffer`
 	
Context: `http,`
`server, location`
	By default, Nginx waits until at least one buffer (defined by `gzip_buffers`) is filled with data before sending the response to the client. Enabling this directive disables buffering.
	
	Syntax: `on` or `off`
	
	Default: `off`

Gzip static

This module adds a simple functionality to the Gzip filter mechanism — when its `gzip_static` directive (`on`, `off`, or `always`) is enabled, Nginx will automatically look for a `.gz` file corresponding to the requested document before serving it. This allows Nginx to send pre-compressed documents instead of compressing documents on the fly at each request. Specifying `always` will force Nginx to serve the gzip version regardless of whether the client accepts gzip encoding.

 This module is not included in the default Nginx build.

If a client requests `/documents/page.html`, Nginx checks for the existence of a `/documents/page.html.gz` file. If the `.gz` file is found, it is served to the client. Note that Nginx does not generate `.gz` files itself, even after serving the requested files.

Gunzip filter

With the *Gunzip filter* module, you can decompress a gzip-compressed response sent from the backend in order to serve it *raw* to the client. For example, in cases where the client browser is not able to process the gzipped files (Microsoft Internet Explorer 6), simply insert `gunzip on;` in a location block to employ this module. You can also set the buffer amount and size with `gunzip_buffers amount size;` where `amount` is the amount of buffers to allocate, and `size` is the size of each allocated buffer.

Charset filter

With the *Charset filter* module, you can control the character set of the response body more accurately. Not only are you able to specify the value of the `charset` argument of the Content-Type HTTP header (such as `Content-Type: text/html; charset=utf-8`), but Nginx can also re-encode the data to a specified encoding method automatically.

Directive	Description
`charset` Context: `http, server, location, if`	This directive adds the specified encoding to the Content-Type header of the response. If the specified encoding differs from the `source_charset` one, Nginx re-encodes the document. Syntax: `charset encoding | off;` Default: `off` Example: `charset utf-8;`
`source_charset` Context: `http, server, location, if`	Defines the initial encoding of the response; if the value specified in the `charset` directive differs, Nginx re-encodes the document. Syntax: `source_charset encoding;`
`override_charset` Context: `http, server, location, if`	When Nginx receives a response from the proxy or FastCGI gateway, this directive defines whether or not the character encoding should be checked and potentially overridden. Syntax: `on` or `off` Default: `off`

`charset_types`
Context: `http, server, location`
	Defines the MIME types that are eligible for re-encoding.
	
	Syntax:
	
	`    charset_types mime_type1 [mime_type2...];`
	`    charset_types * ;`
	
	Default: `text/html, text/xml, text/plain, text/vnd.wap.wml, application/x-javascript, application/rss+xml`

Directive	Description
charset_map Context: http	Lets you define character re-encoding tables. Each line of the table contains two hexadecimal codes to be exchanged. You will find re-encoding tables for the koi8-r character set in the default Nginx configuration folder (koi-win and koi-utf). Syntax: charset_map src_encoding dest_encoding { ... }

Memcached

Memcached is a daemon application that can be connected to via sockets. Its main purpose, as the name suggests, is to provide an efficient distributed key/value memory caching system. The *Nginx Memcached* module provides directives allowing you to configure access to the Memcached daemon.

Directive	Description
memcached_pass Context: location, if	Defines the hostname and port of the Memcached daemon. Syntax: memcached_pass hostname:port; Example: memcached_pass localhost:11211;
memcached_bind Context: http, server, location	Forces Nginx to use the specified local IP address for connecting to the Memcached server. This can come in handy if your server has multiple network cards connected to different networks. Syntax: memcached_bind IP_address; Example: memcached_bind 192.168.1.2;
memcached_connect_timeout Context: http, server, location	Defines the connection timeout in milliseconds (default: 60,000). Example: memcached_connect_timeout 5000;
memcached_send_timeout Context: http, server, location	Defines the data writing operations timeout in milliseconds (default: 60,000). Example: memcached_send_timeout 5,000;
memcached_read_timeout Context: http, server, location	Defines the data reading operations timeout in milliseconds (default: 60,000). Example: memcached_read_timeout 5,000;
memcached_buffer_size Context: http, server, location	Defines the size of the read and write buffer in bytes (default: page size). Example: memcached_buffer_size 8k;

Directive	Description
`memcached_next_upstream` Context: `http, server, location`	When the `memcached_pass` directive is connected to an upstream block (refer to the section on *upstream module*), this directive defines the conditions that should be matched in order to skip to the next upstream server. Syntax: Values selected among `error timeout, invalid_response, not_found,` or `off` Default: `error timeout` Example: `memcached_next_upstream off;`
`memcached_gzip_flag` Context: `http, server, location`	Checks for the presence of the specified flag in the memcached server response. If the flag is present, Nginx sets the `Content-encoding` header to `gzip` to indicate that it will be serving gzipped content. Syntax: numeric flag Default: (none) Example: `memcached_gzip_flag 1;`

Additionally, you will need to define the `$memcached_key` variable, which defines the key of the element that you are placing or fetching from the cache. You may, for instance, use `set $memcached_key $uri` or `set $memcached_key $uri?$args`.

Note that the Nginx Memcached module is only able to retrieve data from the cache; it does not store the results of requests. Storing data in the cache should be done by a server-side script. You just need to make sure to employ the same key-naming scheme in both your server-side scripts and the Nginx configuration. As an example, we could decide to use `memcached` to retrieve data from the cache before passing the request to a proxy if the requested URI is not found (see *Chapter 7, From Apache to Nginx*, for more details about the Proxy module):

```
server {
    server_name example.com;
    [...]
    location / {
        set $memcached_key $uri;
        memcached_pass 127.0.0.1:11211;
        error_page 404 @notcached;
    }
    location @notcached {
        internal;
```

```
            # if the file is not found, forward request to proxy
            proxy_pass 127.0.0.1:8080;
        }
    }
```

Image filter

This module provides image processing functionalities through the *GD Graphics Library* (also known as *gdlib*).

 This module is not included in the default Nginx build.

Make sure to employ the following directives on a `location` block that filters image files only, such as `location ~* \.(png|jpg|gif)$ { ... }`.

Directive	Description
`image_filter` Context: `location`	Lets you apply a transformation on the image before sending it to the client. There are five options available: • `test`: Makes sure that the requested document is an image file, returns a `415 Unsupported media type` HTTP error if the test fails. • `size`: Composes a simple JSON response indicating information about the image such as the size and type (for example, `{ "img": { "width":50, "height":50, "type":"png"}}`). If the file is invalid, a simple `{}` is returned. • `resize width height`: Resizes the image to the specified dimensions. • `crop width height`: Selects a portion of the image of the specified dimensions. • `rotate 90 | 180 | 270`: Rotates the image by the specified angle (in degrees). Example: `image_filter resize 200 100;`
`image_filter_buffer` Context: `http, server, location`	Defines the maximum file size for the images to be processed. Default: `image_filter_buffer 1m;`

Directive	Description
`image_filter_jpeg_quality` Context: `http, server, location`	Defines the quality of the output JPEG images. Default: `image_filter_jpeg_quality 75;`
`image_filter_transparency` Context: `http, server, location`	By default, PNG and GIF images keep their existing transparency during the operations that you perform by using the Image Filter module. If you set this directive to `off`, all existing transparency will be lost, but the image quality will be improved. Syntax: `on` or `off` Default: `on`
`image_filter_sharpen` Context: `http, server, location`	Sharpens the image by the specified percentage (value may exceed 100). Syntax: Numeric value Default: `0`
`image_filter_interlace` Context: `http, server, location`	Enables interlacing of the output image. If the output image is a JPG file, the image is generated in the *progressive JPEG* format. Syntax: `on` or `off` Default: `off`

Please note that when it comes to JPG images, Nginx automatically strips off the metadata (such as EXIF) if it occupies more than five percent of the total space of the file.

XSLT

The Nginx XSLT module allows you to apply an XSLT transform on an XML file or response received from a backend server (proxy, FastCGI, and so on) before serving the client.

 This module is not included in the default Nginx build

Directive	Description
`xml_entities` Context: `http, server, location`	Specifies the DTD file containing symbolic element definitions. Syntax: File path Example: `xml_entities xml/entities.dtd;`

Directive	Description
xslt_stylesheet Context: location	Specifies the XSLT template file path with its parameters. Variables may be inserted in the parameters. Syntax: xslt_stylesheet template [param1] [param2...]; Example: xslt_stylesheet xml/sch.xslt param=value;

xslt_types
 	
Context: http,
server, location
	Defines the additional MIME types, other than text/xml, to which the transforms may apply.
	
	Syntax: MIME type
	
	Example:
	
	  xslt_types text/xml text/plain;
	  xslt_types *;

xslt_paramxslt_ string_param Context: http, server, location	Both the directives allow defining parameters for XSLT stylesheets. The difference lies in the way the specified value is interpreted: the XPath expressions in the value are processed using xslt_param, while xslt_string_param is used for plain character strings. Syntax: xslt_param key value;

About your visitors

The following set of modules provides extra functionality that helps you find out more information about the visitors by parsing client request headers for browser name and version, assigning an identifier to requests presenting similarities, and so on.

Browser

The Browser module parses the User-Agent HTTP header of the client request in order to establish values for the variables that can be employed later in the configuration. The three variables produced are:

- $modern_browser: If the client browser is identified as being a modern web browser, the variable takes the value defined by the modern_browser_value directive.

- $ancient_browser: If the client browser is identified as being an old web browser, the variable takes the value defined by ancient_browser_value.

- $msie: This variable is set to 1 if the client is using a Microsoft IE browser.

To help Nginx recognize the web browsers and for telling the old from the modern, you need to insert multiple occurrences of the `ancient_browser` and `modern_browser` directives:

```
modern_browser opera 10.0;
```

With this example, if the User-Agent HTTP header contains Opera 10.0, the client browser is considered modern.

Map

Just like the Browser module, the Map module allows you to create maps of values depending on a variable:

```
map $uri $variable {
    /page.html   0;
    /contact.html   1;
    /index.html   2;
    default 0;
}
rewrite ^ /index.php?page=$variable;
```

Note that the `map` directive can only be inserted within the `http` block. Following this example, $variable may have three different values. If $uri was set to /page.html, $variable is now defined as 0; if $uri was set to /contact.html, $variable is now 1; if $uri was set to /index.html, $variable now equals 2. For all other cases (default), $variable is set to 0. The last instruction rewrites the URL accordingly. Apart from default, the `map` directive accepts another special keyword: hostnames. It allows you to match the hostnames using wildcards such as *.domain.com.

Two additional directives allow you to tweak the way Nginx manages the mechanism in memory:

- `map_hash_max_size`: Sets the maximum size of the hash table holding a map
- `map_hash_bucket_size`: Sets the maximum size of an entry in the map

Regular expressions may also be used in patterns if you prefix them with ~ (case sensitive) or ~* (case insensitive):

```
map $http_referer $ref {
    ~google "Google";
    ~* yahoo "Yahoo";
    \~bing "Bing"; # not a regular expression due to the \ before the
tilde
    default $http_referer; # variables may be used
    }
```

Geo

The purpose of this module is to provide a functionality that is quite similar to the `map` directive—affecting a variable based on the client data (in this case, the IP address). The syntax is slightly different in that you are allowed to specify IPv4 and IPv6 address ranges (in CIDR format):

```
geo $variable {
  default unknown;
  127.0.0.1    local;
  123.12.3.0/24  uk;
  92.43.0.0/16  fr;
}
```

Note that the preceding block is being presented to you just for the sake of the example and does not actually detect U.K. and French visitors; you'll have to use the GeoIP module if you wish to achieve proper geographical location detection. In this block, you may insert a number of directives that are specific to this module:

- `delete`: Allows you to remove the specified subnetwork from the mapping.

- `default`: The default value given to `$variable` in case the user's IP address does not match any of the specified IP ranges.

- `include`: Allows you to include an external file.

- `proxy`: Defines a subnet of trusted addresses. If the user IP address is among the trusted ones, the value of the `X-Forwarded-For` header is used as an IP address instead of the socket IP address.

- `proxy_recursive`: If enabled, this will look for the value of the `X-Forwarded-For` header even if the client IP address is not trusted.

- `ranges`: If you insert this directive as the first line of your `geo` block, it allows you to specify IP ranges instead of CIDR masks. The following syntax is thus permitted: `127.0.0.1-127.0.0.255    LOCAL;`

GeoIP

Although the name suggests some similarities with the previous one, this optional module provides accurate geographical information about your visitors by making use of the *MaxMind* (`http://www.maxmind.com`) GeoIP binary databases. You need to download the database files from the MaxMind website and place them in your Nginx directory.

This module is not included in the default Nginx build.

All you have to do then is specify the database path with one of the following directives:

```
geoip_country country.dat; # country information db
geoip_city city.dat; # city information db
geoip_org geoiporg.dat; # ISP/organization db
```

The first directive enables several variables: `$geoip_country_code` (two-letter country code), `$geoip_country_code3` (three-letter country code), and `$geoip_country_name` (full country name). The second directive includes the same variables, but provides additional information: `$geoip_region`, `$geoip_city`, `$geoip_postal_code`, `$geoip_city_continent_code`, `$geoip_latitude`, `$geoip_longitude`, `$geoip_dma_code`, `$geoip_area_code`, and `$geoip_region_name`. The third directive offers information about the organization or ISP that owns the specified IP address by filling up the `$geoip_org` variable.

 If you need the variables to be encoded in UTF-8, simply add the `utf8` keyword at the end of the `geoip_` directives.

UserID filter

This module assigns an identifier to the clients by issuing cookies. The identifier can be accessed from the variables `$uid_got` and `$uid_set` further in the configuration.

Directive	Description
`userid` Context: `http, server, location`	Enables or disables issuing and logging of cookies.
	The directive accepts four possible values:
	• on: Enables v2 cookies and logs them
	• v1: Enables v1 cookies and logs them
	• log: Does not send cookie data, but logs the incoming cookies
	• off: Does not send cookie data
	Default value: `userid off;`

Directive	Description
`userid_service` Context: `http, server, location`	Defines the IP address of the server issuing the cookie. Syntax: `userid_service ip;` Default: IP address of the server
`userid_name` Context: `http, server, location`	Defines the name assigned to the cookie. Syntax: `userid_name name;` Default value: The user identifier
`userid_domain` Context: `http, server, location`	Defines the domain assigned to the cookie. Syntax: `userid_domain domain;` Default value: None (the domain part is not sent)
`userid_path` Context: `http, server, location`	Defines the path part of the cookie. Syntax: `userid_path path;` Default value: /
`userid_expires` Context: `http, server, location`	Defines the cookie expiration date. Syntax: `userid_expires date	max;` Default value: No expiration date
`userid_p3p` Context: `http, server, location`	Assigns a value to the P3P header sent with the cookie. Syntax: `userid_p3p data;` Default value: None

Referer

A simple directive is introduced by this module: `valid_referers`. Its purpose is to check the Referer HTTP header from the client request, and possibly, to deny access based on the value. If the referer is considered invalid, `$invalid_referer` is set to 1. In the list of valid referers, you may employ three kinds of values:

- None: The absence of a referer is considered to be a valid referer
- Blocked: A masked referer (such as xxxxx) is also considered valid
- A server name: The specified server name is considered to be a valid referer

Following the definition of the `$invalid_referer` variable, you may, for example, return an error code if the referer was found invalid:

```
valid_referers none blocked *.website.com *.google.com;
if ($invalid_referer) {
  return 403;
}
```

Be aware that spoofing the Referer HTTP header is a very simple process, so checking the referer of client requests should not be used as a security measure.

Two more directives are offered by this module: `referer_hash_bucket_size` and `referer_hash_max_size`, which allow you to define the bucket size and maximum size of the valid referers hash tables respectively.

Real IP

This module provides one simple feature—it replaces the client IP address by the one specified in the *X-Real-IP* HTTP header for clients that visit your website behind a proxy, or for retrieving IP addresses from the proper header if Nginx is used as a backend server (it essentially has the same effect as Apache's `mod_rpaf`; see *Chapter 7, From Apache to Nginx*, for more details). To enable this feature, you need to insert the `real_ip_header` directive that defines the HTTP header to be exploited — either `X-Real-IP` or `X-Forwarded-For`. The second step is to define the trusted IP addresses, in other words, the clients that are allowed to make use of those headers. This can be done thanks to the `set_real_ip_from` directive, which accepts both IP addresses and CIDR address ranges:

```
real_ip_header X-Forwarded-For;
set_real_ip_from 192.168.0.0/16;
set_real_ip_from 127.0.0.1;
set_real_ip_from unix:; # trusts all UNIX-domain sockets
```

 This module is not included in the default Nginx build.

Split Clients

The Split Clients module provides a resource-efficient way to split the visitor base into subgroups based on the percentages that you specify. To distribute the visitors into one group or another, Nginx hashes a value that you provide (such as the visitor's IP address, cookie data, query arguments, and so on), and decides which group the visitor should be affected to. The following example configuration divides the visitors into three groups based on their IP address. If a visitor is affected to the first 50 percent, the value of `$variable` will be set to `group1`:

```
split_clients "$remote_addr" $variable {
    50% "group1";
    30% "group2";
    20% "group3";
}
```

```
location ~ \.php$ {
  set $args "${query_string}&group=${variable}";
}
```

SSL and security

Nginx provides secure HTTP functionalities through the SSL module, but also offers an extra module called *Secure Link* that helps you protect your website and visitors in a totally different way.

SSL

The SSL module enables HTTPS support, HTTP over SSL/TLS in particular. It gives you the option to serve secure websites by providing a certificate, a certificate key, and other parameters defined with the following directives:

 This module is not included in the default Nginx build.

Directive	Description
ssl Context: http, server	Enables HTTPS for the specified server. This directive is the equivalent of listen 443 ssl or listen port ssl more generally. Syntax: on or off Default: ssl off;
ssl_certificate Context: http, server	Sets the path of the PEM certificate. Syntax: File path
ssl_certificate_key Context: http, server	Sets the path of the PEM secret key file. Syntax: File path
ssl_client_certificate Context: http, server	Sets the path of the client PEM certificate. Syntax: File path
ssl_crl Context: http, server	Orders Nginx to load a CRL (Certificate Revocation List) file, which allows checking the revocation status of certificates.
ssl_dhparam Context: http, server	Sets the path of the *Diffie-Hellman* parameters file. Syntax: File path.

Directive	Description
`ssl_protocols` Context: `http, server`	Specifies the protocol that should be employed. Syntax: `ssl_protocols [SSLv2] [SSLv3] [TLSv1] [TLSv1.1] [TLSv1.2];` Default: `ssl_protocols TLSv1 TLSv1.1 TLSv1.2;`
`ssl_ciphers` Context: `http, server`	Specifies the ciphers that should be employed. The list of available ciphers can be obtained by running the following command from the shell: `openssl ciphers`. Syntax: `ssl_ciphers cipher1[:cipher2...];` Default: `ssl_ciphers ALL:!ADH:RC4+RSA:+HIGH:+MEDIUM:+LOW:+SSLv2:+EXP;`
`ssl_prefer_server_ciphers` Context: `http, server`	Specifies whether server ciphers should be preferred over client ciphers. Syntax: `on` or `off` Default: `off`
`ssl_verify_client` Context: `http, server`	Enables verifying certificates to be transmitted by the client and sets the result in the `$ssl_client_verify`. The `optional_no_ca` value verifies the certificate if there is one, but does not require it to be signed by a trusted CA certificate. Syntax: `on | off | optional | optional_no_ca` Default: `off`
`ssl_verify_depth` Context: `http, server`	Specifies the verification depth of the client certificate chain. Syntax: Numeric value Default: `1`
`ssl_session_cache` Context: `http, server`	Configures the cache for SSL sessions. Syntax: `off`, `none`, `builtin:size` or `shared:name:size` Default: `off` (disables SSL sessions)
`ssl_session_timeout` Context: `http, server`	When the SSL sessions are enabled, this directive defines the timeout for using session data. Syntax: Time value Default: 5 minutes

Directive	Description
ssl_password_phrase Context: http, server	Specifies a file containing the passphrases for secret keys. Each passphrase is specified on a separate line; they are tried one after the other when loading a certificate key. Syntax: file name Default: (none)
ssl_buffer_size Context: http, server	Specifies the buffer size when serving requests over SSL. Syntax: Size value Default: 16k
ssl_session_tickets Context: http, server	Enables TLS session tickets, allowing the client to reconnect faster by skipping re-negotiation. Syntax: on or off Default: on
ssl_session_ticket_key Context: http, server	Sets the path of the key file used to encrypt and decrypt the TLS session tickets. By default, a random value is generated. Syntax: file name Default: (none)
ssl_trusted_certificate Context: http, server	Sets the path of a trusted certificate file (PEM format) used to validate the authenticity of client certificates as well as the stapling of OCSP responses. More about SSL stapling can be found later on in the chapter. Syntax: file name Default: (none)

Additionally, the following variables are made available:

- $ssl_cipher: Indicates the cipher used for the current request
- $ssl_client_serial: Indicates the serial number of the client certificate
- $ssl_client_s_dn and $ssl_client_i_dn: Indicates the value of the Subject and Issuer DN of the client certificate
- $ssl_protocol: Indicates the protocol in use for the current request
- $ssl_client_cert and $ssl_client_raw_cert: Returns the client certificate data, which is raw data for the second variable
- $ssl_client_verify: Set to SUCCESS if the client certificate was successfully verified
- $ssl_session_id: Allows you to retrieve the ID of an SSL session

Setting up an SSL certificate

Although the SSL module offers a lot of possibilities, in most cases only a couple of directives are actually useful for setting up a secure website. This guide will help you to configure Nginx to use an SSL certificate for your website (in the example, your website is identified by `secure.website.com`). Before doing so, ensure that you already have the following elements at your disposal:

- A `.key` file generated with the following command: `openssl genrsa -out secure.website.com.key 1024` (other encryption levels work too).

- A `.csr` file generated with the following command: `openssl req -new -key secure.website.com.key -out secure.website.com.csr`.

- Your website certificate file, as issued by the Certificate Authority, for example, `secure.website.com.crt`. (Note: In order to obtain a certificate from the CA, you will need to provide your `.csr` file.)

- The CA certificate file as issued by the CA (for example, `gd_bundle.crt` if you purchased your certificate from `http://www.GoDaddy.com`).

The first step is to merge your website certificate and the CA certificate together with the following command:

```
cat secure.website.com.crt gd_bundle.crt > combined.crt
```

You are then ready to configure Nginx for serving secure content:

```
server {
    listen 443;
    server_name secure.website.com;
    ssl on;
    ssl_certificate /path/to/combined.crt;
    ssl_certificate_key /path/to/secure.website.com.key;
    [...]
}
```

SSL Stapling

SSL Stapling, also called **Online Certificate Status Protocol (OCSP)** Stapling, is a technique that allows clients to easily connect and resume sessions to an SSL/TLS server without having to contact the Certificate Authority, thus reducing the SSL negotiation time. In normal OCSP transactions, the client normally contacts the Certificate Authority so as to check the revocation status of the server's certificate. In the case of high traffic websites, this can cause a huge stress on the CA servers. An intermediary solution was designed—Stapling. The OCSP record is obtained periodically from the CA by your server itself, and is *stapled* to exchanges with the client. The OCSP record is cached by your server for a period of up to 48 hours in order to limit communications with the CA.

Enabling SSL Stapling should thus speed up the communication between your visitors and your server. Achieving this in Nginx is relatively simple: all you really need is to insert three directives in your server block, and obtain a full trusted certificate chain file (containing both the root and intermediate certificates) from your CA.

- `ssl_stapling on`: enables SSL Stapling within the server block
- `ssl_stapling_verify on`: enables verification of OCSP responses by the server
- `ssl_trusted_certificate filename`: where `filename` is the path of your full trusted certificate file (extension should be .pem).

Two optional directives also exist, which allow you to modify the behavior of this module:

- `ssl_stapling_file filename`: where `filename` is the path of a cached OCSP record, overriding the record provided by the OCSP responder specified in the certificate file.
- `ssl_stapling_responder url`: where `url` is the URL of your CA's OCSP responder, overriding the URL specified in the certificate file.

If you are having issues connecting to the OCSP responder, make sure your Nginx configuration contains a valid DNS resolver (using the `resolver` directive).

SPDY

The SPDY module offers support for the SPDY protocol (the SPDY module is not included by default). You can enable SPDY on your server by appending the keyword `spdy` at the end of your `listen` directive.

```
server {
    listen 443 ssl spdy;
    [...]
}
```

Due to the nature of SPDY, it can only be enabled over SSL. Two directives and two variables are brought in by this module:

- `spdy_chunk_size`: sets the size of the SPDY chunks
- `spdy_headers_comp`: sets the compression level for headers (0 to disable, 1 to 9 from lowest/fastest to highest/slowest compression)
- `$spdy`: this variable contains the SPDY protocol version if SPDY is used, an empty string otherwise
- `$spdy_request_priority`: this variable indicates the request priority if SPDY is used, an empty string otherwise

 SPDY is a protocol developed by Google, aiming to improve web latency and security. Although its utility was demonstrated (albeit not always significantly), Google decided to abandon the project after the HTTP/2 standard was ratified. As a result, SPDY support will be officially withdrawn during the first half of 2016.

Secure link

Totally independent from the SSL module, Secure link provides basic protection by checking the presence of a specific hash in the URL before allowing the user to access a resource:

```
location /downloads/ {
secure_link_md5 "secret";
secure_link $arg_hash,$arg_expires;
    if ($secure_link = "") {
        return 403;
    }
}
```

With such a configuration, documents in the /downloads/ folder must be accessed via a URL containing a query string parameter hash=XXX (note the $arg_hash in the example), where XXX is the MD5 hash of the secret you defined through the secure_link_md5 directive. The second argument of the secure_link directive is a UNIX timestamp defining the expiration date. The $secure_link variable is empty if the URI does not contain the proper hash or if the date has expired. Otherwise, it is set to 1.

 This module is not included in the default Nginx build.

Other miscellaneous modules

The remaining three modules are optional (all three need to be enabled at compile time), and provide additional advanced functionality.

Stub status

The Stub status module was designed to provide information about the current state of the server, such as the amount of active connections, the total handled requests, and more. To activate it, place the stub_status directive in a location block. All requests matching the location block will produce the status page:

```
location = /nginx_status {
    stub_status on;
    allow 127.0.0.1; # you may want to protect the information
    deny all;
}
```

 This module is not included in the default Nginx build.

An example result produced by Nginx:

```
Active connections: 1
server accepts handled requests
 10 10 23
Reading: 0 Writing: 1 Waiting: 0
```

It's interesting to note that there are several server monitoring solutions, such as *Monitorix,* that offer Nginx support through the Stub status page by calling it at regular intervals and parsing the statistics.

Degradation

The HTTP Degradation module configures your server to return an error page when your server runs low on memory. It works by defining a memory amount that is to be considered low, and then specifies the locations for which you wish to enable the degradation check:

```
degradation sbrk=500m; # to be inserted at the http block level
degrade 204; # in a location block, specify the error code (204 or
444) to return in case the server condition has degraded
```

Google-perftools

This module interfaces the Google Performance Tools profiling mechanism for the Nginx worker processes. The tool generates a report based on the performance analysis of the executable code. More information can be discovered from the official website of the project http://code.google.com/p/google-perftools/.

 This module is not included in the default Nginx build.

In order to enable this feature, you need to specify the path of the report file that will be generated using the google_perftools_profiles directive:

```
google_perftools_profiles logs/profiles;
```

WebDAV

WebDAV is an extension of the well-known HTTP protocol. While HTTP was designed for visitors to download resources from a website (in other words, reading data), WebDAV extends the functionality of web servers by adding write operations such as creating files and folders, moving and copying files, and more. The Nginx WebDAV module implements a small subset of the WebDAV protocol:

 This module is not included in the default Nginx build.

Directive	Description
dav_methods	Selects the DAV methods you want to enable.
Context: http, server, location	Syntax: dav_methods [off | [PUT] [DELETE] [MKCOL] [COPY] [MOVE]];
	Default: off

Directive	Description
`dav_access` Context: `http, server, location`	Defines access permissions at the current level. Syntax: `dav_access [user:r|w|rw] [group:r|w|rw] [all:r|w|rw];` Default: `dav_access user:rw;`
`create_full_put_path` Context: `http, server, location`	This directive defines the behavior when a client requests creation of a file in a directory that does not exist. If set to on, the directory path is created. If set to off, the file creation fails. Syntax: on or off Default: off
`min_delete_depth` Context: `http, server, location`	This directive defines a minimum URI depth for deleting files or directories when processing the DELETE command. Syntax: Numeric value Default: 0

Third-party modules

The Nginx community has been growing larger over the past few years, and many additional modules have been written by third-party developers. These can be downloaded from the official wiki website `http://wiki.nginx.org/nginx3rdPartyModules`.

The currently available modules offer a wide range of new possibilities, among which are the following:

- An *Access Key* module to protect your documents in a fashion similar to Secure link, by *Mykola Grechukh*
- A *Fancy Indexes* module that improves the automatic directory listings generated by Nginx, by *Adrian Perez de Castro*
- The *Headers More* module, which improves flexibility with HTTP headers, by *Yichun Zhang (agentzh)*
- Many more features for various parts of the web server

To integrate a third-party module into your Nginx build, you need to follow these three simple steps:

1. Download the `.tar.gz` archive associated with the module that you wish to download.

2. Extract the archive with the following command: `tar xzf module.tar.gz`.

3. Configure your Nginx build with the following command:

   `./configure --add-module=/module/source/path [...]`

Once you have finished building and installing the application, the module is available just like a regular Nginx module with its directives and variables.

If you are interested in writing Nginx modules yourself, *Evan Miller* published an excellent walkthrough: *Emiller's Guide to Nginx Module Development*. The complete guide may be consulted from his personal website at `http://www.evanmiller.org/`.

Summary

All throughout this chapter, we have discovered modules that help you in improving or fine-tuning the configuration of your web server. Nginx fiercely stands up to other concurrent web servers in terms of functionality, and its approach towards virtual hosts and the way they are configured will probably convince many administrators to make the switch.

Three additional modules were left out though. The FastCGI module will be approached in the next chapter, as it will allow us to configure a gateway to applications such as PHP or Python. The second one, the proxy module, which lets us design complex setups, will be described in *Chapter 7, From Apache to Nginx*. Finally, *The upstream module* will be detailed in *Chapter 8, Introducing Load Balancing and Optimization*.

PHP and Python with Nginx

5

The first decade of the twenty-first century has been the decade of server-side technologies. Over the past fifteen years or so, an overwhelming majority of websites have migrated from simple static HTML content to highly and fully dynamic pages, taking the Web to an entirely new level in terms of interaction with visitors. Software solutions, including open source ones, emerged quickly and some became mature enough to process high-traffic websites. In this chapter, we will study the ability of Nginx to interact with these applications. We have selected two applications for different reasons. The first one is, obviously, PHP, W3Techs, a website specializing in web technology surveys, reveals that as of June 2015, PHP empowers over 80 percent of the websites designed with a server-side language. The second language in our selection is Python due to the way it is installed and configured to work with Nginx. The mechanism, as we will discover soon, effortlessly applies to other applications such as Perl or Ruby on Rails.

This chapter covers the following topics:

- Discovering the CGI and FastCGI technologies
- The Nginx FastCGI and similar modules
- Setting up PHP and PHP-FPM
- Setting up Python and Django
- Configuring Nginx to work with PHP and Python

An introduction to FastCGI

Before we begin, you should know that, as the name suggests, FastCGI is actually a variation of CGI. Therefore, explaining CGI first is in order. The improvements introduced by FastCGI are detailed in the following sections.

Understanding the CGI mechanism

The original purpose of a web server was merely to respond to requests from clients by serving the files located on a storage device. The client sends a request to download a file, the server processes the request and sends the appropriate response: 200 OK if the file can be served normally, 404 if the file was not found, and other variants.

This mechanism has been in use since the beginning of the World Wide Web. However, as stated before, static websites are being progressively abandoned at the expense of dynamic ones that contain scripts which are processed by applications such as PHP and Python among others. The web-serving mechanism thus evolved into the following:

When a client attempts to visit a dynamic page, the web server receives the request and forwards it to a third-party application. The application processes the script independently and returns the produced response to the web server, which then forwards the response back to the client.

In order for the web server to communicate with that application, the CGI protocol was invented in the early 1990s.

The Common Gateway Interface

As stated in RFC 3875 (CGI protocol v1.1), designed by the **Internet Society (ISOC)**:

> *The Common Gateway Interface (CGI) allows an HTTP server and a CGI script to share responsibility for responding to client requests. [...] The server is responsible for managing connection, data transfer, transport, and network issues related to the client request, whereas the CGI script handles the application issues such as data access and document processing.*

CGI is the protocol that describes the way information is exchanged between the web server (Nginx) and the gateway application (PHP, Python, and so on). In practice, when the web server receives a request that should be forwarded to the gateway application, it simply executes the command corresponding to the desired application, for example, /usr/bin/php. Details about the client request (such as the User Agent and other request information) are passed either as command-line arguments or in environment variables, while actual data from POST or PUT requests is transmitted via the standard input. The invoked application then writes the contents of the processed document to the standard output, which is recaptured by the web server.

While this technology seems simple and efficient enough at first, it comes with a few major drawbacks:

- A unique process is spawned for each request. Memory and other context information are lost from one request to another.

- Starting up a process can be resource-consuming for the system. Massive amounts of simultaneous requests (each spawning a process) could quickly clutter a server.

- Designing an architecture where the web server and the gateway application would be located on different computers seems difficult, if not impossible.

Fast Common Gateway Interface

The issues mentioned in the **Common Gateway Interface (CGI)** section render the CGI protocol relatively inefficient for servers that are subject to heavy loads. In the mid-90s, the will to find solutions led Open Market to develop an evolution of CGI: **Fast Common Gateway Interface (FastCGI)**. It has become a major standard over the past fifteen years, and most web servers now offer the functionality, even proprietary server software such as Microsoft IIS.

Although the purpose remains the same, FastCGI offers significant improvements over CGI with the establishment of the following principles:

- Instead of spawning a new process for each request, FastCGI employs persistent processes that come with the ability to handle multiple requests.

- The web server and the gateway application communicate with the use of sockets such as TCP or POSIX Local IPC sockets. Consequently, the web server and backend processes may be located on two different computers on a network.

- The web server forwards the client request to the gateway and receives the response within a single connection. Additional requests may also follow without needing to create additional connections. Note that on most web servers, including Nginx and Apache, the implementation of FastCGI does not (or at least not fully) support multiplexing.

- Since FastCGI is a socket-based protocol, it can be implemented on any platform with any programming language.

Throughout this chapter, we will be setting up PHP and Python via FastCGI. Additionally, you will find the mechanism to be relatively similar in the case of other applications such as Perl or Ruby on Rails.

Designing a FastCGI-powered architecture is actually not as complex as you might imagine. As long as you have the web server and the backend application running, the only difficulty that remains is to establish the connection between both parties. The first step in that perspective is to configure the way Nginx will communicate with the FastCGI application. FastCGI's compatibility with Nginx is introduced by the FastCGI module, which is included in the default Nginx builds (including the ones that are installed via software repositories). This section details the directives that are made available by the module.

uWSGI and SCGI

Before reading the rest of the chapter, you should know that Nginx offers two other CGI-derived module implementations:

- The **uWSGI** module allows Nginx to communicate with applications through the **uwsgi** protocol, which is derived from **Web Server Gateway Interface (WSGI)**. The most commonly used (if not unique) server implementing the uwsgi protocol is the unoriginally-named uWSGI server. Its latest documentation can be found at `http://uwsgi-docs.readthedocs.org`. This module will prove useful to Python adepts considering that the uWSGI project was designed mainly for Python applications.

- **SCGI**, which stands for Simple Common Gateway Interface, is a variant of the CGI protocol, much like FastCGI. Younger than FastCGI since its specification was first published in 2006, SCGI was designed to be easier to implement and as its name suggests: simple. It is not related to a particular programming language. SCGI interfaces and modules can be found in a variety of software projects such as Apache, IIS, Java, Cherokee, and a lot more.

There are no major differences in the way Nginx handles the FastCGI, uwsgi, and SCGI protocols: each of these have their respective module containing similarly named directives. The following table lists a couple of directives from the FastCGI module, which are detailed in the following sections, and their uWSGI and SCGI equivalents:

FastCGI module	uWSGI equivalent	SCGI equivalent
`fastcgi_pass`	`uwsgi_pass`	`scgi_pass`
`fastcgi_cache`	`uwsgi_cache`	`scgi_cache`
`fastcgi_temp_path`	`uwsgi_temp_path`	`scgi_temp_path`

Directive names and syntaxes are identical. In addition, the Nginx development team has been maintaining all three modules in parallel. New directives or directive updates are always applied to all of them. As such, the following sections will document Nginx's implementation of the FastCGI protocol (since it is the most widely used), but they also apply to uWSGI and SCGI.

The main directives

The FastCGI, uWSGI, and SCGI modules are included in the default Nginx build. You do not need to enable them manually at compile time. The directives listed in the following table allow you to configure the way Nginx *passes* requests to the FastCGI/uWSGI/SCGI application. Note that you will find the fastcgi_params, uwsgi_params, and scgi_params files, which define the directive values that are valid for most situations, in the Nginx configuration folder:

Directive	Description

fastcgi_pass
 	
Context: location, if
	This directive specifies that the request should be passed to the FastCGI server by indicating its location:
	
	• For TCP sockets, the syntax is: fastcgi_pass hostname:port;
	
	• For Unix domain sockets, the syntax is: fastcgi_pass unix:/path/to/fastcgi.socket;
	
	• You may also refer to upstream blocks (read the following sections for more information): fastcgi_pass myblock;
	
	Examples:
	<pre>fastcgi_pass localhost:9000;
	fastcgi_pass 127.0.0.1:9000;
	fastcgi_pass unix:/tmp/fastcgi.socket;
	# Using an upstream block
	upstream fastcgi {
	    server 127.0.0.1:9000;
	    server 127.0.0.1:9001;
	}
	location ~* \.php$ {
	    fastcgi_pass fastcgi;
	}</pre>

Directive	Description

`fastcgi_param`
 	
Context: `http, server, location`
	This directive allows you to configure the request passed to FastCGI. Two parameters are strictly required for all FastCGI requests: `SCRIPT_FILENAME` and `QUERY_STRING`.
	
	Example:
	
	`fastcgi_param SCRIPT_FILENAME /home/website.com/www$fastcgi_script_name;`
	`fastcgi_param QUERY_STRING $query_string;`
	
	As for POST requests, additional parameters are required: `REQUEST_METHOD`, `CONTENT_TYPE`, and `CONTENT_LENGTH`:
	
	`fastcgi_param REQUEST_METHOD $request_method;`
	`fastcgi_param CONTENT_TYPE $content_type;`
	`fastcgi_param CONTENT_LENGTH $content_length;`
	
	The `fastcgi_params` file that you will find in the Nginx configuration folder already includes all of the necessary parameter definitions (except for the `SCRIPT_FILENAME`), which you need to specify for each of your FastCGI configurations.
	
	If the parameter name begins with `HTTP_`, it will override the potentially existing HTTP headers of the client request.
	
	You may optionally specify the `if_not_empty` keyword, forcing Nginx to transmit the parameter only if the specified value is not empty.
	
	Syntax: `fastcgi_param PARAM value [if_not_empty];`

`fastcgi_bind` Context: `http, server, location`	This directive binds the socket to a local IP address, allowing you to specify the network interface you want to use for FastCGI communications. Syntax: `fastcgi_bind IP_address;`
`fastcgi_pass_header` Context: `http, server, location`	This directive specifies the additional headers that should be passed to the FastCGI server. Syntax: `fastcgi_pass_header headername;` Example: `fastcgi_pass_header Authorization;`

Directive	Description
`fastcgi_hide_header` Context: `http, server, location`	This directive specifies the headers that should be hidden from the FastCGI server (headers that Nginx does not forward). Syntax: `fastcgi_hide_header headername;` Example: `    fastcgi_hide_header X-Forwarded-For;`
`fastcgi_index` Context: `http, server, location`	The FastCGI server does not support automatic directory indexes. If the requested URI ends with a /, Nginx appends the value `fastcgi_index`. Syntax: `fastcgi_index filename;` Example: `    fastcgi_index index.php;`
`fastcgi_ignore_ client_abort` Context: `http, server, location`	This directive lets you define what happens if the client aborts their request to the web server. If the directive is turned on, Nginx ignores the abort request and finishes processing the request. If it's turned off, Nginx does not ignore the abort request. It interrupts the request treatment and aborts all related communication with the FastCGI server. Syntax: `on` or `off` Default: `off`
`fastcgi_intercept_ errors` Context: `http, server, location`	This directive defines whether or not Nginx should process the errors returned by the gateway or directly return error pages to the client. (Note: Error processing is done via the `error_page` directive of Nginx.) Syntax: `on` or `off` Default: `off`
`fastcgi_read_timeout` Context: `http, server, location`	This directive defines the timeout for the response from the FastCGI application. If Nginx does not receive the response within this period, the `504 Gateway Timeout` HTTP error is returned. Syntax: Numerical value (in seconds) Default: 60 seconds

Directive	Description
`fastcgi_connect_timeout` Context: `http`, `server`, `location`	This directive defines the backend server connection timeout. This is different from the read/send timeout. If Nginx is already connected to the backend server, the `fastcgi_connect_timeout` is not applicable. Syntax: Time value (in seconds) Default: 60 seconds
`fastcgi_send_timeout` Context: `http`, `server`, `location`	This is the timeout for sending data to the backend server. The timeout isn't applied to the entire response delay but between two write operations. Syntax: Time value (in seconds) Default value: `60` seconds

`fastcgi_split_path_info`
 	
Context: `location`
	A directive particularly useful for URLs of the following form: `http://website.com/page.php/param1/param2/`.
	
	The directive splits the path information according to the specified regular expression:
	
	`fastcgi_split_path_info ^(.+\.php)(.*)$;`
	
	This affects two variables:
	
	• `$fastcgi_script_name`: The filename of the actual script to be executed (in the example: `page.php`)
	
	• `$fastcgi_path_info`: The part of the URL that is after the script name (in the example: `/param1/param2/`)
	
	These can be employed in further parameter definitions:
	
	`fastcgi_param SCRIPT_FILENAME /home/website.com/www$fastcgi_script_name;`
	`fastcgi_param PATH_INFO $fastcgi_path_info;`
	
	Syntax: A regular expression

`fastcgi_store` Context: `http`, `server`, `location`	This directive enables a simple *cache store* where responses from the FastCGI application are stored as files on the storage device. When the same URI is requested again, the document is directly served from the cache store instead of forwarding the request to the FastCGI application. This directive enables or disables the cache store. Syntax: `on` or `off`

Directive	Description
`fastcgi_store_access` Context: `http, server, location`	This directive defines the access permissions applied to the files created in the context of the cache store. Syntax: `fastcgi_store_access [user:r|w|rw] [group:r|w|rw] [all:r|w|rw];` Default: `fastcgi_store_access user:rw;`
`fastcgi_temp_path` Context: `http, server, location`	This directive sets the path of temporary and cache store files. Syntax: The file path Example: `fastcgi_temp_path /tmp/nginx_fastcgi;`
`fastcgi_max_temp_file_size` Context: `http, server, location`	Set this directive to 0 to disable the use of temporary files for FastCGI requests or to specify a maximum file size. Default value: 1 GB Syntax: Size value Example: `fastcgi_max_temp_file_size 5m;`
`fastcgi_temp_file_write_size` Context: `http, server, location`	This directive sets the write buffer size when saving temporary files to the storage device. Syntax: Size value Default value: 8k or 16k
`fastcgi_send_lowat` Context: `http, server, location`	This option allows you to make use of the `SO_SNDLOWAT` flag for TCP sockets under FreeBSD only. This value defines the minimum number of bytes in the buffer for output operations. Syntax: Numerical value (size) Default value: `0`

`fastcgi_pass_request_body`
`fastcgi_pass_request_headers`
Context: `http, server, location`
	This directive defines whether or not the request body and extra request headers should be passed on to the backend server.
	Syntax: on or `off;`
	Default: on

Directive	Description
`fastcgi_ignore_headers` Context: `http, server, location`	This directive prevents Nginx from processing one or more of the following headers from the backend server response: • `X-Accel-Redirect` • `X-Accel-Expires` • `Expires` • `Cache-Control` • `X-Accel-Limit-Rate` • `X-Accel-Buffering` • `X-Accel-Charset` Syntax: `fastcgi_ignore_headers header1 [header2...]`;

`fastcgi_next_upstream`
 	
Context: `http, server, location`
	When `fastcgi_pass` is connected to an upstream block, this directive defines the cases where requests should be abandoned and re-sent to the next upstream server of the block. The directive accepts a combination of values among the following:
	
	• `error`: An error occurs while communicating or attempting to communicate with the server
	• `timeout`: A timeout occurs during transfers or connection attempts
	• `invalid_header`: The backend server returns an empty or invalid response
	• `http_500`, `http_502`, `http_503`, `http_504`, `http_404`: In case such HTTP errors occur, Nginx switches to the next upstream
	• `off`: Forbids the use of the next upstream server
	
	Examples:
	`fastcgi_next_upstream error timeout http_504;`
	`fastcgi_next_upstream timeout invalid_header;`

`fastcgi_next_upstream_timeout` Context: `http, server, location`	Defines the timeout to be used in conjunction with `fastcgi_next_upstream`. Setting this directive to 0 disables it. Syntax: Time value (in seconds)
`fastcgi_next_upstream_tries` Context: `http, server, location`	Defines the maximum number of upstream servers to be tried before returning an error message. This is to be used in conjunction with `fastcgi_next_upstream`. Syntax: Numerical value (default: 0)

Directive	Description
`fastcgi_catch_stderr` Context: `http, server, location`	This directive allows you to intercept some of the error messages sent to `stderr` (the Standard Error stream) and store them in the Nginx error log. Syntax: `fastcgi_catch_stderr filter;` Example: `fastcgi_catch_stderr "PHP Fatal error:";`
`fastcgi_keep_conn` Context: `http, server, location`	When set to `on`, Nginx will conserve the connection to the FastCGI server, thus reducing the overhead. Syntax: `on` or `off` (default: `off`). Note that there is no equivalent directive in the uWSGI and SCGI modules.
`fastcgi_force_ranges` Context: `http, server, location`	When set to `on`, Nginx will enable byte-range support on responses from the FastCGI backend. Syntax: `on` or `off` (default: `off`).
`fastcgi_limit_rate` Context: `http, server, location`	Allows you to limit the rate at which Nginx downloads the response from the FastCGI backend. Syntax: Numerical value (bytes per second)

FastCGI caching and buffering

Once you have correctly configured Nginx to work with your FastCGI application, you may optionally make use of the following directives, which will help you improve the overall server performance by setting up a cache system. Additionally, FastCGI buffering allows you to buffer the responses from the FastCGI backend instead of synchronously forwarding them to the client.

Directive	Description
`fastcgi_cache` Context: `http, server, location`	This directive defines a cache zone. The identifier given to the zone is to be reused in further directives. Syntax: `fastcgi_cache zonename;` Example: `fastcgi_cache cache1;`

Directive	Description
`fastcgi_cache_key` Context: `http, server, location`	This directive defines the cache key. In other words, it is what differentiates one cache entry from another. If the cache key is set to `$uri`, as a result, all requests with a similar `$uri` will correspond to the same cache entry. It's not enough for most dynamic websites; you also need to include the query string arguments in the cache key so that `/index.php` and `/index.php?page=contact` do not point to the same cache entry. Syntax: `fastcgi_cache_key key;` Example: `fastcgi_cache "$scheme$host$request_uri $cookie_user";`
`fastcgi_cache_methods` Context: `http, server, location`	This directive defines the HTTP methods eligible for caching. `GET` and `HEAD` are included by default and cannot be disabled. You may, for example, enable the caching of `POST` requests. Syntax: `fastcgi_cache_methods METHOD;` Example: `fastcgi_cache_methods POST;`
`fastcgi_cache_min_uses` Context: `http, server, location`	This directive defines the minimum number of hits before a request becomes eligible for caching. By default, the response of a request is cached after one hit (further requests with the same cache key will receive the cached response). Syntax: Numerical value Example: `fastcgi_cache_min_uses 1;`

Directive	Description
`fastcgi_cache_path` Context: `http, server, location`	This directive indicates the directory for storing the cached files as well as other parameters. Syntax: `fastcgi_cache_path path [levels=numbers] keys_zone=name:size [inactive=time] [max_size=size] [loader_files=number] [loader_sleep=time] [loader_threshold=time];` The additional parameters are: • `levels`: Indicates the depth of subdirectories (1:2 indicates that subfolders will be created down to two levels) • `keys_zone`: Selects the zone that you previously declared with the `fastcgi_cache` directive, and indicates the size to be occupied in memory • `inactive`: If a cached response is not used within the specified time frame, it's removed from the cache (default: 10 minutes) • `max_size`: Defines the maximum size of the entire cache • `loader_files, loaded_sleep,` and `loader_threshold`: Configures the cache loader: the amount of files it processes in one read cycle (`loader_files`, default: 100 files), the pause time between read cycles (`loader_sleep`, default: 50 ms), and the maximum duration of a read cycle (`loader_threshold`, default: 200 ms) Example: `fastcgi_cache_path /tmp/nginx_cache levels=1:2 zone=zone1:10m inactive=10m max_size=200M;`
`fastcgi_cache_use_stale` Context: `http, server, location`	This directive defines whether or not Nginx should serve stale cached data in certain circumstances (with regard to the gateway). If you use `fastcgi_cache_use_stale timeout`, and if the gateway times out, then Nginx will serve cached data. Syntax: `fastcgi_cache_use_stale [updating] [error] [timeout] [invalid_header] [http_500];` Example: `fastcgi_cache_use_stale error timeout;`

Directive	Description

`fastcgi_cache_valid`
 	
Context: `http, server, location`
	This directive allows you to customize the caching time for different kinds of response code. You may cache responses associated to the `404` error codes for 1 minute, and in the opposite cache, `200 OK` responses for 10 minutes or more. This directive can be inserted more than once, demonstrated as follows:
	
	`fastcgi_cache_valid 404 1m;`
	`fastcgi_cache_valid 500 502 504 5m;`
	`fastcgi_cache_valid 200 10;`
	
	Syntax: `fastcgi_cache_valid code1 [code2...] time;`

`fastcgi_no_cache` Context: `http, server, location`	You may want to disable caching for requests that meet certain conditions. The directive accepts a series of variables. If at least one of these variables has a value (not an empty string and not 0), this request will not be stored in cache. Syntax: `fastcgi_no_cache $variable1 [$variable2] [...];` Example: `fastcgi_no_cache $args_nocaching;`
`fastcgi_cache_bypass` Context: `http, server, location`	This directive functions in a similar manner to `fastcgi_no_cache`, except that it tells Nginx whether or not the request should be *loaded* from cache, if it can be (as opposed to deciding whether to *store* the request result in cache). Syntax: `fastcgi_cache_bypass $variable1 [$variable2] [...];` Example: `fastcgi_cache_bypass $cookie_bypass_cache;`

`fastcgi_cache_lock,`
`fastcgi_cache_lock_timeout, fastcgi_cache_lock_age`
 	
Context: `http, server, location`
	If set to on, `fastcgi_cache_lock` prevents repopulating the existing cache elements for the duration specified by `fastcgi_cache_lock_age` (`fastcgi_cache_lock_timeout` achieves the same result, except the response isn't cached).
	
	Example:
	
	`fastcgi_cache_lock on;`
	`fastcgi_cache_lock_timeout 10s;`

Directive	Description
`fastcgi_cache_revalidate` Context: `http, server, location`	When enabled, Nginx revalidates the expired cache items when instructed to do so by the `If-modified-since` and `If-none-match` headers. Syntax: `fastcgi_cache_revalidate on | off;` Default: off
`fastcgi_buffering, fastcgi_request_buffering` Context: `http, server, location`	Enables or disables the buffering of responses (or client requests, in the case of `fastcgi_request_buffers`) sent by a FastCGI backend. When disabled, Nginx forwards responses to the client synchronously. When enabled, responses are stored in buffers until the backend finishes sending the entire content and then sent to the client. Syntax: `fastcgi_buffering on | off;` Default: on
`fastcgi_buffers` Context: `http, server, location`	This directive sets the amount and size of buffers that will be used for reading the response data from the FastCGI application. Syntax: `fastcgi_buffers amount size;` Default: 8 buffers, 4 k or 8 k each, depending on the platform Example: `fastcgi_buffers 8 4k;`
`fastcgi_buffer_size` Context: `http, server, location`	This directive sets the size of the buffer for reading the beginning of the response from the FastCGI application, which usually contains simple header data. The default value corresponds to the size of 1 buffer as defined by the previous directive (`fastcgi_buffers`). Syntax: Size value Example: `fastcgi_buffer_size 4k;`

The following is a full Nginx FastCGI cache configuration example making use of most of the cache-related directives described in the preceding table:

```
fastcgi_cache phpcache;
fastcgi_cache_key "$scheme$host$request_uri"; # $request_uri includes
the request arguments (such as /page.php?arg=value)
fastcgi_cache_min_uses 2; # after 2 hits, a request receives a cached
response
fastcgi_cache_path /tmp/cache levels=1:2 keys_zone=phpcache:10m
inactive=30m max_size=500M;
fastcgi_cache_use_stale updating timeout;
fastcgi_cache_valid 404 1m;
fastcgi_cache_valid 500 502 504 5m;
```

Since these directives are valid for pretty much any virtual host configuration, you may want to save these in a separate file (fastcgi_cache) that you can include at the appropriate place:

```
server {
    server_name website.com;
    location ~* \.php$ {
        fastcgi_pass 127.0.0.1:9000;
        fastcgi_param SCRIPT_FILENAME /home/website.com/www$fastcgi_
script_name;
        fastcgi_param PATH_INFO $fastcgi_script_name;
        include fastcgi_params;
        include fastcgi_cache;
    }
}
```

PHP with Nginx

We are now going to configure PHP to work together with Nginx via FastCGI. Why FastCGI in particular, as opposed to the other two alternatives SCGI and uWSGI? The answer came with the release of PHP version 5.3.3. As of this version, all releases come with an integrated FastCGI process manager allowing you to easily connect applications implementing the FastCGI protocol. The only requirement is that your PHP build should have been configured with the --enable-fpm argument. If you are unsure whether your current setup includes the necessary components, worry not: a section of this chapter is dedicated to building PHP with everything we need. Alternatively, the php-fpm or php5-fpm packages can be found in most repositories.

Architecture

Before starting the setup process, it's important to understand the way PHP interacts with Nginx. We have established that FastCGI is a communication protocol running through sockets, which implies that there is a client and a server. The client is obviously Nginx. As for the server, well, the answer is actually more complicated than just "PHP".

By default, PHP supports the FastCGI protocol. The PHP binary processes scripts and is able to interact with Nginx via sockets. However, we are going to use an additional component to improve the overall process management: the FastCGI Process Manager, also known as *PHP-FPM*.

PHP-FPM takes FastCGI support to an entirely new level. Its numerous features are detailed in the next section.

PHP-FPM

The process manager, as its name suggests, is a script that manages the PHP processes. It awaits and receives instructions from Nginx, and runs the requested PHP scripts under the environment that you configure. In practice, PHP-FPM introduces a number of possibilities such as:

- Automatically *daemonizing* PHP (turning it into a background process)
- Executing scripts in a *chrooted* environment
- Improved logging, IP address restrictions, pool separation, and much more

Setting up PHP and PHP-FPM

In this section, we will detail the process of downloading and compiling a recent version of PHP. You will need to go through this particular step if you are currently running an earlier version of PHP (<5.3.3).

Downloading and extracting

At the time of writing, the latest stable version of PHP is 5.6.10. Download the tar ball via the following command:

```
[user@local ~]$ wget http://php.net/get/php-5.6.10.tar.gz/from/www.php.
net/mirror
```

Once downloaded, extract the PHP archive with the `tar` command:

```
[user@local ~]$ tar xzf php-5.6.10.tar.gz
```

Requirements

There are two main requirements for building PHP with PHP-FPM: the `libevent` and `libxml` development libraries. If these are not already installed on your system, you will need to install them with your system's package manager.

For Red Hat-based systems and other systems using Yum as the package manager, use the following command:

```
[root@local ~]# yum install libevent-devel libxml2-devel
```

For Ubuntu, Debian, and other systems that use `apt-get` or `aptitude`, the command is as follows:

```
[root@local ~]# aptitude install libxml2-dev libevent-dev
```

Building PHP

Once you have installed all the dependencies, you may start building PHP. Similar to other applications and libraries that were previously installed, you will basically need three commands: `configure`, `make`, and `make install`. Be aware that this will install a new instance of the application. If you already have PHP set up on your system, the new instance will not override it. Instead, it will be installed in a different location that is revealed to you during the `make install` command execution.

The first step (`configure`) is critical here, as you will need to enable the PHP-FPM options in order for PHP to include the required functionality. There is a great variety of configuration arguments that you can pass to the `configure` command; some are necessary to enable important features such as database interaction, regular expressions, file compression support, web server integration, and so on. All the possible configuration options are listed when you run this command:

```
[user@local php-5.6.10]$ ./configure --help
```

A minimal command may also be used, but be aware that a great deal of features will be missing. If you wish to include other components, additional dependencies may be needed, which are not documented here. In all cases, the `--enable-fpm` switch should be included:

```
[user@local php-5.6.10]$ ./configure --enable-fpm [...]
```

The next step is to build the application and install it at the same time:

```
[user@local php-5.6.10]$ make && make install
```

This process may take a while, depending on your system specifications. Take good note of (some of) the information given to you during the build process. If you did not specify the location of the compiled binaries and configuration files, they will be revealed to you at the end of this step.

Post-install configuration

Begin by configuring your newly installed PHP, for example, copying the `php.ini` of your previous setup over to the new one:

Due to the way Nginx forwards the script file and request information to PHP, a security breach might be caused by the use of the `cgi.fix_pathinfo=1` configuration option. It is highly recommended that you set this option to `0` in your `php.ini` file. For more information about this particular security issue, please consult the following article:

http://cnedelcu.blogspot.com/2010/05/nginx-php-via-fastcgi-important.html

The next step is to configure PHP-FPM. Open up the `php-fpm.conf` file, which is located in `/usr/local/php/etc/` by default. We cannot detail all the aspects of the PHP-FPM configuration here (they are largely documented in the configuration file itself anyway), but there are important configuration directives that you shouldn't miss:

- Edit the user(s) and group(s) used by the worker processes and, optionally, the UNIX sockets
- The address(es) and port(s) on which PHP-FPM will be listening
- The number of simultaneous requests that will be served
- The IP address(es) allowed to connect to PHP-FPM

Running and controlling

Once you have made the appropriate changes to the PHP-FPM configuration file, you may start it with the following command (the file paths may vary depending on your build configuration):

```
[user@local ~]# /usr/local/php/sbin/php-fpm -c /usr/local/php/etc/php.ini
--pid /var/run/php-fpm.pid --fpm-config=/usr/local/php/etc/php-fpm.conf
-D
```

The preceding command includes several important arguments:

- `-c /usr/local/php/etc/php.ini` sets the path of the PHP configuration file
- `--pid /var/run/php-fpm.pid` sets the path of the PID file, which can be useful for controlling the process via an init script
- `--fpm-config=/usr/local/php/etc/php-fpm.conf` forces PHP-FPM to use the specified configuration file
- `-D` *daemonizes* PHP-FPM (ensures it runs in the background)

Other command-line arguments can be obtained by running php-fpm -h:

 PHP-FPM can be stopped via the kill or killall commands. Alternatively, you may use an init script to start and stop the process, provided the version of PHP you installed came with one.

Nginx configuration

If you have managed to configure and start PHP-FPM correctly, you are ready to tweak your Nginx configuration file to establish the connection between both parties. The following server block is a simple, valid template on which you can base your own website configuration:

```
server {
    server_name .website.com; # server name, accepting www
    listen 80; # listen on port 80
    root /home/website/www; # our root document path
    index index.php; # default request filename: index.php

    location ~* \.php$ { # for requests ending with .php
        # specify the listening address and port that you configured
previously
        fastcgi_pass 127.0.0.1:9000;
        # the document path to be passed to PHP-FPM
        fastcgi_param SCRIPT_FILENAME $document_root$fastcgi_script_
name;
        # the script filename to be passed to PHP-FPM
        fastcgi_param PATH_INFO $fastcgi_script_name;
        # include other FastCGI related configuration settings
        include fastcgi_params;
    }
}
```

After saving the configuration file, reload Nginx using one of the following commands:

```
/usr/local/nginx/sbin/nginx -s reload
```

Or:

```
service nginx reload
```

Create a simple script at the root of your website to make sure that PHP is being interpreted correctly:

```
[user@local ~]# echo "<?php phpinfo(); ?>" >/home/website/www/index.php
```

Fire up your favorite web browser and load `http://localhost/` (or your website URL). You will see something similar to the following screenshot, which is the PHP server information page:

Note that you may run into the occasional `403 Forbidden` HTTP error if the file and directory access permissions are not properly configured. If that is the case, make sure that you specified the correct user and group in the `php-fpm.conf` file, and that the directory and files are readable by PHP.

Python and Nginx

Python is a popular object-oriented programming language available on many platforms, from Unix-based systems to Windows. It is also available for Java and the Microsoft .NET platform. If you are interested in configuring Python to work with Nginx, it's likely that you already have a clear idea of what Python does. We are going to use Python as a server-side web programming language, with the help of the Django framework.

Django

Django is an open source web development framework for Python that aims to make web development simple and easy, as claimed by its slogan:

> *The Web framework for perfectionists with deadlines.*

More information is available on the project website at `http://www.djangoproject.com`.

Among other interesting features such as a dynamic administrative interface, a caching framework, and unit tests, Django comes with a FastCGI process manager. It's going to make things much simpler for us from the perspective of running Python scripts through Nginx.

Setting up Python and Django

We will now install Python and Django on your Linux operating system, along with their prerequisites. The process is relatively smooth, and mostly consists of running a couple of commands that rarely cause trouble.

Python

Python should be available in your package manager repositories. To install it on Red Hat-based systems and other systems using `yum` as the package manager, use the following command:

```
yum install python python-devel
```

For Ubuntu, Debian, and other systems that use `apt` or `aptitude`, use:

```
aptitude install python python-dev
```

The package manager will resolve dependencies by itself.

Django

In order to install Django, we will use a different approach (although you could skip this entirely and just install it from your usual repositories). We will be downloading the framework with PIP, a tool which simplifies the installation of Python packages. Therefore, the first step is to install PIP; for Red Hat-based systems and other systems using Yum as the package manager, use: `yum install python-pip`

For Ubuntu, Debian, and other systems that use Apt or Aptitude, use:

```
apt-get install python-pip
```

The package manager will resolve the dependencies by itself. Once PIP is installed, run the following command to download and install `Django 1.8.2`, the latest stable version to date:

```
[root@website.com ~]# pip install Django==1.8.2
[...]
[root@website.com ~]# pip install -e django-trunk/
```

Finally, there is one last component required for running the Python FastCGI manager: the `flup` library. This provides the actual FastCGI protocol implementation. For Red Hat-based systems and other systems using Yum as the package manager (the EPEL repositories must be enabled, otherwise you will need to build from source), use:

```
yum install python-flup
```

For Ubuntu, Debian, and other systems that use `apt` or `aptitude`, use:

```
aptitude install python-flup
```

Starting the FastCGI process manager

The process of beginning to build a website with the Django framework is as simple as running the following command:

```
[root@website.com ~]# django-admin startproject mysite
```

Once that part is done, you will find a `manage.py` Python script that comes with the default project template. Open the newly created `mysite` directory containing `manage.py`, and run the following command:

```
[root@website.com mysite]# python manage.py runfcgi method=prefork
host=127.0.0.1 port=9000 pidfile=/var/run/django.pid
```

If everything was configured correctly, and the dependencies are properly installed, running this command should produce no output, which is often a good sign. The FastCGI process manager is now running in the background waiting for connections. You can verify that the application is running with the `ps` command (for example, by executing `ps aux | grep python`). If you don't see any running process, try changing the preceding command slightly by selecting a different port. All we need to do now is set up the virtual host in the Nginx configuration file.

The Nginx configuration

The Nginx configuration is similar to the PHP one:

```
server {
    server_name .website.com;
    listen 80;
    # Insert the path of your Python project public files below
    root /home/website/www;
    index index.html;

    location / {
        fastcgi_pass 127.0.0.1:9000;
        fastcgi_param SCRIPT_FILENAME  $document_root$fastcgi_script_
name;
        fastcgi_param PATH_INFO $fastcgi_script_name;
        include fastcgi_params;
    }
}
```

Summary

Whether you use PHP, Python, or any other CGI application, you should now have a clear idea of how to get your dynamic scripts running with Nginx. There are all sorts of implementations on the Web for mainstream programming languages and the FastCGI protocol. Due to its efficiency, it is rapidly replacing server-integrated solutions such as Apache's mod_php and mod_wsgi, among others.

If you are unsure about connecting Nginx directly to those server applications because you already have a well-functioning system architecture in place (for example, Apache with mod_php), you may want to consider the option offered in the next chapter, *Apache and Nginx Together*.

Apache and Nginx Together 6

If you are reading this book, chances are you have already had to deal with the Apache web server, considering it is still a major player in the market. In fact, a lot of the administrators interested in Nginx are people who have encountered issues with the former: slowdowns, complexity in configuring, lack of responsivity at times, and a variety of other problems. Consequently, the first idea that comes to mind is to replace **Apache** with another web server such as **Nginx**. However, there is an alternative that is not often considered, as it sounds a little far-fetched at first—running both Nginx and Apache at the same time. When you look into it, this solution offers many advantages, especially for administrators looking for a quick and efficient solution to the aforementioned issues.

This chapter covers the following topics:

- An introduction to the reverse proxy mechanism
- The advantages and disadvantages of such an architecture
- Discovering the proxy module of Nginx
- Configuring Nginx to work with Apache
- Reconfiguring Apache to work as a backend server
- Additional tweaks and notes

Nginx as reverse proxy

First, bear in mind that the reverse proxy mechanism that we are going to describe in this chapter should not be considered as a long-term solution. It should be employed as a temporary architecture in problematic cases such as the following:

- When you already have Apache installed with complex configuration files that can hardly be ported to Nginx, or if you do not have the time or the will to completely switch to Nginx

- When your system operates a frontend system management panel such as Parallels Plesk, cPanel, or other solutions that automatically generate Apache configuration files

- When a functionality that your project or architecture requires is available with Apache but not with Nginx

In any other case, a complete switch to Nginx would be a better choice. *Chapter 7, From Apache to Nginx* provides a streamlined description of the process.

Understanding the issue

The reverse proxy mechanism mainly addresses one issue—the overall serving speed of Apache. Due to the massive number of modules and other components that Apache loads in the memory (for each HTTP request that it receives), your server may rapidly get cluttered when it receives massive influxes of requests at the same time. One could say that Apache focuses on functionality at the expense of optimization and processing speeds. In practice, this results in an excessive memory and CPU overhead. Oppositely, Nginx has proven to be both lightweight and stable while serving a larger amount of requests (using less RAM and CPU time in comparison to Apache).

What do we make of that? Before answering this question, it would be interesting to analyze the type of content that will be delivered by your server. Let us visit a regular web page that millions of people load every day: http://www.yahoo.com. While it's not fully representative of the World Wide Web, our analysis will be valid for a large number of websites, and the Yahoo! homepage is the perfect illustration of the problem that we face.

When a regular user visits `http://www.yahoo.com`, the web browser actually needs to download a great amount of data. Here are the different files that the browser downloads:

Media type	File/Request count	Total size	Total Gzipped Size
HTML source code	1	157.6 KB	52.5 KB
JavaScript (`.js`) code files and libraries	6	382.1 KB	112.3 KB
Cascading Style Sheet (`.css`) files	3	256.8 KB	42.8 KB
Flash animations (`.swf`)	2	61.4 KB	61.4 KB
Images linked from CSS files (`.png`, `.gif`)	18	43.0 KB	43.0 KB
Regular images (`.gif`, `.jpg`)	11	73.3 KB	73.3 KB
TOTAL	41	974.2 KB	385.3 KB

 These figures reflect a snapshot taken at the time of writing these lines, as visited by a US-based visitor. Results may differ slightly according to your geographical location, date of visit, and other criteria.

The amount of data that your browser needs to download is relatively low. After all, the 385.3 KB (make that 400-450 KB including cookie data and other overheads) can be transferred in less than a second with the fast Internet connections that are now being offered in many countries.

A much bigger problem, in our case, is the number of requests that the server will have to handle. For all first-time visitors, and for any web browser that does not use cached data to load this page, a minimum of 41 HTTP requests will be processed by the web server. Thankfully, a great number of people will have most of the files cached, but keep in mind that the content changes often, be it news feeds or general website changes. Besides, cached data expires after a while, and people clear their cache every now and then.

Can your web server process 41 HTTP requests in less than a second? Can it process 41,000 (1,000 page views/second)? Can it process 410,000? If so, you probably have the infrastructure to support such a load. Either way, you are better off with Nginx: as you have noticed, 40 out of the 41 requests are for static content—image files, CSS, JavaScript code files, and so on. Given the speed at which Nginx serves those files, we could design an architecture that lets Nginx serve static files and leave Apache to handle the dynamic content.

The reverse proxy mechanism

Somewhat like the FastCGI architecture described in the previous chapter, we are going to be running Nginx as a frontend server. In other words, it will be in direct communication with the outside world, whereas Apache will be running as a backend server and will only exchange data with Nginx:

There are now two web servers running and processing the requests:

- Nginx positioned as a frontend server (in other words, as reverse proxy), receives all the requests coming from the outside world. It filters them, either serving static files directly to the client or forwarding the dynamic content requests to Apache.

- Apache runs as a backend server, and it only communicates with Nginx. It may be hosted on the same computer as the frontend, in which case, the listening port must be edited to leave port 80 available to Nginx. Alternatively, you can employ multiple backend servers on different machines and share the load.

To communicate and interact with each other, neither process will be using FastCGI. Instead, as the name suggests, Nginx acts as a simple proxy server — it receives HTTP requests from the client (acting as HTTP server), and forwards them to the backend server (acting as HTTP client). There is thus no new protocol or software involved. The mechanism is handled by the proxy module of Nginx, as detailed later in this chapter.

Advantages and disadvantages of the mechanism

The main purpose of setting up Nginx as a frontend server and giving Apache a simple backend role is to improve the serving speed. As we established, a great number of requests coming from the clients are for static files, and static files are served much faster by Nginx. The overall performance sharply improves both on the client side and server side.

As a side note, Apache has experienced quite a number of security issues in the past, pushing forward new releases. You are forced to keep your system up to date in order to make sure you have a completely secure web server. It is reasonable to say that the more popular a web server is, the more likely it is that bugs and security issues will be discovered. Oppositely, the stable versions of Nginx have always been relatively secure, and the authors have rarely had to release any critical security fixes.

Eventually, if you adopt this solution, you will find it particularly easy to set up as you have almost no modification to make when it comes to the Apache configuration. All it requires is a simple port change, but even that isn't necessary if you set up Nginx and Apache on different servers. Your setup works as it is, which is particularly useful if you've already spent hours configuring Apache to work with the server-side preprocessors, such as PHP, Python, or others.

On the other hand, you are still deporting the requests for dynamic content to Apache, which is slower than a combination of Nginx and FastCGI most of the time. As we have already stated before, the optimal solution would be to completely switch to Nginx and leave out Apache.

Besides, since Nginx is installed as the frontend, it implies that it receives raw requests from users. This means that the request URI comes in its original form, leading to confusion for Nginx, as it will not be able to differentiate between static and dynamic content. You have two choices to solve this issue. You can either port your rewrite rules to Nginx, or redirect any request that results in a 404 error to the Apache backend.

To illustrate this problem, a request URI such as `/articles/43515-us-economy-strengthens.html` most likely does not correspond to any file on your system — it's meant to be rewritten and turned into a request such as `/article.php?id=43515` or similar. The first solution is to include the rewrite rules directly into your Nginx configuration. The alternative solution is to check for the existence of such a file, and if it doesn't exist, systematically redirect the request to Apache.

Last but not least, and this will be further discussed in the last section of this chapter, there may be some issues with the control panel software such as Parallels Plesk, cPanel, and others. These panels are very useful for administrators, as they automate some of the most bothersome tasks like adding virtual hosts to the Apache configuration, creating e-mail accounts, configuring the DNS daemon, and many more. The two main issues are as follows:

- These control panels allow you to apply changes to the web server configuration, and based on your changes they automatically generate valid configuration files for the server. Unfortunately, so far these control panels offer compatibility only with Apache; they do not generate Nginx configuration files. So any change that you make will have no effect.

- Whether you completely replace Apache with Nginx or go for the reverse proxy mechanism, Nginx usually ends up running on port 80 (and 443 for HTTPS). The control panel software generating the configuration files is unaware of this fact, and might be stubborn. When generating configuration files, it will systematically reset the Apache port to 80, creating conflicts with Nginx.

Both these issues will be discussed again later in the chapter.

The Nginx proxy module

Similarly to the previous chapter, the first step towards establishing the new architecture will be to discover the appropriate module. The default Nginx build comes with the proxy module, which allows forwarding of HTTP requests from the client to a backend server. We will be configuring multiple aspects of the module:

- Basic address and port information of the backend server
- Caching, buffering, and temporary file options
- Limits, timeout, and error behavior
- Other miscellaneous options

All these options are available via directives, which we will learn to configure throughout this section.

Main directives

The first set of directives will allow you to establish the basic configuration, such as the location of the backend server, information to be passed, and how it should be passed.

Directive	Description

proxy_pass
 	
Context: location, if
	Specifies that the request should be forwarded to the backend server by indicating its location:
	
	For regular HTTP forwarding, the syntax is proxy_pass http://hostname:port;
	
	For Unix domain sockets, the syntax is: proxy_pass http://unix:/path/to/file.socket;
	
	You may also refer to upstream blocks: proxy_pass http://myblock;
	
	Instead of http://, you can use https:// for secure traffic. Additional URI parts as well as the use of variables are allowed.
	
	Examples:
	
	proxy_pass http://localhost:8080;
	
	proxy_pass http://127.0.0.1:8080;
	
	proxy_pass http://unix:/tmp/nginx.sock;
	
	proxy_pass https://192.168.0.1;
	
	proxy_pass http://localhost:8080/uri/;
	
	proxy_pass http://unix:/tmp/nginx.sock:/uri/;
	
	proxy_pass http://$server_name:8080;
	
	<pre># Using an upstream block
	upstream backend {
	    server 127.0.0.1:8080;
	    server 127.0.0.1:8081;
	}
	location ~* \.php$
	{
	    proxy_pass http://backend;
	}</pre>

Directive	Description
`proxy_method` Context: `http, server, location`	Allows overriding the HTTP method of the request to be forwarded to the backend server. If you specify POST, for example, all requests forwarded to the backend server will be POST requests. Syntax: `proxy_method method;` Example: `proxy_method POST;`
`proxy_hide_header` Context: `http, server, location`	By default, as Nginx prepares the response received from the backend server to be forwarded back to the client, it ignores some of the headers, such as `Date`, `Server`, `X-Pad`, and `X-Accel-*`. With this directive, you can specify an additional header line to be hidden from the client. You may insert this directive multiple times with one header name for each. Syntax: `proxy_hide_header header_name;` Example: `proxy_hide_header Cache-Control;`
`proxy_pass_header` Context: `http, server, location`	Related to the preceding directive, this directive forces some of the ignored headers to be passed on to the client. Syntax: `proxy_pass_header headername;` Example: `proxy_pass_header Date;`

`proxy_pass_request_body`
 	
`proxy_pass_request_headers`
 	
Context: `http, server, location`
	Defines whether or not the request body and extra request headers should be passed on to the backend server.
	
	Syntax: `on` or `off;`
	
	Default: `on`

Directive	Description

`proxy_redirect`
 	
Context: `http, server, location`
	Allows you to rewrite the URL appearing in the Location HTTP header on redirections triggered by the backend server.
	
	Syntax: `off`, `default`, or the URL of your choice
	
	`off`: Redirections are forwarded *as it is.*
	
	`default`: The value of the `proxy_pass` directive is used as the hostname, and the current path of the document is appended. Note that the `proxy_redirect` directive must be inserted after the `proxy_pass` directive as the configuration is parsed sequentially.
	
	URL: Replace a part of the URL with another.
	
	Additionally, you may use variables in the rewritten URL.
	
	Examples:
	
	`proxy_redirect off;`
	
	`proxy_redirect default;`
	
	`proxy_redirect http://localhost:8080/ http://example.com/;`
	
	`proxy_redirect http://localhost:8080/wiki/ /w/;`
	
	`proxy_redirect http://localhost:8080/ http://$host/;`

`proxy_next_upstream`
 	
Context: `http, server, location`
	When `proxy_pass` is connected to an upstream block, this directive defines the cases where the requests should be abandoned and resent to the next upstream server of the block. The directive accepts a combination of values among the following:
	
	`error`: An error occurred while communicating or attempting to communicate with the server
	
	`timeout`: A timeout occurs during transfers or connection attempts
	
	`invalid_header`: The backend server returned an empty or invalid response
	
	`http_500, http_502, http_503, http_504, http_404`: In case such HTTP errors occur, Nginx switches to the next upstream server
	
	`off`: Forbids the use of the next upstream server
	
	Examples:
	
	`proxy_next_upstream error timeout http_504;`
	
	`proxy_next_upstream timeout invalid_header;`

Directive	Description
`proxy_next_upstream_timeout` Context: `http, server, location`	Defines the timeout to be used in conjunction with `proxy_next_upstream`. Setting this directive to 0 disables it. Syntax: Time value (in seconds)
`proxy_next_upstream_tries` Context: `http, server, location`	Defines the maximum number of upstream servers to be tried before returning an error message; to be used in conjunction with `proxy_next_upstream`. Syntax: `Numeric value` (default: `0`)

Caching, buffering, and temporary files

Ideally, as much as possible, you should reduce the number of requests being forwarded to the backend server. The following directive will help you build a caching system as well as control the buffering options and the way Nginx handles the temporary files:

Directive	Description
`proxy_buffer_size` Context: `http, server, location`	Sets the size of the buffer for reading the beginning of the response from the backend server, which usually contains simple header data. The default value corresponds to the size of 1 buffer, as defined by the directive given previously (`proxy_buffers`). Syntax: `Numeric value` (size) Example: `proxy_buffer_size 4k;`
`proxy_buffering`, `proxy_request_buffering` Context: `http, server, location`	Defines whether or not the response from the backend server should be buffered (or client requests, in the case of `proxy_request_buffering`). If set to `on`, Nginx will store the response data in memory using the memory space offered by the buffers. If the buffers are full, the response data will be stored as a temporary file. If the directive is set to `off`, the response is directly forwarded to the client. Syntax: `on` or `off` Default: `on`

Directive	Description
proxy_buffers Context: http, server, location	Sets the amount and size of buffers that will be used for reading the response data from the backend server. Syntax: proxy_buffers amount size; Default: 8 buffers, 4 k or 8 k each depending on platform Example: fastcgi_buffers 8 4k;
proxy_busy_buffers_size Context: http, server, location	When the backend-received data accumulated in the buffers exceeds the specified value, the buffers are flushed and data is sent to the client. Syntax: Numeric value (size) Default: 2 * proxy_buffer_size
proxy_cache Context: http, server, location	Defines a cache zone. The identifier given to the zone is to be reused in further directives. Syntax: proxy_cache zonename; Example: proxy_cache cache1;
proxy_cache_key Context: http, server, location	This directive defines the cache key; in other words, it differentiates one cache entry from another. If the cache key is set to $uri, as a result all requests with this $uri will work as a single cache entry. But that's not enough for most dynamic websites. You also need to include the query string arguments in the cache key so that /index.php and /index.php?page=contact do not point to the same cache entry. Syntax: proxy_cache_key key; Example: proxy_cache_key "$scheme$host$request_uri $cookie_user";

Directive	Description
`proxy_cache_path` Context: `http`	Indicates the directory for storing the cached files as well as the other parameters. Syntax: `proxy_cache_path path [use_temp_path=on|off] [levels=numbers keys_zone=name:size inactive=time max_size=size];` The additional parameters are: `use_temp_path`: set this flag to `on` if you want to use the path defined via the `proxy_temp_path` directive. `levels`: Indicates the depth level of the subdirectories (usually 1:2 is enough) `keys_zone`: Lets you make use of the zone that you previously declared with the `proxy_cache` directive, and indicates the size that it will occupy in memory `inactive`: If a cached response is not used within the specified time frame, it is removed from the cache `max_size`: Defines the maximum size of the entire cache Example: `proxy_cache_path /tmp/nginx_cache levels=1:2 zone=zone1:10m inactive=10m max_size=200M;`
`proxy_cache_methods` Context: `http, server, location`	Defines the HTTP methods eligible for caching. GET and HEAD are included by default, and cannot be disabled. Syntax: `proxy_cache_methods METHOD;` Example: `proxy_cache_methods OPTIONS;`
`proxy_cache_min_uses` Context: `http, server, location`	Defines the minimum amount of hits before a request is eligible for caching. By default, the response of a request is cached after one hit (subsequent requests with the same cache key will receive the cached response). Syntax: `Numeric value` Example: `proxy_cache_min_uses 1;`

`proxy_cache_valid`
 	
Context: `http, server, location`
	This directive allows you to customize the caching time for different kinds of response codes. You may cache the responses associated with the 404 error codes for 1 minute, and on the opposite cache, 200 OK responses for 10 minutes or more. This directive can be inserted more than once:
	
	`proxy_cache_valid 404 1m;`
	
	`proxy_cache_valid 500 502 504 5m;`
	
	`proxy_cache_valid 200 10;`
	
	Syntax: `proxy_cache_valid code1 [code2...] time;`

Directive	Description
proxy_cache_use_ stale Context: http, server, location	Defines whether or not Nginx should serve stale cached data in certain circumstances (with regard to the gateway). If you use proxy_cache_use_stale timeout, and if the gateway times out, then Nginx will serve cached data. Syntax: proxy_cache_use_stale [updating] [error] [timeout] [invalid_header] [http_500]; Example: proxy_cache_use_stale error timeout;
proxy_max_temp_ file_size Context: http, server, location	Set this directive to 0 to disable the use of temporary files for requests eligible for proxy forwarding, or to specify a maximum file size. Syntax: Size value Default value: 1 GB Example: proxy_max_temp_file_size 5m;
proxy_temp_file_ write_size Context: http, server, location	Sets the write buffer size when saving temporary files to the storage device. Syntax: Size value Default value: 2 * proxy_buffer_size
proxy_temp_path Context: http, server, location	Sets the path of the temporary and cache store files. Syntax: proxy_temp_path path [level1 [level2...]] Examples: proxy_temp_path /tmp/nginx_proxy; proxy_temp_path /tmp/cache 1 2;

Limits, timeouts, and errors

The following directives will help you define the timeout behavior as well as various limitations regarding communication with the backend server:

Directive	Description
proxy_connect_ timeout Context: http, server, location	Defines the backend server connection timeout. This is different from the read/send timeout. If Nginx is already connected to the backend server, the proxy_connect_ timeout is not applicable. Syntax: Time value (in seconds) Example: proxy_connect_timeout 15;

Directive	Description
`proxy_read_timeout` Context: `http, server, location`	The timeout for reading the data from the backend server. This timeout isn't applied to the entire response delay, but between two read operations instead. Syntax: `Time value` (in seconds) Default value: `60` Example: `proxy_read_timeout 60;`
`proxy_send_timeout` Context: `http, server, location`	This timeout is for sending data to the backend server. The timeout isn't applied to the entire response delay, but between two write operations instead. Syntax: `Time value` (in seconds) Default value: `60` Example: `proxy_send_timeout 60;`
`proxy_ignore_ client_abort` Context: `http, server, location`	If set to `on`, Nginx will continue processing the proxy request, even if the client aborts its request. In the other case (`off`), when the client aborts its request, Nginx also aborts its request to the backend server. Default value: `off`
`proxy_intercept_ errors` Context: `http, server, location`	By default, Nginx returns all error pages (HTTP status code 400 and higher) sent by the backend server directly to the client. If you set this directive to `on`, the error code is parsed and can be matched against the values specified in the `error_page` directive. Default value: `off`
`proxy_send_lowat` Context: `http, server, location`	An option allowing you to make use of the `SO_SNDLOWAT` flag for TCP sockets under the BSD-based operating systems only. This value defines the minimum number of bytes in the buffer for output operations. Syntax: `Numeric value` (size) Default value: `0`
`proxy_limit_rate` Context: `http, server, location`	Allows you to limit the rate at which Nginx downloads the response from the backend proxy. Syntax: `Numeric value` (bytes per second)

SSL-related directives

If you are going to be working with SSL backend servers, the following directives will be useful to you:

Directive	Description
proxy_ssl_certificate Context: http, server, location	Sets the path of a PEM file that contains a certificate of authentication to an SSL backend. Syntax: file path Default value: none
proxy_ssl_certificate_ key Context: http, server, location	Sets the path of the secret key file (PEM format) for authentication to an SSL backend. Syntax: file path Default value: none
proxy_ssl_ciphers Context: http, server, location	Sets the ciphers for SSL communication with the backend server. Run the following shell command to get the list of the available ciphers on your server: openssl ciphers. Syntax: cipher names Default value: DEFAULT
proxy_ssl_crl Context: http, server, location	Sets the path of the CRL (Certificate Revocation List) file in the PEM format allowing Nginx to verify the revocation state of the backend server's SSL certificate. Syntax: file path Default value: -
proxy_ssl_name Context: http, server, location	Use this directive to override the server name when verifying the revocation state of the backend server's SSL certificate. Syntax: character string Default value: equal to $proxy_host
proxy_ssl_password_file Context: http, server, location	Sets the path of a file containing passphrases (one per line) which are tried in turn when loading the certificate key. Syntax: file path Default value: -

Directive	Description
proxy_ssl_server_name Context: http, server, location	If you set this directive to on (as it is off by default), your server name will be communicated to the backend server as per the SNI protocol (Server Name Indication). Syntax: on or off Default value: off
proxy_ssl_session_reuse Context: http, server, location	This directive instructs Nginx to reuse the existing SSL sessions when communicating with the backend (thus reducing overhead). The official documentation recommends disabling this if the following errors start to show up in server logs: SSL3_GET_FINISHED:digest check failed. Syntax: on or off Default value: on
proxy_ssl_protocols Context: http, server, location	Sets the protocols to be used when communicating with SSL backends. Syntax: proxy_ssl_protocols [SSLv2] [SSLv3] [TLSv1] [TLSv1.1] [TLSv1.2]; Default value: TLSv1 TLSv1.1 TLSv1.2
proxy_ssl_trusted_certificate Context: http, server, location	Sets the path of your trusted CA certificates (in the PEM format). Syntax: file path Default value: -
proxy_ssl_verify Context: http, server, location	If set to on, Nginx will verify the certificate of the SSL backend server. Syntax: on or off Default value: off
proxy_ssl_verify_depth Context: http, server, location	If the proxy_ssl_verify directive is set to on, this sets the certificate chain verification depth. Syntax: Numeric value Default value: 1

Other directives

Finally, the last set of directives available in the proxy module is uncategorized, and is as follows:

Directive	Description
`proxy_headers_hash_max_size` Context: `http, server, location`	Sets the maximum size for the proxy header's hash tables. Syntax: `Numeric value` Default value: `512`
`proxy_headers_hash_bucket_size` Context: `http, server, location`	Sets the bucket size for the proxy header's hash tables. Syntax: `Numeric value` Default value: `64`
`proxy_force_ranges` Context: `http, server, location`	When set to on, Nginx will enable byte-range support on the responses from the backend proxy. Syntax: on or `off` Default value: `off`
`proxy_ignore_headers` Context: `http, server, location`	Prevents Nginx from processing one of the following four headers from the backend server response: `X-Accel-Redirect, X-Accel-Expires, Expires,` and `Cache-Control.` Syntax: `proxy_ignore_headers header1 [header2...];`
`proxy_set_body` Context: `http, server, location`	Allows you to set a static request body for debugging purposes. Variables may be used in the directive value. Syntax: `String value` (any value) Example: `proxy_set_body test;`
`proxy_set_header` Context: `http, server, location`	This directive allows you to redefine the header values to be transferred to the backend server. It can be declared multiple times. Syntax: `proxy_set_header Header Value;` Example: `proxy_set_header Host $host;`

Directive	Description
proxy_store Context: http, server, location	Specifies whether or not the backend server response should be stored as a file. Stored response files can be reused for serving other requests. Possible values: on, off, or a path relative to the document root (or alias). You may also set this to on and define the proxy_temp_path directive. Examples: proxy_store on; proxy_temp_path /temp/store;
proxy_store_access Context: http, server, location	This directive defines file access permissions for the stored response files. Syntax: proxy_store_access [user:[r|w|rw]] [group:[r|w|rw]] [all:[r|w|rw]]; Example: proxy_store_access user:rw group:rw all:r;
proxy_http_version Context: http, server, location	Sets the HTTP version to be used for communicating with the proxy backend. HTTP 1.0 is the default value, but if you are going to enable keepalive connections, you might want to set this directive to 1.1. Syntax: proxy_http_version 1.0 | 1.1;
proxy_cookie_domain proxy_cookie_path Context: http, server, location	Applies an on-the-fly modification to the domain or path attributes of a cookie (case insensitive). Syntaxes: proxy_cookie_domain off | domain replacement; proxy_cookie_path off | domain replacement ;

Variables

The proxy module offers several variables that can be inserted in various locations, for example, in the proxy_set_header directive or in the logging-related directives such as log_format. The available variables are:

- $proxy_host: Contains the hostname of the backend server used for the current request.

- $proxy_port: Contains the port of the backend server used for the current request.

- `$proxy_add_x_forwarded_for`: This variable contains the value of the `X-Forwarded-For` request header, followed by the remote address of the client. Both values are separated by a comma. If the `X-Forwarded-For` request header is unavailable, the variable only contains the client remote address.

- `$proxy_internal_body_length`: Length of the request body (set with the `proxy_set_body` directive or `0`).

Configuring Apache and Nginx

After having reviewed the proxy module, which allows us to establish our reverse proxy configuration architecture, it's now time to put all these principles into practice. There are basically two main parts involved in the configuration, one relating to Apache and the other to Nginx. The order in which you decide to apply those modifications does not make any difference whatsoever.

Note that while we have chosen to describe the process specifically for Apache, this method can be applied to any other HTTP server. The only point that differs is the exact configuration sections and directives that you will need to edit. Otherwise, the principle of reverse proxy can be applied regardless of the server software you are using.

Reconfiguring Apache

There are two main aspects of your Apache configuration that will need to be edited in order to allow both Apache and Nginx to work together and at the same time. But let us first clarify where we are coming from and where we are going.

Configuration overview

At this point, you probably have the following architecture set up on your server:

- A web server application running on port 80, such as Apache

- A dynamic server-side script processing application such as PHP, communicating with your web server via CGI, FastCGI, or as a server module

The new configuration we are going towards will resemble the following:

- Nginx running on port 80
- Apache (or another web server) running on a different port, accepting requests coming from the local sockets only
- The script processing application configuration (PHP, Python, or the like) will remain unchanged

As you can tell, only two main configuration changes will be applied to Apache (or any other web server that you might be running). The first is changing the listening port number in order to avoid conflicts with Nginx. Secondly, (although this is optional) you may want to disallow the requests coming from outside, and allow only those requests that are forwarded by Nginx. Both configuration steps are detailed in the following sections.

Resetting the port number

Depending on how your web server was set up (manual build or automatic configuration from server panel managers such as cPanel or Plesk), you may find yourself with a lot of configuration files to edit. The main configuration file is often found in /etc/httpd/conf/ or /etc/apache2/, and there might be more depending on how your configuration is structured. Some server panel managers create extra configuration files for each virtual host.

There are three main elements which you need to replace in your Apache configuration:

- The Listen directive is set to listen on port 80 by default. You will have to replace that port by another such as 8080. This directive is usually found in the main configuration file, but in some setups, the directive appears in a separate file called ports.conf.
- You must make sure that the following configuration directive is present in the main configuration file: NameVirtualHost A.B.C.D:8080, where A.B.C.D is the IP address of the main network interface used for server communications.
- The port you just selected needs to be reported in all your virtual host configuration sections.

The virtual host sections must be transformed from the following template:

```
<VirtualHost A.B.C.D:80>
   ServerName    example.com
   ServerAlias   www.example.com
   [...]
</VirtualHost>
```

to the following:

```
<VirtualHost A.B.C.D:8080>
   ServerName    example.com:8080
   ServerAlias   www.example.com
   [...]
</VirtualHost>
```

In this example, `A.B.C.D` is the IP address of the virtual host and `example.com` is the virtual host's name. The port must be edited in the first two lines.

Accepting local requests only

There are many ways by which you can restrict Apache to accept local requests only and deny access to the outside world. But first, why would you want to do that? As an extra layer positioned between the client and Apache, Nginx provides a certain comfort in terms of security. Visitors no longer have direct access to Apache, which decreases the potential risk—no one would be able to exploit the possible new vulnerabilities. Generally speaking, the principle of least privilege should apply.

The first method consists of changing the listening network interface in the main configuration file. The `Listen` directive of Apache lets you specify not only a port, but also an IP address. However, by default, no IP address is selected, which results in communications coming in from all interfaces. All you have to do is replace the `Listen 8080` directive by `Listen 127.0.0.1:8080`; Apache will then only listen on the local IP address. If you do not host Apache on the same server, you will need to specify the IP address of the network interface that can communicate with the server hosting Nginx.

An alternative would be to establish per-virtual-host restrictions, as follows:

```
<VirtualHost A.B.C.D:8080>
   ServerName    example.com:8080
   ServerAlias   www.example.com
   [...]
   order deny,allow
   allow from 127.0.0.1
```

```
        allow from 192.168.0.1
        deny all
</VirtualHost>
```

Using the `allow` and `deny` Apache directives, you are able to restrict the allowed IP addresses accessing your virtual hosts. This allows for a finer configuration, which can be useful in case some of your websites cannot be fully served by Nginx.

Once all your changes are done, don't forget to reload the server using `service httpd reload` or `/etc/init.d/httpd reload` to make sure that the new configuration is applied.

Configuring Nginx

There are only a couple of simple steps to establish a working configuration of Nginx, although it can be tweaked more accurately, as seen in the next section.

Enabling proxy options

The first step is to enable proxying of requests in your location blocks. Since the `proxy_pass` directive cannot be placed at the `http` or server level, you need to include it in every single place that you want it to be forwarded. Usually, a `location / {` fallback block suffices since it encompasses all requests, except those that match the `location` blocks containing a `break` statement.

The following is a simple example using a single static backend hosted on the same server:

```
server {
    server_name .example.com;
    root /home/example.com/www;
    [...]
    location / {
        proxy_pass http://127.0.0.1:8080;
    }
}
```

In the following example, we make use of an `upstream` block allowing us to specify multiple servers:

```
upstream apache {
    server 192.168.0.1:80;
    server 192.168.0.2:80;
    server 192.168.0.3:80 weight=2;
    server 192.168.0.4:80 backup;
```

```
    }
server {
    server_name .example.com;
    root /home/example.com/www;
    [...]
    location / {
        proxy_pass http://apache;
    }
}
```

So far, with such a configuration, all requests are proxied by your backend server(s). We are now going to separate the content into two categories:

- **Dynamic files**: Files that require processing before being sent to the client, such as PHP, Perl, and Ruby scripts, will be served by Apache

- **Static files**: All other content that does not require additional processing, such as images, CSS files, static HTML files, and media, will be served directly by Nginx

Therefore, we somehow need to separate the dynamic from the static content to be provided by either server.

Separating the content

In order to establish this separation, we can simply use two different location blocks, one that will match the dynamic file extensions, and another one encompassing all the other files. This example passes requests for .php files to the proxy:

```
server {
    server_name .example.com;
    root /home/example.com/www;
    [...]
    location ~* \.php.$ {
        # Proxy all requests with an URI ending with .php*
        # (includes PHP, PHP3, PHP4, PHP5...)
        proxy_pass http://127.0.0.1:8080;
    }
    location / {
        # Your other options here for static content
        # for example cache control, alias...
        expires 30d;
    }
}
```

This method, although simple, will cause trouble with websites using URL rewriting. Most *Web 2.0* websites now use links that hide file extensions such as http://example.com/articles/us-economy-strengthens/; some even append artificial extensions such as .html: http://example.com/us-economy-strengthens.html.

If you find yourself in this situation, you will want to employ one of the following solutions:

- The cleaner method is to convert your Apache rewrite rules for Nginx (with Apache, rewrite rules are usually found in the .htaccess file at the root of the website), in order for Nginx to know the actual file extension of the request and proxy it to Apache correctly.

- If you do not wish to port your Apache rewrite rules, you can use the try_files directive to try serving the requested URI, and redirect the request to Apache in case the URI doesn't match any file accessible to Nginx. Or simply let Apache handle the 404 responses via the error_page directive.

The more appropriate method is with try_files: we attempt to serve the requested URI directly, or a corresponding folder, by appending a /, and if all fails we forward the request to Apache:

```
server {
    server_name .example.com;
    root /home/example.com/www;
    [...]
location / {
        # Try serving requested file, or forward to Apache
        try_files $uri $uri/ @proxy;

        # Insert configuration for static files here
        expires 30d;
        [...]
    }
location @proxy {
        # Forwards requests to Apache
        proxy_pass http://127.0.0.1:8080;
    }
}
```

The following is an implementation of this mechanism, using the `error_page` directive:

```
server {
    server_name .example.com;
    root /home/example.com/www;
    [...]
    location / {
        # Your static files are served here
        expires 30d;
        [...]
        # For 404 errors, submit the query to the @proxy
        # named location block
        error_page 404 @proxy;
    }
    location @proxy {
        # Forwards requests to Apache
        proxy_pass http://127.0.0.1:8080;
    }
}
```

Alternatively, making use of the `if` directive from the Rewrite module:

```
server {
    server_name .example.com;
    root /home/example.com/www;
    [...]
    location / {
        # If the requested file extension ends with .php,
        # forward the query to Apache
        if ($request_filename ~* \.php.$) {
            break; # prevents further rewrites
            proxy_pass http://127.0.0.1:8080;
        }
        # If the requested file does not exist,
        # forward the query to Apache
        if (!-f $request_filename) {
            break; # prevents further rewrites
            proxy_pass http://127.0.0.1:8080;
        }
        # Your static files are served here
        expires 30d;
    }
}
```

There is no major performance difference between either of the solutions, as they will transfer the same number of requests to the backend server. For optimal performance, you should work on porting your Apache rewrite rules to Nginx.

Advanced configuration

For now, we have only made use of one directive offered by the proxy module. There are many more features that we can employ to optimize our design. The table that follows lists a handful of settings that are valid for most of your reverse proxy configurations, although they need to be verified individually. Since they can be employed multiple times, you can also place them in a separate configuration file that you will include in your location blocks.

Start by creating a `proxy.conf` text file that you place in the Nginx configuration directory. Insert the directives described in the following table into that file. Then, for each location of your `if` blocks that forwards requests to a backend server or an upstream block, insert the following line after the `proxy_pass` directive:

```
include proxy.conf;
```

Suggested values for some of the settings:

Setting	Description
`proxy_set_header Host $host;`	The Host HTTP header in the request forwarded to the backend server defaults to the proxy hostname, as specified in the configuration file. This setting lets Nginx use the original Host from the client request instead.
`proxy_set_header X-Real-IP $remote_addr;`	Since the backend server receives a request from Nginx, the IP address it communicates with is not that of the client. Use this setting to forward the actual client IP address into a new header, X-Real-IP.
`proxy_set_header X-Forwarded-For $proxy_add_x_forwarded_for;`	Similar to the preceding header, except that if the client already uses a proxy on his/her own end, the actual IP address of the client should be contained in the X-Forwarded-For request header. Using $proxy_add_x_forwarded_for ensures that both the IP address of the communicating socket and possibly the original IP address of the client (behind a proxy) get forwarded to the backend server.

Setting	Description
`client_max_body_size 10m;`	Limits the maximum size of the request body to `10` megabytes. Actually, this setting is referenced here to make sure that you adjust the value to the same level as your backend server. Otherwise, a request that is correctly received and processed by Nginx may not be successfully forwarded to the backend.
`client_body_buffer_size 128k;`	Defines the minimum size of the memory buffer that will hold a request body. Past this size, the content is saved in a temporary file. Adjust this according to the expected size of requests that your visitors will be sending, similarly to `client_max_body_size`.
`proxy_connect_timeout 15;`	If you are working with a backend server on a local network, make sure to keep this value reasonably low (`15` seconds here, but it depends on the average load). The maximum value for this directive is `75` seconds anyway.
`proxy_send_timeout 15;`	Make sure you define a timeout for the write operations (the timeout between two write operations during a communication to the backend server).
`proxy_read_timeout 15;`	Similar to the previous directive, except that this is for read operations.

Many other directives may be configured here. However, the default values are appropriate for most setups.

Improving the reverse proxy architecture

There are a few more additional steps that you may be interested in if you want to perfect your reverse proxy architecture. Three main issues are discussed here: the issue of IP addresses and how to ensure that the backend server retrieves the correct one, how to handle HTTPS requests with such a setup, and finally, a quick word about server control panels (cPanel, Plesk, and others).

Forwarding the correct IP address

Nowadays, a good portion of websites make use of the visitor's IP address for all kinds of reasons:

- Storing the IP address of a visitor posting a comment on a blog or a discussion forum
- Geo-targeted advertising or other services
- Limiting services to specific IP address ranges

Therefore, it is important for those websites to ensure that the web server correctly receives the IP address of the visitor.

As explained before, since Apache, or more generally the backend server, uses the IP address of the socket it communicates with, the IP that will appear in our design will always be the IP of the server hosting Nginx. In the previous section, we discovered a possible solution already—inserting the `proxy_set_header X-Real-IP $remote_addr;` directive in the configuration in order to forward the client IP address in the `X-Real-IP` header.

Unfortunately that is not enough, as some web applications are not configured to make use of the X-Real-IP header. The client remote address needs to be replaced somehow by that value. When it comes to Apache, a module was written to do just that: `mod_rpaf`. Details of how to install and configure it are not discussed here; you may find more documentation over at the official website: `http://stderr.net/apache/rpaf/`.

Alternatively, you could edit the source code of your backend application to take this particular header into consideration. In PHP, the following piece of code would retrieve the correct IP address:

```
$ip_address = $_SERVER["X_REAL_IP"];
```

SSL issues and solutions

If your website is going to serve secure web pages, you need to somehow allow the visitors to connect to your infrastructure via **SSL (Secure Sockets Layer)** on port 443. Two solutions are possible at this point: either you do not make use of Nginx at all and keep your Apache SSL configuration unmodified, or you configure Nginx to accept communications on port 443.

The first solution is clearly the simplest—do not change the port of your virtual hosts as configured in Apache. Your website should still be fully accessible from the outside, unless your backend server is hosted on another computer on the local network.

The alternative is to configure Nginx to accept secure connections via the SSL module, as described in *Chapter 5, PHP and Python with Nginx*. Once your `server` block is correctly configured, you can establish a proxied configuration to forward secure requests to your Apache server. Note that if your backend server is hosted on the same machine, you will need to edit the configuration in order to avoid port conflicts between the frontend and the backend.

Server control panel issues

A lot of server administrators rely on control panel software to simplify many aspects of their work: managing hosted domains, e-mail accounts, network settings, and much more. Advanced software solutions such as Parallels Plesk or cPanel are able to generate configuration files for many server applications (web, e-mail, database, and so on) on the fly. Unfortunately, most of them only support Apache as a unique web server application; Nginx is often left behind.

If you followed the steps of the reverse proxy configuration process, you must've noticed that at some point, the Apache configuration files had to be manually edited. We replaced the listening port, and edited or inserted some configuration directives. Obviously, when the control panel software generates configuration files, it is unaware of the manual changes that we've made. Therefore, it erases our modifications. When you restart Apache, you are greeted with error messages and conflicts.

At this point, there is no other solution than to apply the changes again after each configuration rebuild. With the growing popularity of Nginx, developers will hopefully implement full Nginx support in their software, or at least allow those configuration settings to be edited that are required to use Nginx as a reverse proxy.

 Facing the growing popularity of Nginx, web control panel developers are indeed starting to take steps towards full or partial support of Nginx. As of version 11, Parallels Plesk now offers support for Nginx as a frontend server.

Summary

Configuring Nginx as a reverse proxy for our architecture introduces a lot of advantages in terms of loading speeds and server load as well as overall reliability, since you can use multiple backends. However, a few obstacles might stand in your way, especially if you are running control panel software solutions to manage your services. Moreover, you do not get to make the most of Nginx as you are not using it for all your requests.

If you are seeking to find an even more efficient solution, you may want to look into completely replacing Apache with Nginx. The next chapter will detail this process, step by step, from virtual hosts to rewrite rules and FastCGI.

From Apache to Nginx

Every experienced system administrator will tell you the same story. When your web infrastructure works fine and client requests are served at a good speed, the last thing you want to do is modify the architecture that you have spent days, weeks, or even months putting together. In reality, as your website grows more popular, problems pertaining to scalability tend to occur inevitably (and these problems are not as well documented as the mainstream ones), regardless of the effort that you originally put into your initial server configuration. Eventually, you have to start looking for solutions. In that context, there are multiple reasons why you would want to completely adopt Nginx at the expense of your previous web server application. Whether you have decided that Nginx could be more efficient as a unique server rather than working as a reverse proxy, or simply because you want to get rid of Apache once and for all, this chapter will guide you through the complete process of replacing the latter with the former.

This chapter covers the following topics:

- A quick comparison between Apache and Nginx
- A detailed guide to porting your Apache configuration
- Porting your Apache rewrite rules to Nginx
- Rewrite rules walkthrough for a few popular web applications

Nginx versus Apache

This section will provide answers to the main questions about Nginx—how does it stand apart from the other servers? How does it compare to Apache? Whether you were using Apache before or considered it as a replacement for your current web server, why would you decide to adopt Nginx at the expense of the web server that empowers almost forty percent of websites worldwide?

Features

With the reverse proxy configuration that was elaborated on in the previous chapter, the presence or absence of specific features wasn't much of a problem. This is because Nginx would simply have to differentiate between static and dynamic content, and consequently, serve the static file requests and forward the dynamic file requests to a backend server.

However, when you start considering Nginx as a possible full replacement for your current web server, you better make sure that you know what's in the box. If your projected architecture requires specific components, the first thing you would usually do is check the application features. The following table lists a few of the major features, and describes how Nginx performs in comparison to Apache.

Core and functioning

The features of Nginx and Apache are shown in the following table:

Features	Nginx	Apache
HTTP request management (how the web server processes client requests)	**Event-driven architecture**: In this architecture, requests are accepted using asynchronous sockets, and aren't processed in separate threads to reduce memory and CPU overhead.	**Synchronous sockets, threads, and processes**: In this, each request is in a separate thread or process and uses synchronous sockets.
Programming language (language that the web server is written in)	**C**: The C language is notably low-level and offers more accurate memory management.	**C** and **C++**: Although Apache was written in C, many modules were designed with C++.
Portability (operating systems that are currently supported)	**Multiplatform**: Nginx runs under Windows, GNU/Linux, Unix, BSD, Mac OS X, and Solaris.	**Multiplatform**: Apache runs under Windows, GNU/Linux, Unix, BSD, Mac OS X, Solaris, Novell NetWare, OS/2, TPF, OpenVMS, eCS, AIX, z/OS, HP-UX, and more.
Year of birth	**2002**: While Nginx is younger than Apache, it was intended for a more modern era.	**1994**: Apache is one of the numerous open source projects initiated in the 90s that contributed to making the World Wide Web what it is today.

General functionality

This section mainly focuses on the differences between Apache and Nginx rather than listing all sorts of features that have already been covered in the previous chapters:

Feature	Nginx	Apache
HTTPS support: This specifies whether the web server can deliver secure web pages.	**Supported as a module**: If you require HTTPS support, you need to make sure that you compile Nginx with the proper module.	**Supported as a module**: Apache comes with HTTPS support via a module included by default.
Virtual hosting: This specifies whether the web server can host multiple websites on the same computer.	**Supported natively**: Nginx natively supports virtual hosting, but is not configured by default to accept per-virtual-host configuration files (more details are provided further on in this chapter).	**Supported natively**: Apache natively supports virtual hosting and offers the possibility to include one configuration file per folder (`.htaccess`).
CGI Support: This specifies whether the web server supports CGI-based protocols.	**FastCGI, uWSGI, SCGI**: Nginx supports FastCGI, uWSGI, and SCGI (as well as HTTP proxying) via modules that are included by default at compile time.	**CGI, FastCGI**: Most CGI protocols are exploitable via modules that can be loaded into Apache.
Module system: This specifies how the web server handles the modules.	**Static module system**: Modules are built-in; they must be included at compile time.	**Dynamic module system**: Modules can be loaded and unloaded dynamically from configuration files.

Generally speaking, Apache has a lot to offer, notably a much larger number of modules available. Most of its functionality is modularized, including its core engine. At this time, the official Apache module website references over 500 modules for various version branches, compared to a little more than 100 for Nginx.

Flexibility and community

This is another criterion for establishing an honest comparison between two applications of the likes of Nginx and Apache. In today's information technology industry, you cannot simply look at the raw functionality of a server application without considering questions such as:

- Where am I going to get help if I get stuck?

- Am I going to find documentation about specific features offered by either server?

- Are there going to be more modules in the future?

- Is the project still active and being updated by its developers?

- Has the security of either server been tested by a large enough number of administrators?

These questions generally get answered when the server gets popular enough. In the case of Apache, saying that it is a mainstream application would be an understatement. Documentation is easily found, developers have released hundreds of modules over the years, and it has received regular updates over the past twenty years.

What about Nginx? Where does it stand on those matters? That is definitely a sensitive issue. To begin with, there are some solid websites, centralizing information such as the official documentation reference at `http://www.Nginx.org`. If you have a problem with Apache, a simple search engine query suffices for finding multiple articles, answering the exact question you have been asking yourself. If you have an overly specific problem with Nginx though, you will likely have to resort to newsgroups, mailing lists, or web forums.

On the updates and security side though, Nginx is frequently updated by its author Igor Sysoev and his team. Those updates rarely need to include critical security fixes, as the server has been built on a solid and reliable foundation from the start. Although it doesn't serve as many websites as Apache does, Nginx still empowers some of the most popular online platforms such as Netflix, SourceForge, WordPress, ImageShack, and many more. This contributes in conferring it an undeniable legitimacy in the domain of high-performance web servers.

Performance

While features and community-related matters are important in general, the aspect that can make all the difference is performance. Administrators naturally tend to favor the server that will provide optimal comfort for the end user, characterized by minimal page load times and maximum download speeds.

Chapter 2, Basic Nginx Configuration, provided the first approach to HTTP server performance testing. The same tests can be applied to Apache in order to establish direct performance comparisons. In fact, many admin bloggers and technicians have already done so, and the general trend is unquestionably in favor of Nginx on all aspects such as the following:

- The RPS (requests per second) rate is generally much higher with Nginx, sometimes twice more than Apache. In other words, Nginx is able to serve twice as many pages as Apache in the same amount of time.

- Response times are lower in Nginx. As the request count grows, Apache becomes slower and slower in serving pages.

- Apache tends to use slightly more bandwidth than Nginx for serving the same requests. This can be interpreted in two ways — either Apache generates more traffic overhead, or it is able to transfer the data at a faster rate by better occupying the available bandwidth (it's still not clear as to which of these assumptions is the most valid).

In conclusion, in terms of performance, Nginx wins hands down. It's clearly the main reason why so many have switched to the lightweight Russian web server.

Usage

The reason why Nginx is so far ahead of Apache in terms of performance is because it's precisely the reason it was written for. Originally, Igor Sysoev created Nginx to empower an extremely high-traffic Russian website (`http://www.rambler.ru`), which received hundreds of millions of requests every day. This was probably not part of the original plans of the Apache designers when they initiated the project back in the early 90s.

More generally, it is said that Nginx was designed to address the *C10k problem*. This expression designates a common observation according to which the current state of computer technology and network scalability allows a computer (from the mainstream industry) to maintain only up to 10,000 simultaneous network connections due to operating system and software limitations. While that number isn't representative anymore due to the progress of technology, at the time, the issue was considered very serious, and it triggered the development of major web servers such as Lighttpd, Cherokee, and last but not least: Nginx.

Conclusion

There is one famous quote going around the Nginx community that summarizes the situation pretty accurately:

> *"Apache is like Microsoft Word, it has a million options but you only need six. Nginx does those six things, and it does five of them 50 times faster than Apache."*
> – *Chris Lea,* `https://ChrisLea.com`

Other notable testimonies helped build the reputation of Nginx over time:

> *"I currently have Nginx doing reverse proxy of over tens of millions of HTTP requests per day (that's a few hundred per second) on a single server. At peak load, it uses about 15 MB RAM and 10 percent of my CPU on my particular configuration (FreeBSD 6). Under the same kind of load, Apache falls over (after using 1,000 or so processes and god knows how much RAM), Pound falls over (too many threads, and using 400 MB+ of RAM for all the thread stacks), and Lighty leaks more than 20 MB per hour (and uses more CPU, but not significantly more)."* – *Bob Ippolito,* `http://www.MochiMedia.com`

If you are in the market of high-scale projects with limited resources at your disposal, Nginx comes in as a great solution. Apache is a good option to get your projects started when your knowledge of web servers and hosting is limited, but as soon as you meet success, you, your server, and your visitors may eventually find it inconsistent.

Porting your Apache configuration

That's it. You've had enough of Apache. You have finally decided to make a complete switch to Nginx. There are quite a few steps ahead of you now, the first of which is to adapt your previous configuration in a way that ensures that your existing websites work 1:1 after the switch.

Directives

This section will summarize some of the common Apache configuration directives, and attempt to provide equivalent replacement solutions from Nginx. The following list gives the order of the default Apache configuration file:

Apache directive	Nginx equivalent
ServerTokens: Apache allows you to configure the information transmitted in the request headers regarding the server OS and the software name and versions.	server_tokens: In Nginx, you may enable or disable the transmission of server information by using the server_tokens directive from the main HTTP module.
ServerRoot: This lets you define the root folder of the server, which contains the configuration and the logs folder.	The --prefix build-time option: With Nginx, this option is defined at compile time with the --prefix switch of the configure script, or at execution time with the -p command line option.
PidFile: This defines the path of the application PID file.	pid: The exact equivalent directive is pid.
TimeOut: This directive defines three elements: • The maximum execution time of a GET request. • The maximum allowed delay between two TCP packets in POST and PUT requests. • The maximum allowed delay between two TCP ACK packets.	Multiple directives: There are multiple directives allowing a similar behavior: send_timeout: This defines the maximum allowed delay between two read operations by the client. client_body_timeout: This defines the timeout for reading the client request body. client_header_timeout: This defines the timeout for reading the client request headers.
KeepAlive, MaxKeepAliveRequests, KeepAliveTimeout: These three directives control the keep-alive behavior of Apache.	keepalive_timeout, keepalive_requests: These two directives are the direct equivalents of the Apache ones, except that if you want to completely disable the keepalives, set keepalive_timeout or keepalive_requests to 0.
Listen: This defines the interface and port on which Apache will listen for connections.	listen: In Nginx, this directive is only defined at the virtual host level (server block).
LoadModule: With this directive, Apache offers the possibility to load the modules dynamically.	--with_****_module: Nginx cannot load modules dynamically; these need to be included at compile time. Once incorporated in Nginx, they cannot be disabled.
Include: A file inclusion directive that supports wildcards.	include: The include directive of Nginx is identical.
User, Group: Allows you to define the user and group under which the daemon will be running.	user: The user directive of Nginx lets you specify both the user and the group.

Apache directive	Nginx equivalent
ServerAdmin, ServerSignature: This lets you specify the e-mail address of the server administrator as well as a signature message to be displayed on error and diagnostic pages.	No equivalent As of version 1.8, there is no equivalent in Nginx. Error pages do not show the e-mail address of the server administrator or other information. Use the error_page directive to customize your site's error pages.
UseCanonicalName: This defines how Apache constructs self-referential URLs.	No direct equivalent Although there is no direct equivalent for this Apache directive, the construction of self-referential URLs can be defined via module-specific settings (proxy, FastCGI, and so on).
DocumentRoot: This defines the root folder from which Apache will serve files. The directive can be used at the server and virtual host levels.	root: The root directive can be inserted to define the document root at all levels: http, server, location, and if blocks.
DirectoryIndex, IndexOptions, IndexIgnore: Defines the directory index and file listing options.	index, autoindex, random_index, fancyindex (third party): Nginx also offers a good variety of options for managing indexes.
AccessFileName: Defines the filename of .htaccess files that are included dynamically on page execution.	No equivalent Nginx, as of version 1.8, has no such feature as .htaccess files. Read further sections for more information.
TypesConfig, DefaultType: Defines the MIME type options.	types, default_type: Equivalent directives exist in Nginx, although with a different syntax.
HostNameLookups: This allows looking up of hostnames for client IP addresses for logging or access control purposes.	No equivalent As of Nginx 1.8, there is no equivalent functionality.
ErrorLog, LogLevel, LogFormat, CustomLog: Logging activation and format settings.	access_log, log_format: Nginx also allows a large variety of options, but they are combined in fewer directives.
Alias, AliasMatch, ScriptAlias: Directory aliasing options.	alias: The alias equivalent directive is offered by Nginx, but nothing for the other two.

Modules

As we learned in *Chapter 1, Downloading and Installing Nginx*, modules in Nginx cannot be loaded dynamically, and must be included at compile time. Additionally, they cannot be disabled at runtime, since they are completely compiled and integrated in the main binary. Consequently, you should carefully consider your choice of modules when you build Nginx.

> If you are worried about the impact of the modules you selected on performance, you should be aware that the only noticeable differences will come from the filter modules. This name is given to the modules that apply a filter to the content of requests and/or responses, and therefore, they are always activated. Examples of filter modules: Addition, Charset, Gzip, SSI, and more. In the case of non-filter modules (such as Autoindex, FastCGI, Stub Status, and others), if none of their directives are used, the module handler is never executed.

The following table lists some modules that Apache and Nginx have in common. Note that there might be equivalent modules, but they do not necessarily provide exactly the same functionality, and directives are likely to be different in all cases. You should check the documentation of these modules in their respective chapters:

Apache Module	Nginx Module	Status	Configure switch
mod_auth_basic	auth_basic	Included by default	--without-http_auth_basic_module
mod_autoindex	autoindex	Included by default	--without-http_autoindex_module
mod_charset_lite	charset	Included by default	--without-http_charset_module
mod_dav	Dav	Optional	--with-http_dav_module
mod_deflate	gzip	Included by default	--without-http_gzip_module
mod_expires	headers	Included by default	Cannot be disabled
mod_fcgid	fastcgi	Included by default	--without-http_fastcgi_module
mod_headers	Headers	Included by default	Cannot be disabled
mod_include	Ssi	Included by default	--without-http_ssi_module
mod_log_config	Log	Included by default	Cannot be disabled
mod_proxy	proxy	Included by default	--without-http_proxy_module

Apache Module	Nginx Module	Status	Configure switch
mod_rewrite	rewrite	Included by default	--without-http_rewrite_module
mod_ssl	Ssl	Optional	--with-http_ssl_module
mod_status	stub_status	Optional	--with-http_stub_status_module
mod_substitute	Sub	Optional	--with-http_sub_module
mod_uid	userid	Included by default	--without-http_userid_module

Virtual hosts and configuration sections

Just as Nginx allows you to define the configuration settings at various levels (http, server, location, if), Apache also has its own sections. The section list is described as follows along with a configuration example.

Configuration sections

The following table provides a translation of the Apache sections into Nginx configuration blocks. Some Apache sections have no direct Nginx equivalent, but in most cases, identical behavior can be reproduced with a slightly different syntax:

Apache section	Nginx section	Description
(default)	http	The settings placed at the root of the Apache configuration files correspond to the settings placed at the root of the Nginx configuration file and also to those placed in the http block (as opposed to other blocks such as mail or imap used for the mail server proxying functionality).
<VirtualHost>	server	Apache settings placed in the <VirtualHost> sections should be placed in the server blocks of the Nginx configuration file.
<Location> <LocationMatch>	location	The behavior of the <Location> and <LocationMatch> (regular expression) can be reproduced with the Nginx location block.
None	if	Nginx offers a dynamic conditional structure with the if block. There is no exact equivalent in Apache. The closest equivalent is the RewriteCond directive from the Rewrite module.

Apache section	Nginx section	Description
`<Directory>` `<DirectoryMatch>` `<Files>` `<FilesMatch>`	None	Apache allows you to apply settings to specific locations of the local filesystem, while Nginx only offers per-URI settings.
`<IfDefine>`	None	Applies a set of directives on startup if the specified condition is true. This feature is not available on Nginx.
`<IfModule>`	None	Applies a set of directives on startup if the specified module is loaded. Since Nginx does not support dynamic module loading, this feature is not available.
`<Proxy>` `<ProxyMatch>`	None	Applies a set of directives to proxied resources by specifying a wildcard URI or a regular expression. This section has no equivalent in Nginx.

Creating a virtual host

In Apache, virtual hosts are optional. You are allowed to define server settings at the root of the configuration file:

```
Listen 80
ServerName example.com
ServerAlias www.example.com
DocumentRoot "/home/example.com/www"
[...]
```

However, this behavior is useful only if you are going to host one website on the server, or if you want to define the default settings for incoming requests that do not match other virtual host access rules.

In Nginx, however, all the websites that you will be hosting must be placed in a `server` block which allows the creation of a virtual host, equivalent to the `<VirtualHost>` section in Apache. The following table describes the translation of an Apache `<VirtualHost>` section to an Nginx `server` block:

Apache virtual host	Nginx virtual host equivalent
`<VirtualHost 12.34.56.78:80>`	`server {`
`ServerName example.com:80` `ServerAlias www.example.com`	`listen 12.34.56.78:80;` `server_name example.com www.example.com;`
`UseCanonicalName Off`	# No equivalent

Apache virtual host	Nginx virtual host equivalent
`SuexecUserGroup user group`	# No equivalent
`ServerAdmin "admin@example.com"`	# No equivalent
`DocumentRoot /home/example.com/www`	`root /home/example.com/www;`
`CustomLog /home/example.com/logs/access_log cust`	`access_log/home/example.com/logs/access_log cust;` # Note that the `cust` format must be declared beforehand with `log_format`.
`ErrorLog /home/example.com/logs/error_log`	`error_log /home/example.com/logs/error_log;`

`<Location /documents/>`
`  Options +Indexes`
`</Location>`
	`location /documents/ {`
	`    autoindex on;`
	`}`

`<IfModule mod_ssl.c>`
`SSLEngine off`
`</IfModule>`
	`# there is no equivalent for IfModule.`
	`ssl off;`

`<Directory /home/example.com/www>`
`  <IfModule mod_fcgid.c>`
`  <Files ~ (\.php)>`
`    SetHandler fcgid-script`
`    FCGIWrapper /usr/bin/php-cgi .php`
`    Options +ExecCGI`
`    allow from all`
`  </Files>`
`  </IfModule>`
`  Options -Includes -ExecCGI`
`</Directory>`
	# There is no equivalent to the `Directory` section. The `location` block only applies per-URI settings. The `location` block applies settings for all requests relative to the virtual host root folder. We use it to apply settings to the `.php` files.
	
	`location ~ \.php {`
	`    # Insert your FCGI settings`
	`    fastcgi_pass 127.0.0.1:9000;`
	`    fastcgi_param SCRIPT_FILENAME /home/example.com/ www$fastcgi_script_name;`
	`    fastcgi_param PATH_INFO $fastcgi_script_name;`
	`    include fastcgi_params; # Your additional FastCGI settings`
	`}`
	
	# Other directives have no direct equivalent or are not necessary with Nginx.

`</VirtualHost>`	`}`

This translation guide is valid for regular virtual hosts, serving non-secure web pages. There are a few differences when creating a secure virtual host using SSL. The following table focuses on the SSL-related directives, although directives from the previous table can still be used:

Apache virtual host	Nginx virtual host
`<VirtualHost 12.34.56.78:443>`	`server {`

`ServerName    example.com:443`
`ServerAlias   www.example.com`
	`listen 12.34.56.78:443;`
	`server_name example.com www.`
	`example.com;`

`SSLEngine on`
`SSLVerifyClient none`
`SSLCertificateFile /home/`
`example.com/cert/certchL9435`
	`ssl on;`
	`ssl_verify_client off;`
	`ssl_certificate /home/example.`
	`com/cert/cert.pem;`
	`ssl_certificate_key  /home/`
	`example.com/cert/cert.key;`

`<Directory /home/example.com/`
`www>`
`SSLRequireSSL`
`</Directory>`
	# There is no equivalent required with Nginx.

`</VirtualHost>`	`}`

.htaccess files

This section approaches the tricky problem of `.htaccess` files and the underlying theme of shared hosting. There is indeed no such mechanism in Nginx which, among other reasons, renders shared hosting difficult to achieve.

A recap on Apache .htaccess files

The `.htaccess` files are small independent configuration files that webmasters are allowed to place in every single folder of their website. Upon receiving a request for accessing a particular folder, Apache checks for the presence of such a file and applies it to the request context. This allows the webmasters to apply separate settings at multiple levels. Take a look at the following screenshot:

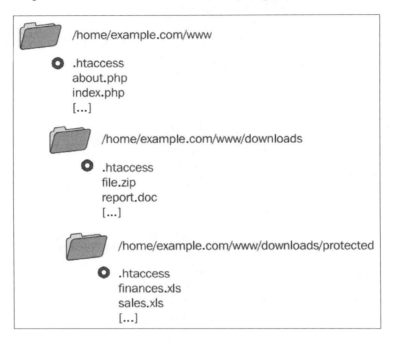

In the case of a client request for `/downloads/protected/finances.xls`, all three `.htaccess` files would be applied in the following order:

1. `/home/example.com/www/.htaccess`

2. `/home/example.com/www/downloads/.htaccess`

3. `/home/example.com/www/downloads/protected/.htaccess`

The settings precedence is given to the last `.htaccess` file read — if the same setting is defined in `/www/.htaccess` and `/www/downloads/.htaccess`, the latter file has priority over the former.

Nginx equivalence

Unfortunately, there is no such mechanism in Nginx. We can, however, find replacement solutions by making the most of the directives that we have at our disposal.

There are three major uses of the `.htaccess` files in Apache:

- Creating access and authentication rules for specific directories
- Defining rewrite rules at the top level (usually not folder-specific)
- Setting flags for modules such as `mod_php`, `mod_perl`, or `mod_python`

 When it comes to the latter, the use of flags is only achievable when the pre-processors are set up as Apache modules. If your server runs PHP through CGI or FastCGI, flags will not be recognized, and generate a `500 Internal Server Error`. In our case, connecting Nginx to such applications can only be done via FastCGI or HTTP; consequently, flags are not allowed.

Depending on the way you declare your virtual hosts, there are two solutions for implementing an `.htaccess`-like behavior or at least something remotely similar.

The first solution, if you are going to list all the virtual hosts from a unique configuration file, is to insert an `include` directive in the `server` block that refers to an extra configuration file located in the `/www/` folder. Do not forget that this configuration file should be hidden and not downloadable by clients:

```
server {
    listen 80;
    server_name .example.com;
    root /home/example.com/www;
    [...]
    # Include extra configuration files
    location / {
        include /home/example.com/www/.ngconf*;
    }
    # Deny access if someone tries to download the file
    location ~ \.ngconf {
        return 404;
    }
}
```

This will include any file with a name starting with `.ngconf` from the `/www/` folder of the virtual host. Note the `*` in the `include` directive. If you specify a filename without a wildcard, Nginx will consider the configuration to be invalid in case the file is missing. If you use the wildcard, the absence of such a file does not generate any error.

The `.ngconf` file would then include directives related to the virtual host itself:

```
autoindex off; # Disable directory listing
location /downloads/ {
    autoindex on; # Allow directory listing in /downloads/
}
[...]
```

This solution seems relatively secure for web-hosting providers, as this only allows the webmasters to define location-related settings (preventing important changes such as using a different port, different host name, and more). However, be aware that if a webmaster creates invalid `.ngconf` files, Nginx will refuse to reload until the issue is fixed. This could be solved by testing the configuration files with the `nginx -t` command in a shell script.

Alternatively, you could decide to place virtual host declarations within separate files located in the root folder of each virtual host. In this case, you would only need the following directive in the main Nginx configuration file:

```
include /home/*/www/.ngconf;
```

The `.ngconf` file then needs to contain the complete virtual host declaration, including the port and server name. This solution should only be considered for the servers that you manage entirely by yourself; you should never allow external webmasters to have so much control over your server.

That being said, there is still one major difference between Apache and Nginx:

- Apache applies the settings from the `.htaccess` files every time a client request is processed
- Nginx applies settings from the `.ngconf` files only when you reload the configuration (such as `service nginx reload`)

At this moment, there is no workaround for this last issue; Nginx does not allow on-the-fly configuration changes.

Administrators of web servers primarily running PHP scripts might be interested in the `htscanner` of the **PECL** package. This extension offers the possibility to process `.htaccess`-like files containing PHP settings. For more details, please refer to the official page of the package: `http://pecl.php.net/package/htscanner`

Rewrite rules

The most common source of worry during an HTTP server switch are the rewrite rules. Unfortunately, Nginx is not directly compatible with the Apache rewrite rules in two regards:

- Usually, rewrite rules are placed within the `.htaccess` files, as discussed in the previous section. Nginx offers no such mechanism, so rewrite rules will have to be placed in a different location.

- The syntax of the rewrite instructions and conditions is quite different, and will need to be adapted. Thankfully, the regular expression syntax itself does not change.

This section will approach some of the issues encountered when porting rules to Nginx, and then will provide some prewritten rules for a couple of major web applications.

General remarks

Before studying some practical examples, let us begin with a couple of important remarks regarding the rewrite rules in Nginx.

On the location

With all that has been said and written about Nginx, we can safely say that it's not the most appropriate web server for web hosting companies that practise shared hosting. The lack of `.htaccess` files renders it practically impossible to host websites that have their own server settings, among which are the rewrite rules. While a replacement solution has been offered in the previous section, it's not optimal as it requires a configuration reload after each change, and to crown it all, reloading is only possible if the entire configuration contains no error.

The consequence of this first issue is that you will have to relocate the rewrite rules. They will have to be placed directly in the `server` or `location` blocks of your virtual host, regardless of which file contains the virtual host configuration. With Apache, rewrite rules will be located somewhere such as `/home/example.com/www/.htaccess`; while with Nginx, you will need to incorporate them into the virtual host configuration file (for example, `/usr/local/nginx/conf/nginx.conf`).

On the syntax

There are two major Apache directives that are important when it comes to porting the rewrite rules to Nginx. Other directives either have no equivalent, are not supported on purpose, or their behavior is already incorporated into the equivalent Nginx directives:

- `RewriteCond`: This allows you to define the conditions that should be matched for the request URI to be rewritten
- `RewriteRule`: This performs the actual request URI rewrite by specifying a regular expression pattern, the rewritten URI, and a set of flags

The first of those directives, `RewriteCond`, is equivalent to Nginx's `if`. It is used for verifying conditions before applying a rewrite rule. The following example ensures that the requested file does not exist (`!-f` flag) before rewriting the URI:

```
RewriteCond %{REQUEST_FILENAME} !-f
RewriteRule . /index.php [L]
```

The Nginx equivalent, using `if` and `rewrite`, would be as follows:

```
if (!-f $request_filename) {
    rewrite . /index.php last;
}
```

It gets a little more complicated when you want to rewrite under multiple conditions. The Nginx `if` statement allows only one condition, and does not allow imbrications of the `if` blocks. Difficulty arises when trying to reproduce a behavior like the following one:

```
RewriteCond %{REQUEST_FILENAME} !-f # File must not exist
RewriteCond %{REQUEST_FILENAME} !-d # Directory must not exist
RewriteRule . /index.php [L] # Rewrites URL
```

There is a simple logical workaround for this particular issue — we will be using multiple `if` blocks, in which we affect a variable. After the two initial `if` blocks, a third comes in to check if the variable was affected by the first two:

```
set $check "";
# If the specified file does not exist, set $check to "A"
if (!-f $request_filename) {
    set $check "A";
}
# If the specified directory does not exist, set $check to $check+B
if (!-d $request_filename) {
    set $check "${check}B";
}
# If $check was affected in both if blocks, perform the rewrite
if ($check = "AB") {
    rewrite . /index.php last
}
```

Note that for those two particular rewrite conditions (`-f` to test file existence and `-d` to test folder existence), Nginx already offers a solution that combines both the tests: `-e`. So, a quicker solution would have been the following:

```
if (!-e $request_filename) {
    rewrite . /index.php last;
}
```

In addition to testing for file and folder existence, `-e` also checks if the specified filename corresponds to an existing symbolic link.

For more information on the `rewrite` module in general, please refer to *Chapter 4, Module Configuration*.

RewriteRule

The `RewriteRule` Apache directive is the direct equivalent to `rewrite` in Nginx. However, there is a subtle difference: URIs in Nginx begin with the / character. Nevertheless, the translation remains simple:

```
RewriteRule ^downloads/(.*)$ download.php?url=$1 [QSA]
```

The preceding Apache rule is transformed into the following:

```
rewrite ^/downloads/(.*)$ /download.php?url=$1;
```

Note that the `[QSA]` flag tells Apache to append the query arguments to the rewritten URL. However, Nginx does that by default. To prevent Nginx from appending the query arguments, insert a trailing `?` to the substitution URL:

```
rewrite ^/downloads/(.*)$ /download.php?url=$1?;
```

The `RewriteRule` Apache directive allows additional flags; these can be matched against the ones offered by Nginx, described in *Chapter 4, Module Configuration*. The following sections walk you through some examples of Nginx rules in famous web applications.

WordPress

WordPress is probably a familiar name to you. As of July 2015, the immensely popular open source blogging application was being used by over 60 million websites worldwide. Powered by PHP and MySQL, it's compatible with Nginx *out of the box*. Well, this statement would be entirely true if it weren't for rewrite rules.

The web application comes with a `.htaccess` file that will be placed at the root of the website:

```
# BEGIN WordPress
<IfModule mod_rewrite.c>
RewriteEngine On
RewriteBase /
RewriteCond %{REQUEST_FILENAME} !-f
RewriteCond %{REQUEST_FILENAME} !-d
RewriteRule . /index.php [L]
</IfModule>
# END WordPress
```

This first example is relatively easy to understand and to translate to Nginx. In fact, most of the rewriting process consists of three steps:

1. Checking if the requested URI corresponds to an existing file, in which case, it is served normally (the request URI is not rewritten).

2. Checking if the requested URI corresponds to a folder, in which case, it is served normally (the request URI is not rewritten).

3. Rewrite to `index.php`, WordPress will then analyze the original URI by itself from within the PHP script (by checking the `$_SERVER["REQUEST_URI"]` variable).

Since there are not a lot of complex rules to take care of, and the URI is analyzed by the PHP script itself, the translation to Nginx is rather easy. Here is a full example of an Nginx virtual host, stripped of all unrelated directives for the sake of simplicity:

```
server {
    listen 80;
    server_name blog.example.com;
    root /home/example.com/blog/www;
    index index.php;
    location / {
    # If requested URI does not match any existing file,
    # directory or symbolic link, rewrite the URL to index.php
       try_files $uri $uri/ index.php;
    }
    # All PHP requests are passed on to PHP-FPM via FastCGI
    # For more information, consult chapter 5
    location ~ \.php$ {
        fastcgi_pass 127.0.0.1:9000;
        fastcgi_param SCRIPT_FILENAME /home/example.com/blog/
www$fastcgi_script_name;
        fastcgi_param PATH_INFO $fastcgi_script_name;
        include fastcgi_params; # include extra FCGI params
    }
}
```

MediaWiki

As its name suggests, MediaWiki is the web engine that empowers the famous Wikipedia online open encyclopedia. It is currently an open source software, and anyone can download and install it on their local server. The application can also be used as a **CMS (Content Management Software)**, and large companies such as Novell have found it to be a reliable solution. Contrary to WordPress, MediaWiki does not come with a prewritten `.htaccess` file for prettying up URLs. Instead, the official MediaWiki website offers a wide variety of methods, which are all documented in the form of wiki articles. Webmasters can implement solutions that go as far as modifying the main Apache configuration file. However, there are simpler solutions that require no such thing. No particular Apache solution has been retained here, as three simple Nginx rewrite rules suffice to do the trick:

- The first one redirects the default requests (for example, / as a request URI) to `/wiki/Main_Page`

- The second one rewrites all the URIs of the `/wiki/abcd` form into the actual URL `/w/index.php?title=abcd`, without forgetting to append the rest of the parameters to the request URL

- The third one ensures that the requests to `/wiki` get redirected to the home page `/w/index.php`

The following is a full virtual host configuration example, including the rewrite rules:

```
server {
    listen 80;
    server_name wiki.example.com;
    root /home/example.com/wiki/www;
    location / {
        index index.php;
        # Permanent redirection to main page
        rewrite ^/$ /wiki/Main_Page permanent;
    }
    # Rewrite /wiki/anything URIs to /w/index.php?title=anything
    rewrite ^/wiki/([^?]*)(?:\?(.*))? /w/index.php?title=$1&$2;
    # Rewrite /wiki to /w/index.php
    rewrite ^/wiki /w/index.php;
    # Your usual FastCGI configuration here
    location ~ \.php$ {
        fastcgi_pass    127.0.0.1:9000;
        fastcgi_index   index.php;
        fastcgi_param   SCRIPT_FILENAME /home/example.com/wiki/
www$fastcgi_script_name;
        include fastcgi_params;
    }
}
```

vBulletin

Discussion forums started blooming at the beginning of the twenty-first century and a lot of popular web applications have appeared such as vBulletin, phpBB, or Invision Board. Most of these forum software platforms have jumped on the bandwagon, and now boast full SEO-friendly URL support. Unfortunately, rewrite rules often come in the form of .htaccess files. Indeed, the vBulletin developers have chosen to provide rewrite rules for Apache 2 and IIS, unsurprisingly forgetting Nginx. Let's teach them a lesson. The following table describes a solution for converting their Apache rewrite rules to Nginx:

Apache rule	Nginx rule
`RewriteEngine on`	`# Not necessary.`

`RewriteCond %{REQUEST_FILENAME} -s [OR]`
`RewriteCond %{REQUEST_FILENAME} -l [OR]`
`RewriteCond %{REQUEST_FILENAME} -d`
`RewriteRule ^.*$ - [NC,L]`
	# Do not rewrite if the requested URI corresponds to an existing file, folder, or link on the system.
	`    if (-e $request_filename) {`
	`        break;`
	`    }`

`RewriteRule ^threads/.* showthread.php [QSA]`	`rewrite ^/threads/.*$ / showthread.php last;`
`RewriteRule ^forums/.* forumdisplay.php [QSA]`	`rewrite ^/forums/.*$ / forumdisplay.php last;`
`RewriteRule ^members/.* member. php [QSA]`	`rewrite ^/members/.*$ /members. php last;`
`RewriteRule ^blogs/.* blog.php [QSA]`	`rewrite ^/blogs/.*$ /blog.php last;`
`ReWriteRule ^entries/.* entry.php [QSA]`	`rewrite ^/entries/.*$ /entry. php last;`

`RewriteCond %{REQUEST_FILENAME} -s [OR]`
`RewriteCond %{REQUEST_FILENAME} -l [OR]`
`RewriteCond %{REQUEST_FILENAME} -d`
`RewriteRule ^.*$ - [NC,L]`
	# For some reason, the same set of rules appears twice in the .htaccess file provided by vBulletin. You do not need to insert the Nginx equivalent a second time.

`RewriteRule ^(?:(.*?)(?:/|$))` `(.*|$)$ $1.php?r=$2 [QSA]`	`rewrite ^/(?:(.*?)(?:/|$))` `(.*|$)$ /$1.php?r=$2 last;`

Summary

Switching from Apache to Nginx may seem complex at first. There are many steps involved in the process, and you may face unsolvable problems if you are not confident and well-prepared. You need to be aware of the current limitations of Nginx: no on-the-fly configuration changes, and thus no `.htaccess` files or any such similar feature. Nginx does not have as many modules as Apache does, at least not yet. Last but not least, you have to convert all your rewrite rules for your websites to be functional under Nginx. So yes, it does take quite a bit of work. But this is a small price to pay to get a server that will ensure long-term stability and scalability. You and your visitors will not regret it, as it generally comes with improved loading and response speeds.

8
Introducing Load Balancing and Optimization

As much as Nginx will help your servers hold the load, there are always limits to what a single machine can process: an aging hard drive or limited bandwidth will eventually induce a bottleneck, resulting in longer request serving times, which in turn leads to disappointment for your visitors.

As your websites grow more popular and your single machine begins to suffer, you will be tempted to simply get a bigger and more expensive server. But this will not be a cost-efficient approach in the long run. Moreover, the more strain a server is exposed to, the more likely it is to suffer from hardware failure.

In this chapter, we will investigate two concepts, the first of which is load balancing: the art of distributing load across several servers and managing this distribution efficiently. The second concept is the subject of thread pools—a new mechanism relieving servers under heavy load (more specifically, load induced by blocking operations) by serving requests in a slightly different manner.

This chapter covers the following topics:

- An introduction to load-balanced architectures
- Common concepts and issues of load balancing
- Dealing with the session affinity problem
- A demonstration of load balancing with MySQL
- Optimizing your setup with the help of thread pools

An introduction to load balancing

All of the most visited websites in the world are built over carefully planned server architectures: fast page loads and download speeds are significant requirements for long-term traffic growth. The concept of load balancing has the potential to solve problems pertaining to scalability, availability, and performance. After a rapid description of the concept, we will elaborate on how Nginx offers to implement such an architecture.

Understanding the concept of load balancing

To put it simply, the concept of load balancing consists of distributing the workload (CPU load, hard disk load, or other forms) across several servers in a manner that is completely transparent to your visitors.

In the case of a single server architecture, client requests are received and processed by one machine. A machine has a limited capacity of operation. For example, suppose a web server is able to respond to 1,000 HTTP requests per second. If the server were to receive more than 1,000 requests per second, the 1,001st client request received in that second would not be served in a timely manner. And from then on, the page's serving time would begin to increase, resulting in a degraded experience for your visitors.

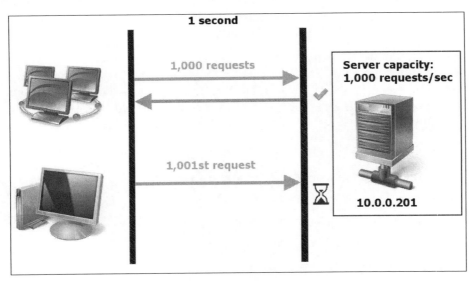

Distributing the load across several servers increases the overall request serving capacity: with two servers at your disposal, you could theoretically allow 2,000 HTTP requests to be served per second. With three servers, you could serve 3,000 requests, and so on.

There are several techniques available for achieving load balancing, the simplest of which is *DNS load balancing*. When a person wishes to visit your website, their web browser will resolve your domain name (example.com) into an IP address (1.2.3.4). To achieve DNS load balancing, simply associate multiple IP addresses with your domain. Upon visiting your website, the operating system of your visitors will select one of these IP addresses by following a simple round-robin algorithm, thus ensuring that on a global scale, all your servers receive more or less the same amount of traffic.

Albeit simple to implement, this load balancing method cannot always be applied to high traffic websites, because it eludes several major issues such as the following:

- What if the IP address selected by a visitor's operating system points to a server that is temporarily unavailable?

- What if your architecture is made up of several types of servers, some of which are capable of handling more requests than the others?

- What if a visitor connects to a particular server and logs in to their user account, only to get switched to another server ten minutes later, and thus losing their session data?

The last of these issues is also known as the *session affinity* problem, and is further detailed in the following section.

Session affinity

Session affinity is an expression that designates the persistent assignment of a client to a particular server in a load-balanced infrastructure. We use the word *session* to describe a set of requests performed by a client on a server. When a visitor browses a website, they often visit more than one page: they log in to their account, they add a product to their shopping cart, they check out, and so on. Until they close their web browser (or a tab thereof), all of their subsequent page views are part of a session, which is most of the time stateful: the server conserves the data related to the operations performed during the visit. In our example, that server would remember the contents of the shopping cart and the login credentials.

If, at some point during the session, the visitor were to switch servers and connect to server B, they would lose any session information contained on server A. The visitor would then lose the contents of their shopping cart as well as their login credentials (they would get logged out).

For that reason, it is of utmost importance to maintain session affinity: in other words, to ensure that a visitor remains assigned to a particular server at all times. The DNS load balancing method does not ensure session affinity, but fortunately, Nginx will help you achieve it.

The upstream module

The implementation of load balancing in Nginx is particularly clever as it allows you to distribute the load at several levels of your infrastructure. It isn't limited to proxying HTTP requests across backend servers: it also offers to distribute requests across FastCGI backends (FastCGI, uWSGI, SCGI, and the like), or even to distribute queries to Memcached servers. Any directive that ends with _pass, such as proxy_pass, fastcgi_pass, or memcached_pass, accepts a reference to a group of servers.

The first step is to declare this group of servers with the help of the **upstream** block, which must be placed within the `http` block. Within the `upstream` block, declare one or more servers with the `server` directive:

```
http {
    upstream MyUpstream {
        server 10.0.0.201;
        server 10.0.0.202;
        server 10.0.0.203;
    }
    [...]
}
```

Now that your server group is declared, you can reference it in your virtual host configuration. For example, you could distribute the incoming HTTP requests across the server group by simply proxying them:

```
server {
    server_name example.com;
    listen 80;
    root /home/example.com/www;
    # Proxy all requests to the MyUpstream server group
    proxy_pass http://MyUpstream;
    [...]
}
```

In this most basic state of configuration, requests are distributed across the three servers of the MyUpstream group according to a simple round-robin algorithm without maintaining session affinity.

Request distribution mechanisms

Nginx offers several ways to solve the problems that we mentioned earlier. The first and simplest of them is the **weight** flag, which can be enabled in the definition of your server group:

```
upstream MyUpstream {
    server 10.0.0.201 weight=3;
    server 10.0.0.202 weight=2;
    server 10.0.0.203;
}
```

By default, servers have a weight of 1, unless you specify otherwise. Such a configuration enables you to give more importance to particular servers: the higher their weight, the more requests they will receive from Nginx. In this example, for every 6 HTTP requests received, Nginx will systematically distribute:

- 3 requests to the 10.0.0.201 server (weight=3)
- 2 requests to the 10.0.0.202 server (weight=2)
- 1 request to the 10.0.0.203 server (weight=1)

For every 12 requests, Nginx will distribute:

- 6 requests to the 10.0.0.201 server (weight=3)
- 4 requests to the 10.0.0.202 server (weight=2)
- 2 requests to the 10.0.0.203 server (weight=1)

Nginx also includes a mechanism that will verify the state of the servers in a group: if a server doesn't respond in time, the request will be re-sent to the next server in the group. There are several flags that can be assigned to the servers in an upstream block that will allow you to better control this mechanism:

- fail_timeout=N where N is the number of seconds before a request is considered to have failed
- max_fails=N where N is the number of attempts that should be performed on a server before Nginx gives up and switches to the next server. By default, Nginx only tries once

- `backup` marks the server as a backup server, instructing Nginx to only use it if another server fails (it is not used otherwise)

- `down` marks the server as permanently unavailable, instructing Nginx not to use it anymore

Finally, Nginx offers plenty of options to achieve session affinity. They come under the form of directives that should be inserted within the upstream block. The simplest of them is `ip_hash`. This directive instructs Nginx to calculate a hash from the first three bytes of the client's IPv4 address (or the full IPv6 address), and based on that hash, keep the client assigned to a particular server. As long as the client's IP address remains the same, Nginx will always forward requests to the same server in the upstream group:

```
upstream {
    server 10.0.0.201 weight=3;
    server 10.0.0.202 weight=2;
    server 10.0.0.203;
    ip_hash;
}
```

Some administrators may deem this method too unreliable, considering the fact that the majority of Internet Service Providers across the globe still provide dynamic IP addresses renewed on a 24-hour basis. So, why not use your own distribution key? Instead of the client's IP address, you could separate the requests based on the criteria of your choice, thanks to the `hash` directive. Since the directive allows variables, you could decide to separate the requests based on a cookie value:

```
upstream {
    server 10.0.0.201;
    server 10.0.0.202;
    hash $cookie_username;
}
```

Based on the data contained in the *username* cookie, your visitors will be assigned to the first or the second server in the upstream group.

Using Nginx as a TCP load balancer

Until recently, the open source version of Nginx would only allow load balancing in the context of HTTP requests. In the meantime, the commercial subscription *NGINX+* took the concept one step further: using Nginx as a TCP load balancer. This would pave the way to much broader possibilities: you could then set up Nginx to distribute load across any form of networked servers—database servers, e-mail servers— literally everything that communicates via TCP. In May 2015, the authors decided that TCP load balancing should be part of the open-source version; as of Nginx 1.9.0 the *Stream module* is included in the source code readily available on Nginx.org.

The Stream module

The way TCP load balancing works in Nginx is remarkably similar to HTTP load balancing. However, since the module that brings forth the new set of directives is not included in the default build, you will need to run the `configure` command with the following flag before building the program: `--with-stream`.

The Stream module offers a new block called *stream* which must be placed at the root of the configuration file (outside of the `http` block). In this block, you must declare two sets of directives:

- `server` declares a TCP server listening on a particular port and optionally a network interface, with or without SSL
- `upstream` defines a server group in a similar manner, as seen previously

In your server blocks, the requests will be sent to the server group with the `proxy_pass` directive.

An example of MySQL load balancing

If you already understand how HTTP load balancing works in Nginx, the following example will look spectacularly simple to you. We will configure Nginx to receive MySQL connections, and balance them across two backend servers, as follows:

```
stream {
    upstream MyGroup {
        # use IP address-based distribution
        hash $remote_addr;
        server 10.0.0.201 weight=2;
        server 10.0.0.202;
        server 10.0.0.203 backup; # use as backup only
    }
```

```
server {
    # listen on the default MySQL port
    listen 3306;
    proxy_pass MyGroup; # forward requests to upstream
}
}
```

That's all there is to it. All directives and options offered by the upstream module are still there. But keep in mind that you won't be able to use HTTP-based variables (such as cookies) to achieve session affinity. The Stream module comes with a lot more options and flags, but they are not detailed here as this falls outside the scope of an HTTP server; additional documentation can be found at http://www.nginx.org.

Thread pools and I/O mechanisms

Before making important financial decisions, such as investing in an additional server or two, you should look to optimize your current setup to make the most of your existing infrastructure.

Relieving worker processes

In the case of websites that require heavy I/O operations, such as file uploads or downloads, the asynchronous architecture of Nginx can present a certain disadvantage: while the master process is able to absorb the incoming connections asynchronously, the worker processes can be blocked for relatively long periods of time by certain tasks (the most common one being reading data from hard disk drives or network drives).

Consider a simplified configuration with two worker processes; each HTTP request received by Nginx gets assigned to either process. Within a process, operations are performed sequentially: receiving and parsing the request, reading the requested file from its storage location, and finally preparing and sending the response to the client. If, for some reason, you were to serve files stored on a network drive with a latency of about 100 ms, both your worker processes would be spending most of their time waiting for the files. As a result, your server would only be able to serve 18 to 20 requests per second.

This isn't a problem that occurs just for network drives: even regular hard disk drives can take a certain amount of time to fetch a file if it isn't in the cache; 10 milliseconds isn't insignificant when you multiply it by 1,000.

The solution that has been made available as of Nginx 1.7.11 is called *thread pools*. The basic principle behind this solution is that instead of reading files synchronously within the worker process, Nginx delegates the operation to a thread. This immediately liberates the worker process, which can then move on to the next request in the queue. Whenever the thread finishes performing the operation, the worker process finalizes and sends the response to the client. It is a pretty simple concept to understand, and thankfully, it's just as simple to configure.

AIO, Sendfile, and DirectIO

In order to enable support for thread pools, Nginx must be built with the `--with-threads` parameter; this functionality doesn't come by default. The first step of the configuration is to define a thread pool with the `thread_pool` directive at the root of your configuration file.

Syntax: `thread_pool name threads=N [max_queue=Q];`

Where `name` is the name you wish to give to the thread pool, `N` is the number of threads that should be spawned, and `Q` the maximum number of operations allowed in the queue. By default, a thread pool exists with the name `default`, coming with 32 threads and a maximum queue of 65,536 operations.

In location blocks that require it, simply insert the `aio` directive and specify the thread pool name:

```
thread_pool MyPool threads=64;
[...]
location /downloads/ {
    aio threads=MyPool;
}
```

Alternatively, insert `aio threads` without a pool name if you want to use the default thread pool. It is also possible to use both `sendfile` and `aio` in the same location:

```
location /downloads/ {
    aio threads;
    directio 8k;
    sendfile on;
}
```

If the file requested by the client is over `8k` (the value specified with the `directio` directive), `aio` will be used. Otherwise, the file will be sent via `sendfile`.

Summary

Before adapting your infrastructure to increasingly high traffic, you should always look for solutions offered by your current set of tools. If traffic causes your server to become unresponsive because of blocking operations such as slow disk reads, you should give thread pools a try. If this turns out to be insufficient, load balancing is the next best thing. Thankfully, as we have discovered in this chapter, implementing a load-balanced architecture is made particularly easy by Nginx; you can even use it to distribute the load of other server applications such as MySQL, e-mail, and more.

Now that we have seen a basic yet comprehensive approach of the most advanced mechanisms offered by Nginx, we will continue by exploring four real-life case studies.

9
Case Studies

The chapters you have read so far have explored the many facets of Nginx: from static web page serving to advanced features such as load balancing. You have learned how to set up Nginx on your server and to configure it to fit the needs of your websites. You've also discovered the numerous advanced modules, which bring forth complex functionality.

We will now make use of the knowledge acquired so far by studying a couple of real-life examples. First, we will set up a complete WordPress site from scratch, approaching all the aspects of configuration including optimization and caching. We will then enable HTTPS support as well as SPDY, and discover how to handle clients who visit your website from a mobile device.

The last part of the chapter will be dedicated to setting up ownCloud — an open source solution allowing you to store documents on your server and retrieve them from a variety of platforms. We will also secure access to your OwnCloud drive by setting up a self-signed certificate.

This chapter covers the following topics:

- An in-depth guide to setting up a WordPress site
- Obtaining and setting up an SSL certificate to enable HTTPS support
- Enabling and testing SPDY on your server
- The basic handling of mobile clients
- Creating a secure cloud drive with ownCloud

Deploying a WordPress site

As stated in *Chapter 7, From Apache to Nginx*, WordPress is currently the most popular content management system on the entire Web. According to a recent survey by `http://www.builtwith.com`, its market share has reached the 50 percent bar, leaving its competitors far behind: Joomla only captures 9 percent of the market, followed by Drupal with just a little over 2 percent. For a lot of web server administrators, setting up WordPress sites or blogs has become a common task, whether it is for personal or professional use.

Preparing your server and obtaining WordPress

In this section, we will get your server ready for downloading and installing the WordPress application. There will be a few configuration files to go through to make sure that WordPress runs smoothly.

System requirements

The first step you need for setting up a WordPress site on a fresh new server is to make sure you have the necessary components installed and up-to-date: it is recommended that you run at least PHP 5.4 and MySQL Server 5. If you haven't done so yet, running the following commands will provide a basic working environment with minimal PHP extensions. Use the following command under a Debian-based Linux operating system:

```
# apt-get install mysql-server php5-fpm php5-mysql php5-gd php5-dev
```

If your server runs a Red Hat-based OS, run the following command:

```
# yum install mysql-server php-fpm php-mysql php-gd php-dev
```

If you have an older version installed on your system, it is recommended that you upgrade it to the latest available version using the `apt-get update && apt-get upgrade` or `yum upgrade` commands.

PHP configuration

After making sure that your server components meet the minimum requirements, you should edit some of the settings if you want WordPress to run smoothly. There are two main aspects of the PHP configuration which you should look into. First, the default PHP configuration file (php.ini) contains the following directives that you will probably want to update:

- cgi.fix_pathinfo: set this value to 0 for security reasons, as we explained in *Chapter 5, PHP and Python with Nginx*.

- post_max_size: by default, the maximum size of the POST request body is 8 megabytes. Increase the value if necessary; keep in mind that file uploads are usually performed via the POST requests.

- upload_max_filesize: set to 2 megabytes by default, this will need to be increased if you want to allow the uploading of large files.

- date.timezone: you will get a warning if you leave this blank. Refer to http://php.net/manual/en/timezones.php to find out the proper value in your situation.

The second aspect of the configuration is the PHP-FPM side. The main php-fpm.conf file does not require immediate changes. However, if you haven't done so yet, you will need to create a *configuration pool*: a set of configuration directives that apply to a particular website or application. This allows you to run the PHP processes under a specific user account, and optionally, configure a specific network interface for communicating with Nginx.

Create a new pool by declaring its name between brackets:

```
[wordpress]
```

Append the following configuration directives:

```
; Specify user account and group for the pool
; We assume that you created a "wordpress" user and group
user=wordpress
group=wordpress
; Network interface and listening port
; Use 127.0.0.1 if Nginx runs on the same machine
listen=127.0.0.1:9000
; Only allow connections from local computer
; Change this value if Nginx runs on a different machine
allowed_clients=127.0.0.1
```

Optionally, you may enable *chrooting*: specify a root directory for the PHP processes of this pool. For example, if you set the chroot to `/home/wordpress/www`, your PHP scripts will only be able to read the files and directories within the specified path (any attempt to read or write a file or directory outside of `/home/wordpress/www` will systematically fail). It is highly recommended that you enable this feature. Should a security breach be discovered in the WordPress code, attackers would only be able to exploit files within the reach of your PHP process; the rest of your server would not be compromised.

```
chroot=/home/wordpress/www;
```

Other configuration directives are documented at length in the default pool file supplied with PHP-FPM; their default values are suitable in most cases.

When it comes to PHP, there is one last bit of configuration that should be performed: enabling *Zend OpCache*. This PHP extension offers an `opcode` caching mechanism that improves script processing times dramatically. This being totally transparent to programmers and visitors, all you have to do is enable it in your `php.ini` configuration file. If you run PHP 5.4, you will have to download and install it with the following command:

```
# pecl install zendopcache
```

Once the command ends, you will be given the full path of the extension. If you run PHP 5.5 or above, the extension is already available in the default extension folder. To enable Zend OpCache, simply add the `extension=path` directive, where `path` is the full path of the extension file (or a path relative to the default extension folder), similar to this:

```
extension=/usr/local/php/lib/php/extensions/no-debug-non-zts-20121212/
opcache.so
```

MySQL configuration

At the time of installing the MySQL server, you were asked to set up the administrator (root) credentials. Since these credentials allow full access to the SQL server including permissions on all databases, you should never use them in any of your PHP applications. The best practice is to create a separate MySQL user, and to assign permissions on the database that will be used by your application. Log in to your local MySQL server with the following command:

```
# mysql -u root -p
```

Create a new SQL database:

```
mysql> CREATE DATABASE wordpress;
```

Create a SQL user and grant all permissions to the wordpress database (don't forget to specify a complex enough password):

```
mysql> GRANT ALL PRIVILEGES ON wordpress.* TO 'wordpress'@'localhost'
IDENTIFIED BY 'password';
```

Now, exit and try logging in to the server using the newly created account:

```
mysql> exit
# mysql -u wordpress -p
mysql> SHOW DATABASES;
```

You should see the wordpress database that you just created.

Downloading and extracting WordPress

The last step is to download the latest version of WordPress, and extract it at the location specified earlier; in our example: /home/wordpress/www. The latest version can always be found at https://wordpress.org/latest.tar.gz:

```
/home/wordpress/www# wget https://wordpress.org/latest.tar.gz
```

```
/home/wordpress/www# tar xzf latest.tar.gz
```

```
/home/wordpress/www# mv ./wordpress/* ./ && rm -r ./wordpress
```

Make sure that the user and group is properly set, and give write permissions over the application files to the wordpress user:

```
/home/wordpress/www# chown -R wordpress ./
```

```
/home/wordpress/www# chgrp -R wordpress ./
```

```
/home/wordpress/www# chmod -R 0644 ./
```

Nginx configuration

Before you can begin setting up WordPress via the user-friendly web installer, you will need to finalize your Nginx server configuration. We will go down to every last detail, and suggest a configuration that would be appropriate for relatively low-end server hardware: eight-core Intel C2750 (Avoton) with 8 GB of RAM and a regular HDD. Directive values should be adjusted depending on your own hardware.

HTTP blocks

We will be going down the blocks starting at the top level: the HTTP blocks, encompassing the directives that affect the entire server. This implies that the directives placed here will affect all the websites served by this instance of Nginx. Open your Nginx main configuration file (`nginx.conf`), and insert or update the following directives:

```
# Sets the user and group under which the worker processes
# will run. The following values are valid assuming your server
# will only be hosting one website.
user wordpress wordpress;
worker_processes 8; # 1 process per core
pid /var/run/nginx.pid;

events {
  # Edit this value depending on your server hardware
  worker_connections 768;
}

http {
  # Core settings affecting I/O
  sendfile on;
  tcp_nopush on;
  tcp_nodelay on;

  # Default Nginx values
  keepalive_timeout 65;
  types_hash_max_size 2048;
  include /etc/nginx/mime.types;
  default_type application/octet-stream;

  # Set access and error log paths
  access_log /var/log/nginx/access.log;
  error_log /var/log/nginx/error.log;

  # Enable gzipping of files matching the given mime types
  gzip on;
  gzip_disable "msie6"; # Disable gzipping for I.E. 6 users
  gzip_types text/plain text/css application/json application/x-
javascript text/xml application/xml application/xml+rss text/
javascript;

  # Include virtual host configuration files;
  # Edit path accordingly
  include /etc/nginx/sites-enabled/*;
}
```

The server block

The following step will require you to create a new file in the directory specified previously. For example, create a file called `wordpress.conf` in the `/etc/nginx/sites-enabled/` folder. Define your virtual host configuration by inserting or updating the following directives:

```
server {
  # Listen on all network interfaces on port 80
  listen 80;

  # Specify the host name(s) that will match the site
  # The following value allows both www. and no subdomain
  server_name .example.com;

  # Set the path of your WordPress files
  root /home/wordpress/www;

  # Automatically load index.php
  index index.php;

  # Saves client request body into files, cleaning up afterwards
  client_body_in_file_only clean;
  client_body_buffer_size 32K;

  # Allow uploaded files up to 300 megabytes
  client_max_body_size 300M;

  # Automatically close connections if no data is
  # transmitted to the client for a period of 10 seconds
  send_timeout 10s;

  # The rest of the configuration (location blocks)
  # is found below
  [...]
}
```

Location blocks

Finally, set up your location blocks: directives that apply to specific locations on your site:

```
# The following applies to static files:
# images, CSS, javascript
location ~* ^.+\.(jpg|jpeg|png|gif|ico|css|js)$ {
```

```
        access_log off; # Disable logging
        # Allow client browsers to cache files
        # for a long period of time
        expires 180d;
    }


    # The following applies to every request
    location / {
      # Try serving the requested URI:
      # - If the file does not exist, append /
      # - If the directory does not exist,
      # redirect to /index.php forwarding the request URI
      # and other request arguments
        try_files $uri $uri/ /index.php?q=$uri&$args;
    }


    # The following applies to every PHP file
    location ~ \.php$ {
      # Ensure file really exists
      if (!-e $request_filename) {
        return 404;
      }
      # Pass the request to your PHP-FPM backend
      fastcgi_pass 127.0.0.1:9000;
      fastcgi_index index.php;
      fastcgi_param PATH_INFO $fastcgi_script_name;
      include fastcgi_params;
    }
```

WordPress configuration

Once your Nginx configuration is finalized and saved, make sure that you reload the Nginx configuration, either via the service Nginx reload or the `/usr/local/nginx/sbin/nginx -s` reload (or your usual Nginx binary location).

If all goes well, you should be able to run the web-based WordPress installer by visiting `http://example.com/wp-admin/install.php` (replacing `example.com` with your own domain name). You will be prompted for:

- The name of the database you created earlier, in our example: `wordpress`
- The SQL user name you created earlier, in our example: `wordpress`
- The password associated with the user

- The database host: `127.0.0.1` if your MySQL server is hosted on the same server
- A prefix for all the SQL tables created by WordPress

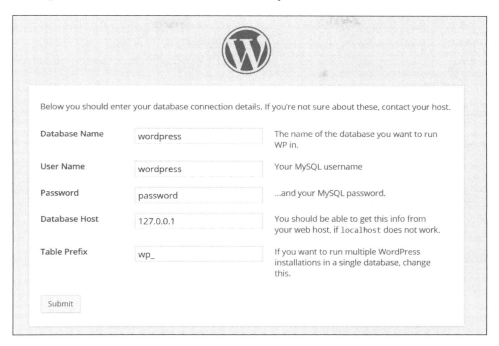

Once the installer completes, you can begin configuring and preparing your WordPress site. In order to enable pretty URLs, you should check the **Settings > Permalinks** section. Several URL schemes, such as `http://example.com/post-name/` or `http://example.com/year/month/post-name/`, are offered.

Securing communications with HTTPS

Implementing HTTPS support is becoming an increasingly important requirement in the modern Web. Visitors no longer trust online stores that don't secure communications, and all of the major actors of the industry are slowly eradicating plain-text transmissions. Facebook, Google, and Twitter all default to HTTPS now. Google has even announced that their search engine will promote websites that offer HTTPS support. There isn't any reason left to skip this part, and Nginx makes it particularly easy. We will thus expand on the example in the previous section, and enable HTTPS support on our WordPress site; please note however that the guide remains valid regardless of the application you are securing.

Self-signed certificates and certificate authorities

In order to enable HTTPS, we have to obtain an SSL certificate which will contain information pertaining to the domain name that we wish to secure. There are two types of certificates that you may set up for your website:

- Self-signed certificates: you can generate a certificate all by yourself on your own server
- Certificates signed by a trusted certificate authority offer an additional level of security: a third party ascertains the authenticity of your server as visitors connect to your website

For testing environments or websites that are meant for a restricted amount of visitors, self-signed certificates can be an option; however, bear in mind that web browsers will display a warning message when visitors browse your site.

The site's security certificate is not trusted!

You attempted to reach **192.168.17.129**, but the server presented a certificate issued by an entity that is not trusted by your computer's operating system. This may mean that the server has generated its own security credentials, which Chrome cannot rely on for identity information, or an attacker may be trying to intercept your communications.

You should not proceed, **especially** if you have never seen this warning before for this site.

[Proceed anyway] [Back to safety]

▶ Help me understand

In the case of our WordPress example site, the best option is to set up a certificate that is signed by a third party (self-signed certificates are covered further on in this chapter) seeing as we intend it to be visited by as many people as possible.

In order to obtain a trusted certificate, you must rely on paid services, which can be found online rather easily. Pricing may vary depending on the number of domains you wish to secure: for a single domain (without any subdomains) 70 US dollars per year is considered a fair price.

Obtaining your SSL certificate

After purchasing the plan of your choice, there are a few steps to perform before you can enable HTTPS in your Nginx configuration. The first of these is to generate a private encryption key that must be kept as safe as possible (any attacker that gets hold of this key would theoretically be able to impersonate your server). This key will be generated with a program called `openssl`, which must be installed on your system. Install it with the following command:

```
# apt-get install openssl
```

Alternatively, for Red Hat-based operating systems, use the following command:

```
# yum install openssl
```

Run the following command to generate your 2048-bit RSA private key, replacing `example.com` with your actual domain name:

```
# openssl genrsa –out example.com.key 2048
```

A file called *example.com.key* is now present in the current directory. Before you move the file to a secure location, you must generate a *Certificate Signing Request* file which will be transmitted to the certificate authority. The following command will take care of it:

```
# openssl req -new -key example.com.key -out example.com.csr
```

As you execute this command, you will be prompted to enter details about your company or organization; the most important part is *Common Name* (for example, *server FQDN* or *YOUR name*): this is where you should enter your actual domain name, in our case, `example.com`. Once this is done, you are left with a `.csr` file containing the information required by the Certificate Authority to generate your certificate. Log in to your account on the Certificate Authority website, and upload the `.csr` file (or its contents). Your certificate signing request will be verified and processed by the certificate authority, and the certificate files will be provided to you immediately or after a short period of time, depending on the Certificate Authority you selected.

Enabling HTTPS in your Nginx configuration

At this point, you should have received two files from your Certificate Authority: your site's certificate file (`.crt`), and an additional certificate file containing information relative to the Certificate Authority itself. These two files must be concatenated into one by using the following command:

```
# cat your_site_certificate.crt certificate_authority.crt > example.com.
crt
```

The order is important: your site's certificate first, followed by your CA's certificate. Now that this is done, two files are required to finalize your Nginx configuration:

- Your private key file generated during the first step (example.com.key)
- The certificate file that we just generated (example.com.crt)

Store them in a secure location, but keep in mind Nginx must have the read permission in order to function properly. We will now edit the Nginx configuration to enable HTTPS.

Open the existing server block for your domain, and append the following directives below the listen 80; line:

```
# Listen on port 443 using SSL and make it the default server
listen 443 default_server ssl;

# Specify the path of your .crt and .key files
ssl_certificate      /etc/ssl/private/example.com.crt;
ssl_certificate_key /etc/ssl/private/example.com.key;

# Enable session caching, increase session timeout
ssl_session_cache shared:SSL:20m;
ssl_session_timeout 60m;

# Disable SSL in favor of TLS (safer)
ssl_protocols TLSv1 TLSv1.1 TLSv1.2;
```

Save your configuration and reload Nginx. At this point, you are able to browse your site via HTTPS (while HTTP is still enabled). However, we must inform WordPress that the site URL has changed. Open your WordPress site control panel; go to **Settings** > **General**, and update the site address:

General Settings

Site Title	My Site Name
Tagline	My Site Tagline
	In a few words, explain what this site is about.
WordPress Address (URL)	https://www.example.com
Site Address (URL)	https://www.example.com
	Enter the address here if you want your site home page to be different from your WordPress installation directory.

Furthermore, if your custom theme includes elements linked statically, you will want to update the URLs by replacing `http` with `https` (or better still, removing the protocol altogether, since modern web browsers are clever enough to use the correct one automatically).

Setting up and testing SPDY

As detailed in *Chapter 4, Module Configuration*, the SPDY protocol was designed by Google in order to improve the page loading time for visitors through various techniques (data compression, multiplexing of requests, and so forth). SPDY can be enabled quite simply by making sure that the module exists in your Nginx build, and appending a flag to your `listen` configuration directive.

If you are unsure whether you included the SPDY module in your Nginx build, run the `nginx -V` command to find out. If you did not include it, you should rebuild Nginx with the `--with-http_spdy_module` command-line argument. Once SPDY is available, open up your server block configuration and update the `listen` directive:

```
listen 443 default_server ssl spdy;
```

Reload Nginx, and visit your website again from a web browser that supports SPDY (Google Chrome or Firefox, among others). You may or may not notice an improvement in speed; if you want to make sure that SPDY is correctly enabled, you can use a browser extension that will provide indications. In Google Chrome, you can download an extension called *HTTP/2 and SPDY indicator*, available on the Chrome Web Store free of charge. The following screenshot displays what you will see if everything has been set up correctly:

However, be aware that the SPDY support will progressively be dropped over time in favor of HTTP 2, which will encompass all the improvements brought forth by SPDY.

Creating your ownCloud drive

By now, everyone must have heard of Dropbox and similar services that allow you to store files online and retrieve them easily from all sorts of devices, including mobile phones and tablets. While Dropbox is well known for being easy to use and safe enough to store important files, it comes with a price and a limited storage size. The servers that your files are stored on don't belong to you, and recent events have shown that third parties (that is, government agencies) are sometimes allowed to go through your documents if they can provide valid justification. Parallel to Dropbox and other commercial services, a free open source platform was developed: ownCloud. In this chapter, we will set up ownCloud on your Nginx-powered server, and secure communications with the help of a self-signed certificate.

Getting ownCloud

Before installing ownCloud on your server, you should follow the steps that we covered in the previous section:

1. Make sure your server runs PHP 5.4 or greater, as well as at least version 5 of MySQL server.

2. Update your PHP configuration file accordingly, taking particular care of the directives regarding the maximum file upload size.

3. Create a PHP-FPM pool dedicated to ownCloud.

4. Set up a SQL database and user.

Once all the preceding steps have been covered, you are ready to begin downloading and extracting ownCloud. Head over to `http://www.ownCloud.org` and obtain the URL of the latest version; then, run the following commands:

- `/home/owncloud/www# wget https://download.owncloud.org/community/owncloud-8.1.1.zip`

- `/home/owncloud/www# unzip owncloud-8.1.1.zip`

- `/home/owncloud/www# mv ./owncloud/{.[!.],}* ./ && rm -r ./owncloud`

Make sure that the user and group are properly set, and give write permissions over the application files to the `owncloud` user:

- `/home/owncloud/www# chown -R owncloud ./`

- `/home/owncloud/www# chgrp -R owncloud ./`

- `/home/owncloud/www# chmod -R 0644 ./`

Nginx configuration

You are ready to configure Nginx to host your ownCloud drive. This time, the configuration appears slightly more complex due to the nature of the application and its multiple access mechanisms. Initially, we will be accessing our ownCloud instance via HTTP; the final section is dedicated to implementing a self-signed SSL certificate allowing us to browse our cloud drive over HTTPS.

Begin by creating a new configuration file in the virtual host configuration folder—in our example, /etc/nginx/sites-enabled/. Insert the following set of directives (or obtain the default Nginx configuration supplied with ownCloud, and edit it to suit your needs):

```
server {
  # For now, we won't be enabling HTTPS
  listen 80;

  # Insert your host name and document root here
  server_name cloud.example.com;
  root /home/owncloud/www;

  # Set the maximum allowed file upload size
  client_max_body_size 42G;

  # Disable gzip to avoid the removal of the ETag header
  gzip off;

  # Rewrite rules for DAV access
  rewrite ^/caldav(.*)$ /remote.php/caldav$1 redirect;
  rewrite ^/carddav(.*)$ /remote.php/carddav$1 redirect;
  rewrite ^/webdav(.*)$ /remote.php/webdav$1 redirect;

  # Set index and error pages
  index index.php;
  error_page 403 /core/templates/403.php;
  error_page 404 /core/templates/404.php;

  # Deny access to the following files and folders
  location ~ ^/(?:\.htaccess|data|config|db_structure\.xml|README){
    deny all;
  }

  location / {
    # OwnCloud rewrite rules
```

```
        rewrite ^/.well-known/host-meta /public.php?service=host-meta
last;
        rewrite ^/.well-known/host-meta.json /public.php?service=host-
meta-json last;
        rewrite ^/.well-known/carddav /remote.php/carddav/ redirect;
        rewrite ^/.well-known/caldav /remote.php/caldav/ redirect;
        rewrite ^(/core/doc/[^\/]+/)$ $1/index.html;

        # Attempt to serve requested URI
        # or redirect request to index.php
        try_files $uri $uri/ /index.php;
    }

    # The following applies to URIs ending with .php
    location ~ \.php(?:$|/) {
      # Prepare URI path info
      fastcgi_split_path_info ^(.+\.php)(/.+)$;
      # Load default FastCGI parameters
      include fastcgi_params;
      fastcgi_param SCRIPT_FILENAME $document_root$fastcgi_script_name;
      fastcgi_param PATH_INFO $fastcgi_path_info;
      # Important: set HTTPS to off for the time being
      fastcgi_param HTTPS off;
      fastcgi_buffers 64 4K;
      fastcgi_pass 127.0.0.1:9000;
    }

    # Allows visitors to cache static files
    location ~* \.(?:jpg|jpeg|gif|bmp|ico|png|css|js|swf)$ {
      expires 30d;
      access_log off;
    }
}
```

After saving your configuration and reloading Nginx, open your web browser and load the main ownCloud page—in our example, `http://cloud.example.com`. You should now see a setup page inviting you to create an administrator account and define storage settings.

Proceed with the installation of ownCloud. After the initial setup screen, you will be prompted to enter the SQL database information and credentials. Past this point, you should be able to enjoy your online drive straight away, but remember that the communication between you and the server isn't secure yet. Proceed to the next step to begin setting up a self-signed certificate.

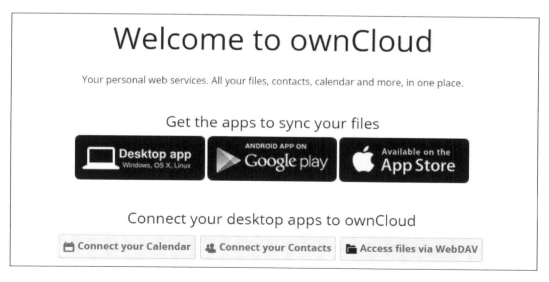

Setting up a self-signed certificate

Since our ownCloud drive is meant for personal use, and for the sake of example, we will resort to a self-signed certificate: the procedure is relatively hassle-free, and it doesn't cost a thing. Run the following commands to generate your certificate:

```
# openssl genrsa -out owncloud.key 2048

# openssl req -new -key owncloud.key -out owncloud.csr

# openssl x509 -req -days 1000 -in owncloud.csr -signkey owncloud.key
-out owncloud.crt
```

Now that you have the required files at your disposal, open your virtual host configuration file (containing your server block), and make the following changes:

- Replace `listen 80` with `listen 443 ssl`
- Insert `ssl_certificate /etc/cert/owncloud.crt;` (use your actual certificate file path) after the `listen` directive
- Insert `ssl_certificate_key /root/cert/owncloud.key;` (use your actual private key file) after the above directive
- Replace `fastcgi_param HTTPS off;` with `fastcgi_param HTTPS on;`

Save your configuration file and reload Nginx. You are now able to browse your ownCloud drive over HTTPS, but since the certificate is self-signed, you will see a warning screen before you can access the application.

Summary

As you may have noticed in the cases we studied in this chapter, the process of setting up a web application can sometimes be long and complex. But when it comes to the part that concerns Nginx, configuration is usually pretty simple and straightforward: a couple of directives in a server block, reloading the server, and you're done.

Unfortunately, in some cases, while your initial configuration seems to do the trick, you realize over time that your visitors run into a variety of problems, or are presented with unexpected error pages. The next chapter will prepare you to face such issues by exploring several leads should you ever need to troubleshoot your web server.

10
Troubleshooting

Even if you read every single word of this book with the utmost attention, you are unfortunately not sheltered from all kinds of issues, ranging from simple configuration errors to the occasional unexpected behavior of one module or another. In this chapter, we attempt to provide solutions for some of the common problems encountered by administrators who are just getting started with Nginx.

The appendix covers the following topics:

- A basic guide containing general tips on Nginx troubleshooting
- How to solve some of the most common install issues
- Dealing with `403 Forbidden` and `400 Bad Request` HTTP errors
- Why your configuration does not appear to apply correctly
- A few words about the `if` block behavior

General tips on troubleshooting

Before we begin, whenever you run into some kind of problem with Nginx, you should make sure to follow the recommendations given in the following sections, as they are generally a good source of solutions.

Checking access permissions

A lot of errors that Nginx administrators are faced with are caused by invalid access permissions. On two separate occasions, you are offered to specify a user and a group for the Nginx worker processes to run:

- When configuring the build with the `configure` command, you are allowed to specify a user and a group that will be used by default (refer to *Chapter 1, Downloading and Installing Nginx*).

- In the configuration file, the `user` directive allows you to specify a user and a group. This directive overrides any value you may have defined during the `configure` step.

If Nginx is supposed to access files that do not have the correct permissions — in other words, which cannot be read (and by extension cannot be written, for directories that hold temporary files, for example) by the specified user and group — Nginx will not be able to serve the files correctly. Additionally, should your web application encounter an error related to file or directory access permissions, the user and group under which your FastCGI or other backend runs should also be investigated.

Testing your configuration

A common mistake is often made by administrators showing a little too much self-confidence: after having modified the configuration file (often without a backup), they reload Nginx to apply the new configuration. If the configuration file contains syntax or semantic errors, the application will refuse to reload. Even worse, if Nginx is stopped (for example, after a complete server reboot), it will refuse to start at all. In all such cases, remember to follow these recommendations:

- Always keep a backup of your working configuration files in case something goes wrong

- Before reloading or restarting Nginx, test your configuration with a simple command — `nginx -t` — to test your current configuration files, or run `nginx -t -c /path/to/config/file.conf`

- Reload your server instead of restarting it — by preferring `service nginx reload` over `service nginx restart` (`nginx -s reload` instead of `nginx -s stop && nginx`), as it will keep the existing connections alive, and thus won't interrupt ongoing file downloads

Have you reloaded the service?

You would be surprised to learn how often this happens: the most complicated situations have the simplest solutions. Before tearing your hair out, before rushing to the forums or asking IRC for help, start with the most simple of verifications.

You just spent two hours creating your virtual host configuration. You've saved the files properly, and fired up your web browser to check the results. But did you remember that one additional step? Nginx, unlike Apache, does not support on-the-fly configuration changes in `.htaccess` files or similar. So take a moment to make sure you did reload Nginx with `service nginx reload`, `/etc/init.d/nginx reload` or `/usr/local/nginx/sbin/nginx -s reload` without forgetting to test your configuration beforehand!

Checking logs

There is usually no need to look for the answer to your problems on the Internet. Chances are that the answer is already given to you by Nginx in the log files. There are two variations of log files you may want to check. First, check the access logs. These contain information about the requests themselves: the request method and URI, the HTTP response code issued by Nginx, and more depending on the log format you defined.

```
error log
1  2015/09/12 06:46:19 [error] 10164#0: *221161 open() "/home/example.com/wp-content/plugins/contactformgenerator/documentati
2  2015/09/12 06:46:25 [error] 10164#0: *221162 open() "/home/example.com/wp-content/plugins/seo-interlinking/js/quicksearch.
3  2015/09/12 06:46:25 [error] 10164#0: *221163 open() "/home/example.com/wp-content/plugins/Premium_Gallery_Manager/sprites/
4  2015/09/12 06:46:30 [error] 10164#0: *221164 open() "/home/example.com/wp-content/plugins/rock-form-builder/admin/js/rock-
5  2015/09/12 06:46:30 [error] 10164#0: *221165 open() "/home/example.com/wp-content/plugins/maxbuttons-pro/js/maxbuttons.js"
6  2015/09/12 07:32:23 [error] 10164#0: *221206 open() "/home/example.com/robots.txt" failed (2: No such file or directory),
7  2015/09/12 07:44:08 [error] 10164#0: *221207 open() "/home/example.com/robots.txt" failed (2: No such file or directory),
8  2015/09/12 10:05:14 [error] 10164#0: *221298 open() "/home/example.com/favicon.ico" failed (2: No such file or directory),
```

More importantly, the error log is a goldmine of information for troubleshooting. Depending on the level you defined (see the `error_log` and `debug_connection` directives for more details), Nginx will provide details on its inner functioning. For example, you will be able to see the request URI translated to an actual file system path. This can be a great help for debugging the rewrite rules. The error log should be located in the `/logs/` directory of your Nginx setup, which, by default, is `/usr/local/nginx/logs` or `/var/log/nginx`.

Install issues

There are typically four sources of errors when attempting to install Nginx or to run it for the first time:

- Some of the prerequisites are missing or an invalid path to the source was specified. More details about prerequisites can be found in *Chapter 1, Downloading and Installing Nginx*.

- After having installed Nginx correctly, you cannot use the SSL-related directives to host a secure website. Have you made sure to include the SSL module correctly during the `configure` step? More details in *Chapter 1, Downloading and Installing Nginx*.

- Nginx refuses to start and outputs a message similar to `[emerg] bind() to 0.0.0.0:80 failed (98: Address already in use)`. This error signifies that another application is utilizing the network port 80. This could either mean that another web server such as Apache is already running on the machine, or that you don't have the proper permissions to open a server socket on this port. This can happen if you are running Nginx from an underprivileged system account.

- Nginx refuses to start and outputs a message similar to `[emerg] 3629#0: open() "/path/to/logs/access.log" failed (2: No such file or directory)`. In this case, one of the files that Nginx tries to open, such as log files, cannot be accessed. This could be caused by invalid access permissions or by an invalid directory path (for example, when specifying log files to be stored in a directory that does not exist on the system).

The 403 Forbidden custom error page

If you decide to use the `allow` and `deny` directives to respectively allow or deny access to a resource on your server, clients who are being denied access will usually fall back on a `403 Forbidden` error page. You carefully set up a custom, user-friendly 403 error page for your clients to understand why they are denied access. Unfortunately, you cannot get that custom page to work, and clients still get the default Nginx `403` error page. You have provided the following code for doing do:

```
server {
    [...]
    allow 192.168.0.0/16;
    deny all;
    error_page 403 /error403.html;
}
```

The problem is simple: Nginx also denies access to your custom 403 error page! In such a case, you need to override the access rules in a location block specifically matching your page. You can use the following code to allow access to your custom 403 error page only:

```
server {
    [...]
    location / {
        error_page 403 /error403.html;
        allow 192.168.0.0/16;
        deny all;
    }
    location = /error403.html {
        allow all;
    }
}
```

If you are going to have more than just one error page, you could specify a location block matching all the error page filenames:

```
server {
    [...]
    location / {
        error_page 403 /error403.html;
        error_page 404 /error404.html;
        allow 192.168.0.0/16;
        deny all;
    }
    location ~ "^/error[0-9]{3}\.html$" {
        allow all;
    }
}
```

All your visitors are now allowed to view your custom error pages.

400 Bad request

Occasionally, you may run into a recurring issue with some of your websites: Nginx returns `400 Bad Request` error pages to random visitors, and this only stops happening when visitors clear their cache and cookies. The error is caused by an overly large header field sent by the client. Most of the time, this occurs when cookie data exceeds a certain size. In order to prevent further trouble, you may simply increase the value of the `large_client_header_buffers` directive in order to allow larger cookie data size:

```
large_client_header_buffers 4 16k;
```

Truncated or invalid FastCGI responses

When setting up an Nginx frontend for a website that heavily relies on AJAX (Asynchronous JavaScript and XML) along with a FastCGI backend such as PHP, you may run into different sorts of problems. If your server returns truncated AJAX responses, invalid JSON values, or even empty responses, you may want to check your configuration for the following elements:

- Have you set up a writable directory for the temporary FastCGI files? Make sure you do so via the `fastcgi_temp_path` directive.

- If `fastcgi_buffering` is set to `off`, all FastCGI responses are forwarded to the client synchronously, in chunks of a certain size (determined by `fastcgi_buffer_size`).

- In some cases, increasing the size and number of buffers allocated to storing FastCGI responses prevents the responses from getting truncated. For example, use `fastcgi_buffers 256 8k;` for 256 buffers of 8 kilobytes each.

Location block priorities

A problem that occurs frequently when using multiple location blocks in the same server block is that the configuration does not apply as you thought it would.

As an example, say you want to define a behavior to be applied to all the image files that are requested by the clients:

```
location ~* \.(gif|jpg|jpeg|png)$ {
    # matches any request for GIF/JPG/JPEG/PNG files
    proxy_pass http://imageserver; # proxy pass to backend
}
```

Later on, you decide to enable the automatic indexing of the /images/ directory. Therefore, you decide to create a new location block matching all the requests starting with /images/:

```
location ^~ /images/ {
    # matches any request that starts with /images/
    autoindex on;
}
```

With this configuration, when a client requests for downloading the /images/ square.gif file, Nginx applies the second location's block only. Why not the first one? That is because location blocks are processed in a specific order. For more information about location block priorities, refer to *The Location block* section in *Chapter 3, HTTP Configuration*.

If block issues

In some situations, if not most, you should avoid using if blocks. There are two main issues that occur if you do so, regardless of the Nginx build you are using.

Inefficient statements

There are some cases where if is used inappropriately, in a way that risks saturating your storage device with useless checks:

```
location / {
    # Redirect to index.php if the requested file is not found
    if (!-e $request_filename) {
        rewrite ^ index.php last;
    }
}
```

With such a configuration as the preceding one, every single request received by Nginx will trigger a complete verification of the directory tree for the requested filename, thus requiring multiple storage disk access system calls. If you test /usr/local/nginx/html/hello.html, Nginx will check /, /usr, /usr/local, /usr/local/nginx, and so on. In any case, you should avoid resorting to such a statement by filtering the file type beforehand (for instance, by making such a check only if the requested file matches specific extensions):

```
location / {
    # Filter file extension first
    if ($request_filename !~ "\.(gif|jpg|jpeg|png)" {
        break;
```

```
    }
    if (!-f $request_filename) {
        rewrite ^ index.php last;
    }
}
```

Unexpected behavior

The `if` block should ideally be employed for simple situations, as its behavior might be surprising in some cases. Apart from the fact that the `if` statements cannot be nested, the following situations may present issues:

```
# Two consecutive statements with the same condition:
location / {
    if ($uri = "/test.html") {
        add_header X-Test-1 1;
        expires 7;
    }
    if ($uri = "/test.html") {
        add_header X-Test-1 1;
    }
}
```

In this case, the first `if` block is ignored, and only the second one is processed. However, if you insert a *Rewrite module* directive in the first block, such as `rewrite`, `break`, or `return`, the block will be processed, and the second one will be ignored.

There are many other cases where the use of `if` causes problems:

- Having `try_files` and the `if` statements in the same location block is not recommended as the `try_files` directive will, in most cases, be ignored.
- Some directives are theoretically allowed within the `if` block, but can create serious issues—for instance, `proxy_pass` and `fastcgi_pass`. You should keep those within the `location` blocks.
- You should avoid using the `if` blocks within a `location` block that captures regular expression patterns from within its modifier.

These issues originate from the fact that, while the Nginx configuration is written in what appears to be a declarative language, directives from the Rewrite module such as `if`, `rewrite`, `return`, or `break` make it look like event-based programming. In general, you should try to avoid using directives from other modules within the `if` blocks as much as possible.

Summary

Most of the problems you run into occur during the early configuration stages while you test your server before production. These problems are usually easier to deal with, because you are mentally prepared for the challenge and, more importantly, because Nginx points out syntax or configuration errors on start-up. It is, on the other hand, much more difficult to identify the cause of malfunctions while your websites are actually in their production stages. But once again, Nginx saves the day: if you properly configure the log files (both access and error logs), and make a habit of reading them regularly, you will find that problem solving is made easy.

This concludes our journey with Nginx, during which we have been through a large number of subjects: from basic mechanisms of the HTTP server to web application deployment and troubleshooting. If you are interested in becoming a true Nginx expert, we recommend further reading: *Mastering Nginx*, by *Dimitri Aivaliotis*, and *NGINX High Performance*, by *Rahul Sharma*. You could even develop your own Nginx modules: *Nginx Module Extension* (by *Usama Dar*) is an excellent book that will help you get started.

Index

Symbols

A

B

C

W

web-based WordPress installer
  URL 262
WebDAV module
  about 157
  directives 157, 158
Web Server Gateway Interface (WSGI) 166
website access
  Autoindex module 126, 127
  Index module 126
  Log module 128, 129
  Random index module 128
weight flag 248
WordPress
  about 238
  rewrite rules 239
WordPress site
  communications, securing with HTTPS 263
  deploying 256
  MySQL, configuring 258

Nginx, configuring 259
PHP configuration 257, 258
server, preparing 256
system requisites 256
WordPress configuration 262, 263
WordPress, downloading 259
WordPress, extracting 259
WordPress, obtaining 256
World Wide Web (WWW) 5

X

XSLT module
  about 143, 144
  directives 144

Z

zlib library 4

Thank you for buying
Nginx HTTP Server
Third Edition

About Packt Publishing

Packt, pronounced 'packed', published its first book, *Mastering phpMyAdmin for Effective MySQL Management*, in April 2004, and subsequently continued to specialize in publishing highly focused books on specific technologies and solutions.

Our books and publications share the experiences of your fellow IT professionals in adapting and customizing today's systems, applications, and frameworks. Our solution-based books give you the knowledge and power to customize the software and technologies you're using to get the job done. Packt books are more specific and less general than the IT books you have seen in the past. Our unique business model allows us to bring you more focused information, giving you more of what you need to know, and less of what you don't.

Packt is a modern yet unique publishing company that focuses on producing quality, cutting-edge books for communities of developers, administrators, and newbies alike. For more information, please visit our website at www.packtpub.com.

About Packt Open Source

In 2010, Packt launched two new brands, Packt Open Source and Packt Enterprise, in order to continue its focus on specialization. This book is part of the Packt Open Source brand, home to books published on software built around open source licenses, and offering information to anybody from advanced developers to budding web designers. The Open Source brand also runs Packt's Open Source Royalty Scheme, by which Packt gives a royalty to each open source project about whose software a book is sold.

Writing for Packt

We welcome all inquiries from people who are interested in authoring. Book proposals should be sent to author@packtpub.com. If your book idea is still at an early stage and you would like to discuss it first before writing a formal book proposal, then please contact us; one of our commissioning editors will get in touch with you.

We're not just looking for published authors; if you have strong technical skills but no writing experience, our experienced editors can help you develop a writing career, or simply get some additional reward for your expertise.

Mastering Nginx

ISBN: 978-1-84951-744-7   Paperback: 322 pages

An in-depth guide to configuring NGINX for any situation, including numerous examples and reference tables describing each directive

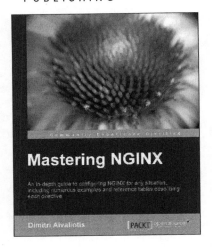

1. An in-depth configuration guide to help you understand how to best configure NGINX for any situation.

2. Includes useful code samples to help you integrate NGINX into your application architecture.

3. Full of example configuration snippets, best-practice descriptions, and reference tables for each directive.

Nginx Essentials

ISBN: 978-1-78528-953-8   Paperback: 150 pages

Excel in Nginx quickly by learning to use its most essential features in real-life applications

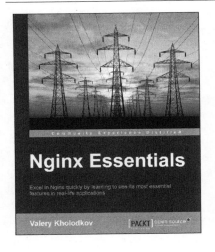

1. Learn how to set up, configure, and operate an Nginx installation for day-to-day use.

2. Explore the vast features of Nginx to manage it like a pro, and use them successfully to run your website.

3. Example-based guide to get the best out of Nginx to reduce resource usage footprint.

Please check **www.PacktPub.com** for information on our titles

NGINX High Performance

ISBN: 978-1-78528-183-9   Paperback: 168 pages

Optimize NGINX for high-performance, scalable web applications

1. Configure Nginx for best performance, with configuration examples and explanations.

2. Step–by-step tutorials for performance testing using open source software.

3. Tune the TCP stack to make the most of the available infrastructure.

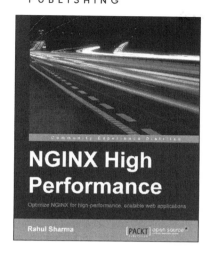

Nginx Module Extension

ISBN: 978-1-78216-304-6   Paperback: 128 pages

Customize and regulate the robust Nginx web server, and write your own Nginx modules efficiently

1. Install Nginx from its source on multiple platforms.

2. Become acquainted with core Nginx modules and their configuration options.

3. Explore optional and third party module extensions along with configuration directives.

Please check **www.PacktPub.com** for information on our titles

16068834R00176

Printed in Great Britain
by Amazon